Communitarianism and its C

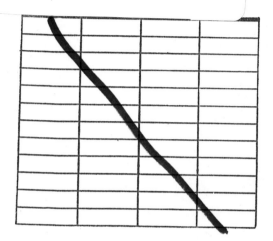

Communitarianism and its Critics

Daniel Bell

CLARENDON PRESS · OXFORD
1993

Oxford University Press, Walton Street, Oxford OX2 6DP

Oxford New York Toronto
Delhi Bombay Calcutta Madras Karachi
Kuala Lumpur Singapore Hong Kong Tokyo
Nairobi Dar es Salaam Cape Town
Melbourne Auckland Madrid
and associated companies in
Berlin Ibadan

Oxford is a trade mark of Oxford University Press

Published in the United States
by Oxford University Press Inc., New York

British Library Cataloguing in Publication Data
Data available

Library of Congress Cataloging in Publication Data
Bell, Daniel, Dr.
Communitarianism and its critics / Daniel Bell.
Includes bibliographical references.
1. Social ethics.   2. Community.   3. Liberalism.   I. Title.
HM131.B3948 1993   303.3'72—dc20   93–10518
ISBN 0–19–827877–2
ISBN 0–19–827922–1 (Pbk. USA only)

10 9 8 7 6 5 4 3 2 1

Typeset by Hope Services (Abingdon) Ltd.
Printed in Great Britain
on acid-free paper by
Biddles Ltd., Guildford and King's Lynn

For Song Bing

Acknowledgements

THIS book is a revised version of a doctoral thesis submitted to Oxford University in February 1991. Not surprisingly, I received a lot of help along the way, but I am most indebted to my thesis supervisor, David Miller of Nuffield College. If progress is the reason that I'm thoroughly embarrassed by earlier drafts of this work, then much of the credit should go to him.

I owe much to my doctoral thesis examiners, G. A. Cohen and Raymond Plant, for their many written and oral comments (special thanks to fellow Montrealer G. A. Cohen, for his inspiringly high academic standards and excellent sense of humour). At McGill, Charles Taylor helped by leading an illuminating seminar on Heidegger, and conversations with James Booth deepened my interest in political theory. I'd also like to thank Daniel Weinstock, who read and helpfully commented on the whole thesis. Needless to say, I am especially grateful to OUP referee Will Kymlicka, whose critical report on the thesis was so insightful I felt it had to be included in this book (see Appendix 1).

A note of appreciation to my friends at St Antony's College. The cosmopolitan atmosphere did not provide an ideal environment for work on communitarianism in Western societies—discussion topics ranged from Chinese dumpling recipes at mealtime to Middle Eastern politics over Turkish coffee—but St Antony's is the best place for anyone who wants to learn about communities far away from home.

A very special thanks to my parents—Maman, Papa, Anthony, and Odile—for their love and inspiration.

Finally, I'd like to thank OUP editor Tim Barton for his patience and encouragement, Karen Janes (Oxford) and Rohani bte Jantan (Singapore) for their technical help, as well as the Quebec and British governments for financial assistance during the course of my graduate studies.

Contents

Introduction

American men, women, and children are members of many communities—families; neighbourhoods; innumerable social, religious, ethnic, work place, and professional associations; and the body politic itself. Neither human existence nor individual liberty can be sustained for long outside the interdependent and overlapping communities to which we all belong. Nor can any community long survive unless its members dedicate some of their attention, energy, and resources to shared projects. The exclusive pursuit of private interest erodes the network of social environments on which we all depend, and is destructive to our shared experiment in democratic self-government. For these reasons, we hold that the rights of individuals cannot long be preserved without a communitarian perspective. A communitarian perspective recognizes both individual human dignity and the social dimension of human existence.[1]

So begins the preamble to 'The Responsive Communitarian Platform: Rights and Responsibilities', a fourteen-page document endorsed by over fifty signatories united in their 'conviction that a communitarian perspective must be brought to bear on the great moral, legal, and social issues of our time'.[2] Many of us worried by unshackled greed, rootlessness, alienation from the political process, rises in the rate of divorce, and all the other phenomena related to a centring on the self and away from communities in contemporary Western societies will be heartened by the appearance of this platform—it seems to outline the moral basis for measures aimed at dealing with such problems, a basis absent from the dominant liberal individualist discourse of the day. None the less, a platform is a platform, and communitarian ideas propagated by political thinkers need to be intellectually appealing as well as politically relevant. Hence, the reason for this book—I try to provide a more systematic statement of the communitarian position from which one can derive certain political measures meant to stem the erosion of communal life and nurture the fragile communities that still bind us together.

Before we get on to that, however, it is worth recalling that communitarians have criticized liberal political theorists for not being up to this task, and an overview of the debate between liberals and their communitarian critics,[3] referred to as 'the central debate in Anglo-American political theory during the 1980s',[4] will prepare us for a look at the communitarian position itself. What follows is a brief discussion of the historical importance and core tenets of (Rawlsian) liberalism, a review of the central criticisms advanced in the 1980s by prominent communitarian critics and the various ways that liberals have dealt with those criticisms, and finally, I provide a sketch of my own argument, noting how that argument fits into (and moves beyond) the aforementioned debate.

'Left Neo-Kantian Liberalism'

Most contemporary liberals[5] work within the theoretical framework established by John Rawls in his landmark 1971 book *A Theory of Justice*,[6] a framework which can be termed 'left neo-Kantian liberalism'. Rawls reformulated and systematized liberal theory, almost single-handedly answering two seemingly fatal objections to liberal theory advanced in the 1960s.

The first objection was that utilitarianism, the dominant justification for liberal politics before the publication of *A Theory of Justice*, might require sacrificing some people's rights for the greater benefit of others. John Stuart Mill thought that he could defend liberal justice in the name of producing the greatest happiness for the members of society,[7] but surely there were times when 'the greatest happiness for the greatest number' calls for morally noxious acts. To borrow an extreme example from Alasdair MacIntyre:

> If in a society of twelve people, ten are sadists who will get great pleasure from torturing the remaining two. Does the principle of utility enjoin that the two should be tortured?[8]

If the sum total of happiness is greater when the two are tortured, the utilitarian has very little choice but to go along with the torture. Utilitarian philosophy, it would seem, is an inadequate foundation for even the most basic individual rights and liberties.[9]

Critics on the political left argued that liberal 'bourgeois freedoms' need a material basis, the second major objection to pre-*A Theory of Justice* liberalism. It's all very nice to defend liberal values such as the right to free speech and equal citizenship, but so long as liberalism had nothing to say about the social and economic conditions that allow for substantive realization of those values, progressive forces can be forgiven for suspect-

ing that liberal ideology was devised and maintained largely for the purpose of perpetuating the rule of the propertied class.[10]

By reformulating liberalism on a Kantian basis, Rawls successfully
answered the first group of critics. That is, he offered a defence of liberal
freedoms so basic that they could not be overridden by the good of society as a whole. The crucial move was to found liberalism on the capacity
(and responsibility) we have to exercise our Kantian moral powers of
shaping, pursuing, and revising (if need be) our own life-plans, and to
respect the exercise of these same powers of self-determination on the part
of other persons. Everybody has a 'highest-order interest' in making use of
his or her powers of self-determination, powers which can only be exercised in the context of available civil and political freedoms.[11] These freedoms, in other words, have value because they enable individuals to
exercise their powers of self-determination, and not because they maxi-
mize social utility.

To meet the objection from the political left, Rawls argued that since
no one deserves his or her natural assets, liberal equality requires at least
partial compensation for unequal talents and abilities. That is, inequalities
cannot be justified by an appeal to unequal endowments, for the following reason: we reject as unjust special advantages that accrue from one's
social background on the grounds that undeserved social circumstances
do not entitle one to extra rewards and resources, and since natural talents
and abilities are also undeserved, it seems equally unfair when people's
fate is made better or worse off as a result of differences in natural endowments.[12] While this might lead one to the conclusion that no one should
benefit from their natural talents, Rawls added the insight that it is not
unfair to allow inequalities if the social system is arranged so that they
work for the good of the least fortunate in the genetic lottery. In short,
Rawls pushed liberal equality beyond its traditional preoccupation with
civil and political rights, arguing that liberalism also requires government
intervention to ensure a just distribution of material resources.
Individuals have an equal right not just to civil and political freedoms
they need to form, pursue, and revise their own conceptions of the good
life, but also to an equal share of social and economic resources needed
for that same purpose, unless inequalities benefit the least fortunate.

Along with this new justification for the redistributive functions of the
state, 'left neo-Kantian liberals' have also defended the principle of official
state neutrality.[13] On this view, the state may not seek to promote any

conception of the good life, for only then can it respect the equal freedom that all persons should have to pursue their freely chosen conceptions of the good life. The government should provide a fair framework for individuals to seek the good in their own way, but it acts unjustly when it presumes to say what is valuable in life, thus restricting people's capacity for self-determination.

Communitarian Criticisms of 'Left Neo-Kantian Liberalism'

First, a word of caution. Those typically put forward as communitarian critics of liberal political theory—Alasdair MacIntyre, Michael Sandel, Charles Taylor, and Michael Walzer—have yet to identify themselves with the 'communitarian movement'.[14] None of them endorsed the manifesto mentioned at the beginning of this introduction, perhaps disturbed by some of the ideas their 'followers' advocate. What does unite them, however, is the view that liberalism does not sufficiently take into account the importance of community for personal identity, moral and political thinking, and judgements about our well-being in the contemporary world. Many particular objections along these lines have been raised, but one can distinguish between claims of three sorts.

THE LIBERAL SELF

The first claim is that liberalism rests on an overly individualistic conception of the self. Liberal justice, above all, is intended for rational individuals who freely choose their own way of life, on the assumption that we have a 'highest-order interest' in choosing our central projects and life-plans, regardless of what it is that is chosen. Presumably, it ought to follow that there is something fundamentally wrong with unchosen attachments and projects.[15] But does this view capture our actual self-understandings? We ordinarily think of ourselves, Michael Sandel says, 'as members of this family or community or nation or people, as bearers of this history, as sons or daughters of that revolution, as citizens of this republic',[16] social attachments that more often than not are involuntarily picked up during the course of our upbringing, rational choice having played no role whatsoever. I didn't choose to love my mother and father, to care about the neighbourhood in which I grew up, to have special feelings for the people of my country, and it is difficult to understand why anyone would think that I have chosen those attachments, or that I ought to have done so.

Even so, the liberal might reply, surely it is important to make some choices in life, such as choosing one's career and marriage mate, and hence the government should provide individuals with the rights and resources that enable them to make those choices. This assumption (and the political implication), however, can also be contested. Compare two persons, unimaginatively named *A* and *B*. *A*, aware of the importance of exercising her moral powers of self-determination, decides early on to set her own life-plan. Already in high school, she evaluates various career options, thinks about the costs and benefits associated with each one, and chooses to become a corporate lawyer. Subsequently, she selects a university programme that helps her achieve that end, treats most people she meets as potential 'contacts' that can help her find a job with a good law firm, and generally behaves in a very calculating way towards the things and people that cross her path. Fortunately, *A* knows how to turn situations to her advantage, and she eventually succeeds in her goal. As far as marriage is concerned, *A* decides she won't get serious with anyone until she is well-established in her career, and she shuns intimacy, occasionally fighting off what her instincts tell her. By her mid-30s, *A* has reached that stage in her career plan where she can search for a marriage partner, but here too she decides to be careful, and not only because she has inherited a big trust-fund she doesn't want to share with just anyone. Her partner, she reasons, must be good-looking, intelligent, and independently established in his career, among other criteria she has in mind. Once again, *A* succeeds in getting what she wants, and she ends up marrying a man she had originally met by means of an advertisement she had placed in the classified section of the *New York Review of Books*.

B, in contrast, never does get the chance to exercise his moral powers of choice. In high school, he doesn't quite know what to do with himself until he is pressured by his father to do some community work at a local centre for handicapped people. He finds it hard going at first, but ends up feeling quite devoted to his work, to the point that he has very little free time to think about his own career. He does eventually get accepted by a university (not a very good one, however), and takes several courses here and there because he doesn't know what he wants to specialize in. Come his last year, he reluctantly takes a course in photography (he has few free time slots due to his continued involvement with handicapped people), but to his surprise discovers that he really enjoys it. He will end up taking a job as a photographer, but *B*'s career is side-tracked for a while—soon after graduation, he is called up by the military to defend his country from an invasion by a Nazi-like foreign power, and the following year he falls madly in love with a woman he met by chance, temporarily drops all dealings with the bourgeois world, and marries her shortly thereafter. His friends ask him why he is so completely infatuated with his wife, but he cannot answer with more than a self-satisfied smile (*B* was never very good with words).

The moral of this story is that people do not necessarily have a 'highest-order interest' in rationally choosing their career and marriage partner, as opposed to following their instincts, striving for ends and goals set for them by others (family, friends, community groups, the government, God), and letting fate do the rest of the work (is *A*'s life better than *B*'s?). This, combined with an awareness of the unchosen nature of most of our social attachments, undermines those justifications for a liberal form of social organization founded on the value of reflective choice (see Act I for more details).

LIBERAL UNIVERSALISM

Even if there is nothing incoherent or undesirable about the liberal conception of the choosing self, say the second type of 'communitarian critics', liberals are none the less insufficiently sensitive to the importance of community or social context for their theory to have practical force. Modern liberal individualism, writes Alasdair MacIntyre, requires that we 'abstract ourselves from all those particularities of social relationship in terms of which we have been accustomed to understand our responsibilities and interests [so as to] arrive at a genuinely neutral, impartial, and, in this way, universal point of view, freed from the partisanship and the partiality and onesidedness that otherwise affect us'.[17] The most famous contemporary application of this method is Rawls's argument that his principles of justice would have been chosen by hypothetical individuals in an 'original position', a position whose special virtue is that it allows us to regard the human situation 'from the perspective of eternity',[18] from all social and temporal points of view. But why should real-life individuals living in specific times and places find anything plausible about a political morality conceived for idealized 'free and equal persons'? Here in Singapore, most of my students seem quite satisfied with their relatively benign paternalistic regime, and while I do my best (when I lecture on Rawls) to explain to them that they should feel a sense of moral outrage at a government which curtails liberal freedoms and tells them how they should lead their lives, that many Singaporeans are not starting their lives with an equal share of society's resources and that quite radical government policies such as 'nationalizing wealth, affirmative action, worker self-ownership, payment to homemakers, public health care, [and] free university education'[19] might be required to remedy unfairness in their society, I am told in response that I have to understand Singapore's particular history and special circumstances. Your theory is not suitable for a little city-state devoid of natural resources, surrounded by potentially hostile neighbours, and with a recent history of crippling poverty and brutal ethnic conflict, they say, and at that point there is nothing left to do but to go on to the next subject, (my presentation of) Rawls's theory of justice having had no more impact than their previous class on Bulgarian theatre.[20]

Michael Walzer offers a more promising approach to moral and political thinking in his book *Spheres of Justice*. Instead of devising principles from an objective and universal standpoint, he argues, we should stay rooted in our traditions, interpreting 'to one's fellow citizens the world of meanings that we share'.[21] People will be motivated by ideas and values that stem from the self-understandings and lived experiences of the society in which they find themselves, and hence philosophers concerned with moral persuasion should ground their theories in historically contingent social norms and intuitions rather than search for eternal principles of justice (see Act II for more details).

LIBERAL ATOMISM

Critics of the third type argue that liberal theory may well have practical force, but that its effects are partly if not wholly detrimental to our wellbeing. Liberalism, it is claimed, contributes to, or at least does not sufficiently take account of, the negative social and psychological effects related to the atomistic tendencies of modern liberal societies. There is undoubtedly a worrying trend in contemporary societies towards a callous individualism that ignores community and social obligations, and liberal theory does not seem up to the task of dealing with this problem.

On the one hand, liberalism allows for too much governmental intervention, legitimizing policies that have undermined and continue to undermine our communal attachments. The state can and should intervene to protect civil and political liberties and to ensure a fair distribution of economic goods, according to Rawlsian liberals, regardless of the consequences. But in an age of flattened lives and widespread social malaise, Charles Taylor asks, should we resort to the state 'to rectify any deviation from the strict principles of justice, no matter what the cost in such goods as community spirit, friendship, or traditional identity?'[22] Swedes are currently discovering to their dismay that their over-enthusiasm for the welfare state, perhaps the closest approximation anywhere of Rawls's theory of justice, has eroded not only their economic competitiveness, but also family and social ties outside the umbrella of their all-embracing state.

On the other hand, liberal theory, with its insistence on state neutrality, unduly constrains the legitimate sphere of governmental action, barring from consideration policies aimed at developing or restoring some sense of community. The state should stay out of the business of telling citizens what constitutes a valuable life, the theory goes, hence it cannot justify policies by an appeal to the value of community. But this view leads to strange and possibly undemocratic consequences—should we (or a Supreme Court) strike down all 'non-neutral' policies meant to increase social responsibility and sustain the communal attachments that give meaning to our lives, even if such policies have the overwhelming support of the citizenry and no matter how trivial the objection from someone who happens to prefer leading a life of rootlessness and anti-social behaviour? (See Acts III to V and Appendix II for more details.)

The 'Communitarianization' of Liberalism

Communitarian criticisms have had an immense impact on liberal theory. Notwithstanding the unwillingness of prominent critics to identify themselves with the 'communitarian camp', liberal theorists have felt a great need to (re)interpret their theory so that it can withstand communitarian objections. Other critiques (e.g. libertarian) of 'left neo-Kantian liberalism' which on the face of it pose an equally serious challenge to liberal theory have not caused liberal theorists to refine, reconsider, and amend their assumptions to nearly the same extent. While I suspect this may have more to do with contemporary moral and political concerns than anything else—more people seem worried about the breakdown of community in the modern world than, say, violations of absolute property rights—the liberal response has thus far taken place almost wholly at the level of theory. That is, rather than think about how traditional liberal institutions and practices have legitimized the uninhibited pursuit of self-interest characteristic of the Reagan/Thatcher years, or how liberal politics can be reformed so as to deal with the atomistic tendencies of our age, contemporary liberal theorists have more often than not withdrawn from the real world, focusing their energies on cleansing liberal theory of overly individualistic or universalist presuppositions.[23] If I'm right that the decline of community in the modern world and the 1980s in particular motivated communitarian criticisms in the first place and helps to explain why liberals felt the force of such criticisms, clearly a liberal response which disavows any responsibility for, or even interest in, the excessive atomism of actual liberal societies will not be sufficient. But differences also remain at the level of principle, as I argue below.

THE LIBERAL SELF RECONSIDERED

In response to the objection that liberalism is premised on an overly individualistic theory of the person, Rawls himself has denied that liberal justice appeals to that or any other 'metaphysical' conception of human nature. Justice as fairness, he says, 'is intended as a political conception, [framed to apply to] society's main political, social, and economic institutions, and how they fit together into one unified system of cooperation'. This conception of justice does not depend 'on philosophical claims I should like to avoid, for example, claims to universal truth, or claims about the essential nature and identity of persons'.[24] Thus he now rejects Kant's ideal of self-determination,[25] and any other philosophical warrant for his (unchanged) political position. Liberal politics with new foundations turns out to be liberal politics with no foundations.

Rawls's concession to the communitarians has not gone undisputed in the liberal camp, however. For one thing, it raises a serious problem—if people's private self-understandings conflict with what they are to do in the political sphere according to Rawls's principles of justice, how can they be motivated to subordinate what's important to them in their everyday lives to what they should do *qua* participants in the political arena? Moreover, and there seems to be an emerging liberal consensus on this point, communitarian objections to the choosing self can be rebutted. Most important, liberals now emphasize, is not choosing our own life-plans, or thinking of ourselves as unencumbered by social ties and commitments; rather, liberalism founded on the value of self-determination requires only that we be able critically to evaluate our ends, hence that 'no end or goal is exempt from possible re-examination'.[26] It may well be that we initially came to value certain attachments without having exercised the powers of choice, and that we cannot entirely escape our socialization, but that does not mean that we can't engage in autonomous deliberation as a piecemeal process, 'akin to repairing Neurath's boat at sea',[27] if we have valid reasons for doing so.

What are we to make of this response? If the choice is between a picture of a self totally immersed in its social world and incapable of any critical distance whatsoever, and one partially immersed but able to distance itself from any one particular attachment it chooses to focus on, the liberal suggestion admittedly appears more plausible. But is there not another alternative, one that perhaps better captures the way we think of ourselves and our core commitments? I have in mind the idea that we are indeed able to re-examine some attachments, but that there are others so fundamental to our identity that they cannot be set aside, and that an attempt to do so will result in serious and perhaps irreparable psychological damage. Can I choose to shed the attachment I feel for the family which brought me up, or will such an attempt lead to perverse and unintended consequences? Is it possible for an Inuit person from Canada's far North suddenly to decide to stop being an Inuit, or is the only sensible response to recognize and accept this constitutive feature of her identity? For most of us, our identities are necessarily bound up with at least some of what I call 'constitutive communities', however free and rational we might otherwise be (constitutive communities are defined and distinguished from contingent attachments in Act III). Such communities present a problem for a liberalism which denies the existence of constitutive ends.

LIBERAL UNIVERSALISM RECONSIDERED

Responding to the charge that liberal justice lacks relevance for actual people living at specific times in particular communities, Rawls has downplayed the significance of the original position and the claim that his principles of justice are universally valid because they would be agreed to by all rational agents in a pre-social state without any knowledge of what life-plan they will have.[28] Instead, he now argues that the task of political philosophy is 'to articulate and to make explicit those shared notions and principles thought to be latent in common sense', and that his principles of justice derive their validity from their 'congruence with our deeper understanding of ourselves and our aspirations'. The liberal conception of justice may not be 'suitable for all societies regardless of their particular social or historical circumstances,'[29] he concedes, but it does seem to be the most appropriate political morality, the one most likely to gain consensus, for those of us living in modern constitutional democracies like the United States, given our traditions and current political dilemmas.

Rawls's approach to political philosophy, it appears, does not depart significantly from the communitarian approach. Both are concerned with interpreting the community's shared understandings, and their dispute would seem to turn on who provides a better account of them. As was the case with Rawls's shift in response to the communitarian critique of the liberal self, however, few liberal theorists have wholeheartedly endorsed Rawls's other concession to the communitarian critics of liberal theory (it is also a matter of dispute to what extent Rawls has actually been 'communitarianized' in this respect). Reasons include the obvious problem that much empirical evidence contradicts Rawls's implication that his theory provides an accurate account of our beliefs regarding distributive justice.[30] More fundamentally, perhaps, many liberal theorists have objected to 'communitarian' methodology on the grounds that it has conservative implications and endorses moral relativism. If what is just is defined in terms of a community's deepest understandings, does that mean that I can never criticize what is approved in my community, or what is approved in other communities, no matter how abhorrent the practice and the justification for it? (I try to respond to such questions in Act II, and the issue is further taken up in the two appendices.)

LIBERAL ATOMISM (NOT) RECONSIDERED

As we have seen, liberal premises have been significantly 'communitarianized',[31] by Rawls himself and (arguably) less so by other liberal theorists. When it comes to liberal conclusions, however, there has been very little movement. Liberals have heard communitarian concerns about loneliness, divorce, deracination, political apathy, and everything else connected with the breakdown of community in contemporary Western societies, but this has not, by and large, caused them to consider the need to modify traditional liberal institutions and practices so as to incorporate the value of community.[32] Some simply concede that the 'liberal vision of the good community' in practice would probably mean living in a fairly narcissistic, superficial world without really deep or persistent commitments, a price presumably worth paying:

[Liberal society] would probably pay for this diversity, tolerance, and experimentation with a degree of superficiality, the consequence of a lack of depth or persistence in commitments. There might be a certain amount of feigned or affected eccentricity. And with all the self-critical, self-shaping introspection, perhaps also a degree of self-absorption or even narcissism . . .

Liberalism holds out the promise, or the threat, of making all the world like California. By encouraging tolerance or even sympathy for a wide array of lifestyles and eccentricities, liberalism creates a community in which it is possible to decide next week I might quit my career in banking, leave my wife and children, and join a Buddhist cult.[33]

Others, more sensitive to the value of community, feel the force of communitarian concerns about actual liberal societies. Just try to imagine a society without community in which no one does more or less than respect everyone else's liberal rights, Amy Gutmann asks:

People do not form ties of love and friendship (or they do so only in so far as necessary to developing the kind of character that respects liberal rights). They do not join neighbourhood associations, political parties, trade unions, civic groups, synagogues, or churches. This might be a perfectly liberal, arguably even a just society, but it is certainly not the best society to which we can aspire.[34]

A very unattractive society it would be (worse than California), and if it even begins to approximate the world we are heading towards, we should do more to encourage fellow citizens to join and participate in the various forms of community that give meaning to our lives—so far there is no disagreement. But, liberals say, the buck stops prior to the state—government officials can hear our complaints about loneliness, deracination, divorce, and so on, but doing anything about it would involve unjustifiable restrictions on people's capacity for leading autonomous lives. Family units may be breaking down, but individuals have made those choices, and that's that.[35] There may be relatively innocuous ways of dealing with such problems—say, divorce could be made a more time-consuming procedure, thus allowing for a certain period of reflection before the knot is permanently untied—but the government cannot presume to say that family life is a good worthy of our allegiance. More important, always, is the preservation of our basic liberties and a just distribution of resources.

Liberal neutrality, in short, proscribes any sort of state tampering with questions of value, but there is another reason why liberal theorists want to keep the government out of the business of promoting community. This is the view that liberal individual rights in fact protect and facilitate genuinely communal ways of life. The rights to freedom of association, expression, and religion, Allen Buchanan writes, 'allow individuals to partake of the alleged essential human good of community by protecting existing communities from interference from without and by giving individuals the freedom to live with like-minded others to create new communities'.[36] But this is a peculiar response—liberal individual rights seem alive and well in contemporary Western societies, and yet atomistic tendencies seem to be getting stronger as well, communal relationships not coming about as a happy by-product of individual rights any more than socially desirable results have inevitably come about as a result of the (now largely lost) liberal faith in the unhampered workings of the free market.

For those deeply concerned about the breakdown of community in the modern world, liberalism will not have been sufficiently 'communitarianized', if not at the level of principle, then certainly at the level of political practice. Alienation, rootlessness, the lack of shared projects, and so on, will seem to require serious thinking about plausible and justifiable political measures that can deal with such problems, measures which may conflict with (what will look like) liberalism's absurd and counter-intuitive restrictions on the legitimate functions of government. There would appear to be a need, then, to articulate a theory, or at least to provide the outlines of a theory, meant to address the concerns of such people. At this point, I can return to what this book aims to do—to present and defend a communitarian theory from which one can derive 'pro-community' political measures such as local veto power over building projects that fail to respect existent architectural styles, special protection for single-industry communities, producer-oriented economics, mandatory civilian national service, political support for threatened linguistic communities, stricter divorce laws, and co-operation-producing education. (See Acts III to V for more details on practices and policies derived from communitarian premisses; several examples from Singapore are discussed in Appendix 2.)

What Communitarianism Is

My statement of the communitarian position is divided into three parts, similar to the typology I employed in this introduction (claims about the self, appropriate methodology in political theory, and the value of community), but of course the focus is on communitarian arguments, relevant aspects of liberal theory being brought up principally to clarify and refine those arguments. Two things should be noticed: (1) I employ the dialogue form to present and defend my interpretation of communitarianism, with the protagonist, Anne De la Patrie, expounding a recently completed doctoral thesis entitled 'What Communitarianism Is' against the objections of a liberal critic, named Philip Schwartzberg (the choice of the dialogue form is explained in the next section); and (2) I spend the most time on the least-discussed (third) part of the liberal–communitarian debate, namely, questions about which communities we are to value and the political implications that flow therefrom (strangely enough, no word has been so ill defined in this whole debate as the word 'community').[37] To summarize:

In the first part of the book (Act I), De la Patrie develops the idea that we are, first and mostly, social beings, deeply bound up in the social world in which we happen to find ourselves. This section serves three purposes: (1) it states in clear language what communitarians mean when they say that we are social beings, that community matters whether we like it or not, whether we know it or not; (2) it undermines those interpretations of liberalism founded on a highly individualistic view of the person; and (3) it calls attention to the importance of Heidegger for communitarian thinkers, complementing the more usual references (found in the works of Charles Taylor, Alasdair MacIntyre, and Michael Sandel, among others) to Aristotle and Hegel.

Next, in the second part (Act II), De la Patrie and Schwartzberg turn to the methodological issue of how best to carry out political reasoning. This section aims to defend Michael Walzer's idea that political thinking involves the interpretation of shared understandings bearing on the political life of one's community, as opposed to those who would derive universally applicable political principles starting from a more abstract specification of individuals and their needs, interests, and moral claims. De la Patrie argues that Walzer's approach need not be conservative and/or relativistic in a way that damages communitarianism.

In the third part (Acts III, IV, and V), De la Patrie presents and defends an argument in favour of communal life from which she draws political implications appropriate for those of us living in the modern world. She posits a need to experience our lives as bound up with the good of the communities out of which our identity has been constituted, and she distinguishes between three kinds of 'constitutive communities': (1) communities of place, or communities based on geographical location (Act III); (2) communities of memory, or groups of strangers who share a morally significant history (Acts IV and V); and (3) psychological communities, or communities of face-to-face personal interaction governed by sentiments of trust, co-operation, and altruism (Act V). The dialogue ends with another argument in favour of valuing 'constitutive communities', namely, the idea that we would care about them more than anything else on our deathbed.

Appendix 1 is a mini-dialogue written by a real-life liberal critic, Will Kymlicka, and Appendix 2 is my response to Kymlicka's criticisms. The appendices highlight points of contention between liberals and communitarians, and address several issues (e.g. feminism, legalization of gay marriages, communitarian politics in Asian societies) neglected or inadequately dealt with in the original dialogue.

Notes

I am particularly indebted to Will Kymlicka for coming up with the idea that this book needs an introduction, as well as for his extensive comments on an earlier draft of this introduction. I would also like to thank David Miller and OUP editor Tim Barton for their comments on an earlier draft.

1. From the preamble to 'The Responsive Communitarian Platform: Rights and Responsibilities', in the *Responsive Community* (Winter 1991/2), 4, a new quarterly journal dedicated to exploring the relationship between individual rights and community obligations.

2. Ibid. 5; 'Our time' refers to the contemporary American context, but the same can be said of the contemporary West as a whole.

3. Recent overviews of the liberal–communitarian debate include Shlomo Avineri and Avner de-Shalit's introduction to their edited collection of readings entitled *Communitarianism and Individualism* (Oxford: Oxford University Press, 1992); Simon Caney's article, 'Liberalism and Communitarianism: A Misconceived Debate', *Political Studies* (June 1992); and the most thorough review to date, Stephen Mulhall and Adam Swift's book *Liberals and Communitarians* (Oxford: Blackwell, 1992). Michael Zilles has prepared a biographical guide to the relevant literature in pt. 6 of David Rasmussen, ed., *Universalism vs. Communitarianism* (Cambridge, Mass.: MIT Press, 1990).

4. Susan Moller Okin, 'Humanist Liberalism', in Nancy Rosenblum, ed., *Liberalism and the Moral Life* (Cambridge, Mass.: Harvard University Press, 1989), 46.

5. Not including 'libertarian liberals' such as Robert Nozick and (the late) Friedrich Hayek who oppose any attempts by the government to rectify unequal social and natural disadvantages.

6. John Rawls, *A Theory of Justice* (Cambridge, Mass.: The Belknap Press of Harvard University Press, 1971).

7. Mill tries to derive a liberal conception of justice from considerations of social utility in ch. 5 of *Utilitarianism* (see the selection in James Sterba, ed., *Justice: Alternative Political Perspectives* (Belmont, Calif.: Wadsworth Publishing Co., 1980)).

8. Alasdair MacIntyre, *A Short History of Ethics* (London: Routledge, 1967), 238.

9. For more elaborate arguments showing that even the most sophisticated forms of utilitarianism cannot at the end of the day provide the necessary underpinnings for the protection of individual rights and liberties, see Will Kymlicka, *Contemporary Political Philosophy: An Introduction* (Oxford: Clarendon Press, 1990), ch. 2 and Raymond Plant, *Modern Political Thought* (Oxford: Basil Blackwell, 1991), ch. 4.

10. The classic statement of this argument can be found in Karl Marx's essay 'On the Jewish Question'.

11. Rawls spells out what he means by 'highest-order interests' (that parties in the original position have) in developing and exercising Kantian moral powers of self-determination in his article 'Kantian Constructivism in Moral Theory', *Journal of Philosophy* (Sept. 1980), esp. 524–7. Some have seen here a significant departure from the argument in *A Theory of Justice*, but Chandran Kukathas and Philip Pettit argue that the priority given by the parties in the original position to their interests in developing and exercising their Kantian moral powers should be interpreted as an attempt to strengthen and refine the Kantian basis of Rawls's endeavours. An (unwelcome, in their view) 'important qualitative change in the character of Rawls's political theory' only took place after 1982, when Rawls rejected Kant's moral philosophy in response to communitarian criticisms (see their book *Rawls: A Theory of Justice and its Critics* (Cambridge: Polity Press, 1990), 142 and ch. 7, generally).

12. On the importance of this intuition for Rawls's argument (more important than Rawls himself recognizes), see Kymlicka, *Contemporary Political Philosophy: An Introduction*, 55–8. In his famous 'Critique of the Gotha Program', Marx also criticized the distributive principle 'to each according to his contribution' on the grounds that it allows for the influence of unequal (undeserved) individual endowments. Working with different notions of what is feasible in capitalist societies, however, Marx thought that such unfairness (income injustices caused by unequal talents) was an inevitable defect even in 'the first phase of communist society, as it is when it has just emerged after prolonged birth pangs from capitalist society' (from David McLellan, ed., *Karl Marx: Selected Writings* (Oxford: Oxford University Press, 1977), 569).

13. See e.g. Bruce Ackerman, *Social Justice in the Liberal State* (New Haven, Conn.: Yale University Press, 1981); Ronald Dworkin, 'Liberalism', in Stuart Hampshire, ed., *Public and Private Morality* (Cambridge: Cambridge University Press, 1978), 113–43; Will Kymlicka, 'Liberal Individualism and Liberal Neutrality', *Ethics* (July 1989), esp. 883–5; and Charles Larmore, *Patterns of Moral Complexity* (Cambridge: Cambridge University Press, 1987), ch. 3.

14. Taylor begins his article 'Cross-Purposes: The Liberal–Communitarian Debate' by noting that 'We often hear talk of the difference between "communitarians" and "liberals" in social theory, and in particular in the theory of justice. Certainly a debate seems to have been engaged between two "teams", with people like Rawls, Dworkin, Nagel, and Scanlon on one side (team L), and Sandel, MacIntyre, and Walzer on the other (team C)' (from Nancy Rosenblum, ed., *Liberalism and the Moral Life*, 159), leaving himself out of 'team C'; in his article 'The Communitarian Critique of Liberalism', Walzer criticizes 'current American versions' of the 'communitarian critique' and offers a weaker ('less powerful') version of his own, one 'more available for incorporation within liberal (or social democratic) politics' (*Political Theory* (Feb. 1990), 7), a task similar to that embarked upon by 'communitarianized' liberals (see section on 'The "Communitarianization" of Liberalism', below). Most peculiar is that Walzer avoids any mention in this article of the 'communitarian' critique of 'universalist' liberal methodology that is normally associated with his own book *Spheres of Justice* (Oxford: Basil Blackwell, 1983); MacIntyre opens a letter to the periodical *The Responsive Community* (Summer 1991), 91 with the following sentences: 'In spite of rumours to the contrary, I am not and never have been a communitarian. For my judgement is that the political, economic, and moral structures of advanced modernity in this country, as elsewhere, exclude the possibility of realizing any of the worthwhile types of political community which at various times in the past have been achieved, even if always in imperfect forms. And I also believe that attempts to remake modern societies in systematically communitarian ways will always be either ineffective or disastrous'; Sandel has come closest to placing himself in the 'communitarian camp' by including a selection of his writings in the second part of a book he edited on the 'liberal–communitarian debate', but it is important to note that he entitled the collection *Liberalism and its Critics* (Oxford: Basil Blackwell, 1984), which suggests that he is presenting leading statements of liberal theory and some largely negative challenges to it, as opposed to contrasting two fully developed theories.

15. Those who do not choose their own plan of life, says John Stuart Mill, are no better than apes:

> The human faculties of perception, judgement, discriminative feeling, mental activity, and even moral preference, are exercised only in making a choice . . .
>   He who lets the world, or his own portion of it, choose his plan of life for him, has no need of any other faculty than the ape-like one of imitation. ('On Liberty', in *Three Essays* (Oxford: Oxford University Press, 1975), 72–3.)

16. Michael Sandel, *Liberalism and the Limits of Justice* (Cambridge: Cambridge University Press, 1981), 179.
17. Alasdair MacIntyre, *Whose Justice? Which Rationality?* (London: Duckworth, 1988), 3.
18. This is the language Rawls employs on the last page of *A Theory of Justice.*
19. Some of the possible political implications of liberal equality, according to Will Kymlicka (in *Contemporary Political Philosophy*, 86).
20. A minority of students, it should be said, do respond positively to Rawls's arguments.
21. Michael Walzer, *Spheres of Justice*, p. xiv.
22. Charles Taylor, 'Comments and Replies' (to critics of *Sources of the Self*), *Inquiry: An Interdisciplinary Journal of Philosophy* (June 1991), 244 (but without the premiss about flattened lives and social malaise; for Taylor's views on those issues, see his recent book *The Malaise of Modernity* (Concord, Ontario: Anansi, 1991)).
23. As Patrick Neal and David Paris put it:

> One cannot imagine Hobbes arguing that the adequacy of his theory is to be divorced from the practical effects of that theory as it was embodied in the self-understandings and lived experiences of a society in which it was practised. Yet, by contrast, contemporary liberal theorists frequently respond to communitarian criticism of the substantive character of life in liberal societies by dismissing it as irrelevant, as sociological criticism which 'misses the point'. Even though liberal societies are increasingly populated with possessive individualists (or worse), we are nevertheless reminded that liberal theory has advanced to the point of being thoroughly cleansed of such presuppositions. In this situation, one suspects that liberal theory's 'advance' has been attained only by denying the very real, practical implications of its 'Hobbesian' forebears ('Liberalism and the Communitarian Critique: A Guide for the Perplexed', *Canadian Journal of Political Science* (Sept. 1990), 430).

24. John Rawls, 'Justice as Fairness: Political not Metaphysical', *Philosophy and Public Affairs* (Summer 1985), 224–5, 223. This article has been widely interpreted as Rawls's response to Sandel's criticisms, even though Sandel is mentioned by name only once in a dismissive footnote on p. 239. In the same vein, this time more explicitly in response to Sandel's criticisms, Charles Larmore provides a defence of liberalism as a political doctrine that does not depend on a theory of the person in his book *Patterns of Moral Complexity.*
25. See Rawls's article 'The Idea of an Overlapping Consensus', *Oxford Journal of Legal Studies*, 7 (1987), 6.
26. Will Kymlicka, *Liberalism, Community and Culture* (Oxford: Clarendon Press, 1989), 52; see also Ronald Dworkin's article 'Liberal Community',

California Law Review, 77 (1989), 489, and Stephen Macedo, *Liberal Virtues: Citizenship, Virtue and Community in Liberal Constitutionalism* (Oxford: Clarendon Press, 1990), 247.

27. Caney, 'Liberalism and Communitarianism', 277.

28. It should be noted that Rawls had already backed away from the 'universalism' of *A Theory of Justice* prior to communitarian objections in the 1980s, so it would be misleading to claim that communitarian critics *caused* Rawls to become 'communitarianized' in this respect.

29. Rawls, 'Kantian Constructivism in Moral Theory', *Journal of Philosophy*, 518, 519, 518.

30. Several experiments have been devised to test Rawls's claims against popular opinion, and in particular how people respond to Rawls's difference principle. If people endorsed this principle, one would expect them to support it from behind a simulated veil of ignorance—in fact, however, subjects reject the difference principle on the grounds that it emphasizes their concern that no one should live in poverty to the entire exclusion of their other concern that the able and hardworking should have the chance to reap large rewards (most favour a system which imposes an income floor and then maximizes the average salary that individuals could receive above it). More generally, David Miller comments that:

> The evidence surveyed throughout this article [a review of the empirical literature on distributive justice] highlights popular attachment to desert as a major criterion for income distribution and suggests that a distribution based on this criterion is potentially more stable than one that aims to raise the position of the worst off group regardless of considerations of desert and need. ('Distributive Justice: What the People Think', *Ethics* (Apr. 1992), 580.)

31. Liberal purists such as Simon Caney argue that liberalism had already been 'communitarianized' after its encounter with Hegel, and hence that every attractive argument advanced by 1980s communitarians had already been incorporated into liberal premises (see his article 'Liberalism and Communitarianism', esp. 289). The implication of this argument, backed up with quotes from the collected works of J. S. Mill and the more obscure sections of *A Theory of Justice*, is that Taylor, Sandel, MacIntyre, *et al.* have been wasting their time.

32. Will Kymlicka's book *Liberalism, Community and Culture* is an important exception to this trend. Appealing to the value of cultural community, Kymlicka constructs an argument for minority rights from which he derives the political implication that temporary illiberal measures can be justified when the very existence (as opposed to the character) of the community is at stake. This argument, however, relies on a (to my mind) contestable premiss

about the importance of self-determination, applies a universal standard for evaluating minority rights claims, and remains a long way from meeting communitarian concerns about excessive atomism in liberal societies, concerns relevant not just for vulnerable minorities.

33. Macedo, *Liberal Virtues,* 278.

34. Amy Gutmann, 'Communitarian Critics of Liberalism', *Philosophy and Public Affairs* (Summer 1985), 320.

35. Notwithstanding Stephen Macedo's claim that liberal justice gives him the unconditional right to leave his (hypothetical?) wife and children, most contemporary liberals do allow for the state to intervene in parental decisions about divorce if the interests of children are at stake. If not, however, it is presumed that the liberal state can and should pass laws that allow for shotgun divorces. Perhaps the state can pass two sorts of divorce laws, chosen by individuals when they decide to get married: one for liberal couples who prefer to have the absolute freedom to dump their marriage partner (so long as the interests of children are not at stake), and another for communitarians who recognize the advantages of being bound by a law that allows for a certain period of reflection before the marriage contract is torn up.

36. Allen Buchanan, 'Assessing the Communitarian Critique of Liberalism', *Ethics* (July 1989), 858.

37. That I had largely to leave behind (or go beyond) the liberal–communitarian debate can be confirmed by a glance at the endnotes for Acts III to V—there are more references to the *Guardian* and the *New York Review of Books* than to *Political Theory* and *Philosophy and Public Affairs*.

In Defence of the Dialogue Form

I haven't changed my mind about any of the arguments I invoked to justify my having adopted the dialogue form for my doctoral thesis, so they are reproduced here without changes of any substance.

It will be noticed that I have adopted the dialogue form for my D.Phil. thesis. It may seem presumptuous to have opted for such an unusual thesis form without having proved myself in the standard thesis form. I cannot answer this criticism satisfactorily. None the less, I believe that the following nine arguments in favour of the dialogue form carry sufficient weight to justify my having adopted it:

1. Whereas the author of an analytical philosophy essay tends to anticipate objections to her arguments by invoking such seeming afterthoughts as 'a critic might argue that . . .' and then proceeding to show why that critic would be misguided if he in fact argued that, the dialogue form allows for more systematic treatment of a contrasting position in the form of a person who continually presses his objections to the protagonist's case. (Thrasymachus in Plato's *Republic* comes to mind as a successful realization of this possibility.) The protagonist's responses, it goes without saying, need not leave the critic completely satisfied. In the context of this thesis, a critic of a liberal orientation challenges the communitarian ideas I am trying to present, and the reader is invited to choose sides.[1] If I have succeeded in creating a compelling critic, the reader may well side with the critic in the final analysis.

2. The ongoing communitarian–liberal debate in Anglo-American political theory seems especially amenable to the dialogue form, one interlocutor representing my interpretation of communitarian ideas currently floating in the air, the other drawing on relevant aspects of the works of liberal theorists.

3. The constraint of creating a plausible dialogue has compelled me into cleaning up the academic jargon that would not have passed in a conversation between two old friends who meet by chance some years later. As a by-product, the ideas expressed in the dialogue should be

readily grasped by the non-expert. The specialist in political theory, if he is so inclined, can turn to the endnotes for references, technical elaboration of arguments, and marginal commentary.

4. The constraint of creating a plausible dialogue does not allow for quotations from the works of relevant authorities that would buttress the interlocutors' points (no one quotes at length from books in actual conversations). The result is a shortish thesis that can be read in a single sitting without inducing excess drowsiness.

5. The dialogue form allows for a self-referential thesis. That is, my D.Phil. thesis is a dialogue about a D.Phil. thesis, which is an advantage in the sense of providing the examiners with a glimpse of what we ordinarily think of as a doctoral thesis, hence facilitating comparative grading. (Of course, this is only an advantage as compared to a D.Phil. thesis written in dialogue form that is not about a D.Phil. thesis.)

6. In common with many other undergraduates, I first came across philosophy by means of Plato's dialogues. Utterly enchanted by Plato's style, and the implication that philosophic inquiry is pursued by means of a conversation between friends seeking truth, I was both surprised and disappointed to find out that the dialogue form in philosophy has all but died out. There have been some post-Plato efforts at writing philosophy in dialogue form—twentieth-century examples include Heidegger's fictionalized account of a dialogue on language between himself and a Japanese friend,[2] Wittgenstein's *Philosophical Investigations*, which often assumes the form of imaginary dialogues or conversations,[3] and Maurice Cranston's *Political Dialogues*[4]—but this way of writing philosophy is still, I think, badly in need of resuscitation. Hence my effort.[5]

7. A dialogue that resembles an actual conversation can hint at the way that speech is affective as well as cognitive in politically relevant ways.[6] That is, simulating real-life linguistic interaction can illuminate the ways that factors not having to do with interest calculation and bargaining come to bear on political discussion.

8. A conversation between two friends in a realistic setting forces the reader to re-create in her mind the context in which the ideas are discussed, thus aiding retention of the material presented in this thesis.

9. The dialogue form, if done well, makes for more entertaining reading than the often dry analytical essay. I can only hope that my thesis will not prove to be an exception to this general rule.

Notes

1. For a book-length defence of the 'dialectical' literary presentation on the grounds that the author, rather than preaching the truth, asks readers to discover the truth for themselves, see Stanley Fish, *Self-Consuming Artifacts: The Experience of Seventeenth Century Literature* (Berkeley, Calif.: University of California Press, 1972).

2. See his 'A Dialogue on Language' in Martin Heidegger, *On The Way to Language* (New York: Harper and Row, 1982), 1–54.

3. John W. Danford writes:

   both [Plato and Wittgenstein] approach philosophical questions in a dialectical spirit. For both Plato and Wittgenstein, philosophic enquiry is dialectical because it goes on between friends seeking truth. As such it has the tentative character, the lack of compulsion so characteristic of Wittgenstein's later philosophy, which in fact is often pursued by means of imaginary dialogues or conversations. (*Wittgenstein and Political Philosophy* (Chicago: Chicago University Press, 1978), 197.)

4. See Maurice Cranston, *Political Dialogues* (London: BBC, 1968).

5. Writing from the position of having completed my doctoral thesis, I think I may have an explanation for why the dialogue form in philosophy has all but died out—the task of combining philosophy and literature is an immensely difficult one for minds not as great as Plato's. I fear that my effort at resuscitating the dialogue form in philosophy may well have the unintended effect of deterring future upstarts from even attempting this task.

6. Benjamin Barber makes the same point in *The Conquest of Politics* (Princeton: Princeton University Press, 1988), ch. 5, esp. 'Scene 10: A Dialogue about the Affective Potential of Dialogue'.

Act I: A Communitarian Critique of Liberal Foundations

SCENE: *May, 1990.* La Coupole *café in Montparnasse, Paris. The Louis Armstrong/Duke Ellington duo 'Solitude' fades out. A dishevelled but potentially good-looking young man, named Philip Schwartzberg, is seated alone at a small square table. Next to him is a large, round table with the De la Patrie family—the mother a confident, distinguished-looking professional type, the father unable to suppress an air of reluctant resignation that suggests he regrets the passing of the time when he would have been the undisputed master of his family, and their twin daughters of 26. Both tables are illuminated.*

[*A tuxedoed waiter is taking Philip's order*]

PHILIP [*heavy Anglophone accent*] Une soupe à l'oignon gratinée, une choucroute garnie, et un café maintenant s'il-vous-plaît.

WAITER [*patronizing tone*] *Un café maintenant?* Monsieur, le café vient *après* le repas.

[*At this point, one of the twins at the De la Patrie table, named Anne, catches sight of Philip*]

PHILIP [*unsuccessfully searching for appropriate words*] Quoi? Mais, mais, *je veux* un café maintenant!

WAITER Monsieur, ça ne se fait pas.

PHILIP [*giving up*] Bon, d'accord, d'accord.

[*The waiter sneers, then leaves. Philip picks up the monthly newspaper* Le Monde diplomatique *to read an article with the headline 'Le Sionisme en crise'. Anne gets up, and walks over to Philip's table*]

ANNE Hello Philip!

[*Philip puts down his newspaper, looks up at Anne, and smiles, surprised*]

PHILIP Hello Anne! Fancy seeing you here . . . please sit down.

[*She takes up his offer*]

ANNE [*teasingly*] I can remember that, in our undergraduate days, you'd regularly seem to find a subject of dispute with old ladies working the cash register of the McGill cafeteria. Next time I see you, five or six years later, I find you arguing with a waiter in a Paris café! *Plus ça change, plus c'est pareil...*

PHILIP [*excitedly*] Did you see that! Am I not allowed to have a coffee *before* my meal? What kind of country is this?

ANNE They're very attached to their mealtime practices here.

PHILIP [*not appeased*] But who's serving who? Who's the paying customer? Why can't I have a coffee now if I want one now? Why should I be forced to have it his way?

ANNE [*patiently*] It should be noted that you spoke in French to the waiter. Did you feel forced to do that?

PHILIP No, but I had to communicate to him the information necessary for us to successfully enact our market transaction.

ANNE He may speak English . . . Why didn't you test that possibility by addressing him in English?

PHILIP Well, as you know, being in Paris, it would have been rude to do so.

ANNE Ah, interesting. So you think it's important to make an effort to adapt one's language to fit the linguistic context. So not everything is up to the discretion of the customer, then.

PHILIP No, of course not, I never said that. A visitor should respect the local culture.

ANNE Yes, but perhaps if you take your commitment to respecting the local culture seriously, this would imply both respect for the French language *and* respect for the mealtime practices of French culture.

PHILIP OK, enough sermonizing. As it turns out, I did it his way anyway.

ANNE I'm not sermonizing. I'm suggesting that if you had consistently applied the principle that underlies your practice of switching to French in a French context—namely, that one ought to adapt to the practices of the local culture to the extent that this is possible—you wouldn't have objected to the practice of having a coffee *after* one's meal.

PHILIP [*sighs*] OK, thank you for your help. Let's get off this topic—why don't you tell me what you've been up to.

ANNE Well, you probably know that I stayed on at McGill to do some graduate work—I mentioned that in a letter to which you never responded.

PHILIP Oh, I'm sorry. Believe it or not, you're still on a list of friends that I meant to get back to.

ANNE [*sardonically*] That's good to know. You obviously abide by the principle that it is best to maintain contact with one's academic colleagues. You never know who can come in handy when it comes to career opportunities.

PHILIP Please, Anne, we're not getting off to a very good start here. Let's try being nice to each other.

ANNE I agree. So why don't you tell me what you've been doing with yourself first. You went off to Oxford to do graduate work in philosophy . . .

PHILIP Yes, and for debating, but I've since found out that those pursuits are incompatible. One aims at truth, the other, victory.

ANNE The pursuit of truth sounds more challenging. How did you fare on that score?

PHILIP Not well. I've taken some time off to travel on the Continent.

ANNE [*pause*] You seem reluctant to tell me about your recent experiences.

PHILIP Suspect the worst, and you'll probably be right.

ANNE You haven't lost that droll side of yours, I notice. Self-deprecation was your forte, however sincere it may have been.

PHILIP It's sincere, believe me. I have a very low opinion of myself . . . Of course, it's also true that I have an even lower opinion of everyone else.

ANNE [*not amused*] I suggest we go on to something easier—why did you come to *La Coupole?*

PHILIP That, I can answer. Being in Paris, I was curious to see the café where Jean Paul Sartre and Simone de Beauvoir nourished what they called their essential love.

ANNE With all due respect, I hope you had a better reason for coming here. This notion of essential love must have been a Sartrian joke. You'll recall that Sartre, for whom the self was detachable from its social roles and statuses, from its history, hated essences, which he saw as crystallizations of bad faith. Rather, Sartre sought absolute, and ever-renewed, freedom.[1] Besides, even if you assumed that Sartre seriously maintained that necessary relationships are important, you could not, as the liberal you once were and may still be, accept his argument that both members of a necessary relationship should experience contingent loves too. After all, Sartre, by approaching women with the assumption 'I already have a necessary relationship, but if you don't mind being contingent for a while, I would like to sleep with you', violated the liberal dictum that individuals be treated as ends in themselves, deserving of respect.

PHILIP [*slightly taken aback*] Um, that 'liberal dictum' only applies to the way that a government should treat its citizens . . . Maybe you should tell me what you're doing here.

ANNE I came to *La Coupole* for a seemingly more prosaic reason than the one you offered—I like the food.

PHILIP I'm about to find out if I like the food, but I ordered a meal primarily to avoid the evil that afflicts such a large portion of humanity—going to bed with a stomach that's not pacified.

ANNE If you aim low, you've a greater likelihood of success.

PHILIP [*looking over at the De la Patrie table*] Tell me, Anne, why did you come here with your whole family?

ANNE [*lowers voice*] I had a grandmother in Paris, but she's dead . . .

PHILIP [interrupting] What?

ANNE [*raises voice, apparently surprised by Philip's lack of sensitivity*] I said she's dead. We came for the funeral.

PHILIP Oh, I'm sorry.

ANNE Well, it was inevitable. She led a good life . . . [*the lights illuminating the De la Patrie table are dimmed*] . . . But I do have something joyous to celebrate—I've just completed my doctoral thesis!

PHILIP Congratulations! Do you mind telling me about it, or have you had enough?

ANNE I'd be happy to talk about it. Not only have I not had enough, but I'm busy applying its implications in my own life, and in society at large . . . [*Philip looks upward, assuming an 'I wouldn't have asked that question if I knew what I was getting into' air*] . . . My thesis is entitled 'What Communitarianism Is'—what I've done, as the title suggests, is to lay bare the constitutive principles of communitarianism.

PHILIP Mmmh . . . it sounds like you took on quite a challenge. I've come across the term 'communitarianism' occasionally, but still am not at all clear as to what it is, other than a vague affirmation of the need for community.

ANNE Yes, well, there's a reason for that. One of the central debates in Anglo-American political theory during the 1980s has been between defenders of liberalism and its communitarian critics, but communitarians have so far failed to come up with even the outlines of a theory of their own[2]—until my thesis, that is. If I've succeeded in weaving together a coherent and appealing theory, drawing from the works of those who have been labelled 'communitarians', this would have been a most significant achievement, a great contribution to political theory.

PHILIP [*looks in vain for waiter with his* soupe à l'oignon; *resigns himself to pursuing the conversation*] Please refresh my memory. Who are these 'communitarians'?

ANNE Well, as I implied, there's no easy answer to that question. It is one of the peculiarities of the communitarian movement that its purported proponents have yet, as far as I know, to explicitly identify themselves in their written works with this movement—the communitarian label has been foisted upon them by others, usually critics.

PHILIP Interesting. A non-existing theory advocated by nobody.

ANNE Of course, there does exist a substantial corpus of distinctly 'communitarian' ideas in the works of those who have been labelled communitarians, and it is from this corpus of ideas that I drew my inspiration.

PHILIP So tell me, who exactly are the proponents of these 'communitarian' ideas?

ANNE Among contemporary thinkers, we have Charles Taylor, Michael Walzer, Michael Sandel, Alasdair MacIntyre, and others I can't think of at the moment.

PHILIP All men, I notice.

ANNE Yes, but perhaps only a woman could have focused on the positive as I have, shifting the debate from ontology to advocacy. Whereas the authors I named have been more successful at making use of communitarian ideas about the social constitution of the self to criticize liberal foundations, I articulated a communitarian moral vision, a stand in favour of community life most appropriate for the modern world . . .

PHILIP Perhaps you'd have done better to focus on the politics of the communitarian movement. What I do know about the communitarian movement is that it's often criticized for being insufficiently specific with respect to political proposals.[3]

ANNE Actually, I did draw some political consequences that flow from my communitarian moral vision. But we had better begin with the communitarian critique of liberal foundations, for this is the level at which the debate has been carried on thus far.

PHILIP [*not expecting to be convinced*] Tell me, then, what's wrong with liberal foundations?

ANNE The deepest problem, as I see it, is that liberal theory continues to pay homage to the enlightenment ideal of the autonomous subject who successfully extricates herself from the immediate entanglements of history and the characteristics and values that come with that entanglement.

PHILIP Are you thinking of Rawls's original position, the procedure he uses to develop his theory of justice?[4]

ANNE That is the most notorious contemporary application of this ideal. Rawls, as you know, asks us to imagine an individual behind what he calls a 'veil of ignorance', by which he means a self unencumbered by the particularities of history, circumstance, and conceptions of the good life for human beings to live.

PHILIP So what's the criticism?

ANNE To think of individuals with no knowledge about their particular situation in society—of selves as socially disembodied beings—makes no sense.

PHILIP [*irritated by Anne's smug dismissal*] What do you mean, *it makes no sense*? I read *A Theory of Justice*, and it makes perfect sense to me.

ANNE Of course, one can always *imagine* individuals as such. Wim Wenders, in his latest film *The Wings of Desire*, also imagines socially disembodied beings.

PHILIP Well, there you have it.

ANNE Perhaps not unexpectedly, however, the socially disembodied beings of Wenders' film seem distinctly German—angst-ridden, melancholic, dour, humourless, and so on. We know the type.[5]

PHILIP I could think of more sinister character traits that may apply to Germans. But in any case, I haven't seen that film, so let's get back to Rawls's original position.

ANNE There too. Where you see self-interested individuals engaged in strategic thinking to develop principles of justice that govern social co-operation, read the career-minded North-Eastern liberal with a guilty social conscience. He wants to devise a political scheme that grants to the marginalized sectors of society the same kinds of career opportunities he had.[6]

PHILIP [*testily*] Why don't you address Rawls's arguments, instead of speculating about his psychological motivation?

ANNE I'm not just speculating about his psychological motivation. I'm pointing out that even when socially disembodied beings are imagined, these tend to reflect the characteristics and values of the milieu in which they're imagined.

PHILIP [*his frustration not alleviated*] OK, fine. You still haven't said what's allegedly wrong with the original position.

ANNE Essentially, the problem is that to imagine individuals as socially disembodied beings is so far removed from people's intuitions that liberal theory can never get off the ground. Whether or not Rawls successfully derives his two principles of justice, actual individuals would only endorse these if they fit with their intuitions.[7]

PHILIP But Rawls doesn't say that we should abstract from *all* intuitions. In fact, he emphasizes in a subsequent article that what gives his principles of justice their force is that they fit with the intuitions of individuals who share a public tradition committing them to liberal democracy.[8]

ANNE That reformulation fails, I think, for the intuitions Rawls invokes are still too thin to give his theory sufficient force. Even if we grant the assumption that Rawls accurately captures the intuitions that citizens share as members of a liberal democratic polity, he doesn't explain why obligations that arise from the political sphere should have priority over other commitments.[9] Why, say, should I act from principles of justice worked out on the basis of my political intuitions instead of conforming to what I think I should do *qua* woman?

PHILIP I guess it depends on the context. Act like a woman if I kiss you, a Rawlsian if I vote for you.[10]

ANNE You missed my point. By excluding 'thick' intuitions about one's identity and sense of the good from the original position,[11] Rawls implicitly assumes that citizens would agree to give up what he calls 'private self-understandings' in the public sphere were there to be a conflict between one's 'private' commitments and one's obligations *qua* citizen. But Rawls gives us no reason for thinking that,[12] and moreover action which flows from intuitions about one's identity and sense of the good—in my case, what I would do *qua* woman, Catholic, member of the De la Patrie family, just to name a few of my 'private' commitments—would in all likelihood trump demands arising from intellectually agreed upon principles of justice.[13]

PHILIP My own view is that people acting from their class position poses a more serious problem for the actual implementation of Rawls's theory, but let's leave that for later—here comes that enforcer of French mealtime practices . . .

[*Waiter arrives with a* soupe à l'oignon gratinée, *which he serves to Philip*]

PHILIP [*reluctantly*] Merci.

[*Waiter frowns, then leaves the stage*]

PHILIP [*tastes soup*] Ahhh! Ahhhh! [*flings spoon back in bowl*]

ANNE Too hot, I gather. You should have postponed your urge to sample your soup.

PHILIP Thank you for your sympathy . . . Perhaps this is the proof that we're not socially disembodied beings—we are, at minimum, feeling selves.

ANNE We're much more than that. We are, first and mostly, social beings, embodied agents 'in the world' engaged in realizing a certain form of life.

PHILIP I don't understand . . .

ANNE Before I go on, I should note that we're moving on to an ontological question, a question concerning what factors you will invoke to account for social life. The communitarian idea is that 'society' is ultimate in the order of explanation—whether we like it or not, whether we know it or not, we're deeply bound up in the social world in which we happen to find ourselves.

PHILIP Oh, oh. Here it comes, the philosopher who tells you that you ought to subordinate your individuality to the good of the community.

ANNE No, no. I want to emphasize that an ontological thesis does not amount to advocating anything *per se*. A good ontological thesis can do no more than structure the field of possibilities in a more perspicuous way, helping to define the options which it is meaningful to support by advocacy.[14]

PHILIP [*makes another attempt at tasting the soup*] I don't quite grasp the relevance of what you're saying.

ANNE Well, I haven't quite finished with my critique of liberal foundations. If your justification for liberalism is that a liberal form of social organization facilitates a highly individualistic life-form, and my ontological thesis shows that a highly individualistic life-form is an impossibility, then you have to reconsider your justification for liberalism.

PHILIP I never said that the justification for liberalism is that it facilitates 'a highly individualistic life-form'. What does this mean, 'a highly individualistic life-form'?

ANNE I have in mind the idea of the self-sufficient subject who chooses a life-plan and then impinges her will on the world so as to realize that life-plan. This idea rests on the assumption that we can do what we do largely as a result of individual decisions about what to do, an erroneous assumption if there ever has been one . . .

PHILIP [*incredulous*] Are you denying that I'm the one who normally chooses what I do, when I do it, and how I do it?

ANNE Precisely. But let's not proceed too quickly, for the very obviousness of what I'm about to say makes it hard to grasp. I will point to 'the hidden hand of the community', if you will, the way that social practices guide most of what we do, most of the time, without our even noticing the fact. Specifically, I'll defend the thesis that 'the normal mode of existence is that of unreflectively acting in a way specified by the practices of one's social world.'[15]

PHILIP Please be more clear. What do you mean by 'the practices of one's social world'?

ANNE I'm referring to the everyday coping skills into which we've been socialized and which tell us what should be done in a given situation. Such practices—I'll call them 'social practices', since they're supplied by the social world in which we happen to find ourselves—include ways of sitting, standing, dressing, pronouncing, walking, greeting, playing sports, and more generally, encountering objects and people . . .

PHILIP [*interrupting*] So I've learned certain ways of sitting, standing, and so on, from my social world. So what?

ANNE I want to stress that social practices, these everyday coping skills which tell us what to do in a given situation, normally operate 'behind our backs', as it were—when acting in a way specified by social practices, we need not have plans and goals, let alone the long-range life-plans that, say, Rawls would suppose.

PHILIP I don't understand.

ANNE Take the following example—when riding a bicycle, you wouldn't think of yourself as a self-sufficient subject who has the experience of riding a bicycle and thereby causing the bicycle-riding; you just do what's appropriate as prescribed by the structure of the situation. The same is true, I venture, when you walk, dress, play games, and so on— you would normally just do what you have to do without having formulated any goals or made any choices. You let yourself be guided by the relevant social practices that you've learned, and that's that . . . [*short pause*] . . . We should try to impress on ourselves what a huge amount of our lives is spent in this state, and how little is spent in the deliberate, effortful, choosing subject mode.[16]

PHILIP So all these practices are supplied by one's social world, we learn them and act according to them, no questions asked. You make life sound easy.

ANNE For the most part, that's true. Did you ever ask yourself, 'why do I sometimes stand when I ride a bicycle?' You might well have done so, for there's a different way of doing this task in another community—Chinese people, more concerned with stability, almost never stand on their bicycles.[17]

PHILIP Interesting difference, but I was wondering about your premiss that we have easy access to practices which tell us what should be done in a given situation . . . Do such practices include ways of eating?

ANNE Yes. Eating, drinking—all comportment at mealtime. We learned what to do at mealtime—which utensils to use for what purpose, how far to sit from other people, when to look and speak to others, the whole structure of mealtime practices—and we usually do what needs to be done in a given situation, without thinking about it.

PHILIP [*struggling with a half-metre long cord of melted* gruyère] I wonder about that. There's no obvious way of eating this soup, for example.

ANNE I don't think that a French person would be having such a hard time of it. You haven't been brought up in a French culture, which helps to explain your current predicament.

PHILIP Even if I was French, I might be having this trouble—I've yet to master the table manners of my own culture.

ANNE Yes, well, I suppose you have individual differences in this respect . . . But there's a more pertinent response to your point about your not knowing how to eat *soupe à l'oignon gratinée*. This breakdown from the normal, everyday mode of existence forces you into a state where you have to think of yourself as a subject struggling with a certain object, having the experience of selecting the goal of eating *soupe à l'oignon* properly, formulating various ways of executing the goal, choosing from among those ways, and accepting responsibility for the outcome of your action. In other words, traditional intentionality is introduced at the point where there's a breakdown, where our ordinary way of coping with things is insufficient.[18] Of course, it's this 'breakdown' mode which we tend to notice, and which has therefore been studied in detail by many philosophers who have then gone on mistakenly to define all action as occasioned by processes of reflection.[19] Liberals have picked up this assumption, positing the idea of a self-sufficient subject who seeks to realize an autonomously arrived-at life-plan,[20] losing sight of the fact that critical reflection upon one's ends is nothing more than one possibility that arises when our ordinary way of coping with things is insufficient to get things done!

PHILIP I didn't know that my problems with onion soup could have such momentous implications . . . But in any case, let me address your argument. The liberal need not posit a self-sufficient subject standing over against an external world who always, or even mostly, impinges his will upon that world. You see, once you've granted the possibility of critical reflection upon one's ends, that's all that's needed . . .

ANNE [*interrupting*] Critical reflection, it should be pointed out, presupposes a taken-for-granted background that itself cannot be reflected upon. That you even noticed a breakdown from the normal mode of existence, and sought to make sense of the situation in a way that, say, a nineteenth-century Papua New Guinean couldn't have, presupposes some sort of background familiarity with the context within which the breakdown manifests itself.[21]

PHILIP [*raises voice*] Look, I've already accepted that a defence of liberalism doesn't require a decontextualized self who sets aside the whole kit and caboodle he's picked up since day one so as to create a world which is uniquely his. You see, the justification for a liberal politics concerned primarily with securing the conditions for individuals to lead autonomous lives rests on the possibility and desirability of *normative* self-determination,[22] not complete construction of one's identity from scratch. By 'normative self-determination', I mean the exercise of the capacity to choose one's conception of the good life, the importance of making one's own choices with respect to things of *value* . . . [*short pause*] . . . And what you said about certain communal practices often, or even mostly, guiding our behaviour without our being aware of this fact doesn't show why those practices ought to be valued, or reflectively endorsed in 'non-ordinary moments of existence', much less why the government ought somehow to promote these practices . . .

ANNE You're hinting at a fact/value distinction, what is and what ought to be, and, following Hume, assuming that the latter cannot be derived from the former. However, I don't think that this is an accurate way to dichotomize the social practices which ordinarily guide our behaviour, for social practices contain both elements.[23] Social practices, that is, have standards of correctness built into them—one can distinguish between a right and a wrong way of following social practices . . . Let's go back to eating practices. It's descriptively true that we've learned how to use forks, knives, and so on, but such practices are also norm-governed—we follow norms that tell us how these eating practices ought to be carried out. Of course, norms governing practices are frequently violated, as we saw with your inability to eat *soupe à l'oignon* in the proper way, but . . .

PHILIP [*interrupting*] Not again with that *oignon* soup! Next time I see you, I'll pay more attention to my table manners.

ANNE I was about to say—although norms are frequently violated, there's a tendency to conform to these norms, like it or not. This comes out most clearly when we look at how language works, the way that we're all engaged in the subtle task of ensuring conformity to the norms of pronunciation and grammar that we've learned. If I pronounce a word or name incorrectly, say, others will pronounce the word correctly with a light stress on what I've mispronounced and often I'll correct myself without even noticing.[24]

PHILIP If someone points to what he thinks is a mistake of mine on the grounds that what I do doesn't conform to what the community does, I'll try to evaluate his claim on its own merits, rather than 'automatically' conforming to the community's practices.

ANNE I'm not sure what you mean by 'evaluating a claim on its own merits'. If I try to explain some of my community's practices to someone— why we pronounce words the way we do, why we prefer sitting on chairs instead of the floor, why we eat with knives and forks whereas another community uses chopsticks, and so on—I just say 'this is what we do.' Once a practice and its standards of correctness have been explained by what we in fact do, no more basic explanation is possible. Giving grounds must come to an end somewhere.[25]

PHILIP [*pause*] Let me try to summarize your argument. We learn certain norm-governed practices from the social world in which we happen to find ourselves, we spend most of our time blindly following these practices, and if we somehow fail to conform to those practices, we have a moral obligation to conform to those practices because community agreement is the final source of justification for those practices.

ANNE [*raises voice*] Oh no! When I speak of social practices with their own standards of correctness built into them, I'm not referring to morality. Most practices—eating, pronouncing, dressing, and distance-standing practices, for example—have nothing to do with moral imperatives.

PHILIP Well, in that case, you're completely missing the point of what I'm saying. You see, what justifies a liberal form of social organization isn't that human activity and social resources will be directed towards the overriding goal of exercising the capacity to choose trivial things like table manners or pronunciation norms; rather, it's the protection and the cultivation of the human capacity to choose *what is worth* doing, achieving, or being. It may well be, then, that our behaviour is ordinarily guided by trivial norm-governed practices whose ultimate justification rests on communal agreement; but that doesn't show why we shouldn't have the rights, powers, and opportunities to develop and exercise our capacity to freely determine our own conception of the good, our own conception of a life worth pursuing.[26]

ANNE Let me ask you something, Philip—what's your conception of the good life?

PHILIP [*nervous laughter*] Well . . . [*pause*] . . . good food, fine wine, scintillating conversation, and divine sex as an afterthought.

ANNE You joke around, but there was a serious point to that question. The term 'conception of the good life' lacks substance; it's not a coincidence that liberal theorists are hard pressed to offer compelling examples of what they mean by that term. Very few of us think of ourselves as individuals with our own, autonomously arrived at conception of the good life. As a matter of fact, I don't know of anyone who has autonomously developed their own theory of how to live well, and then chosen between alternatives in a manner completely consistent with that life-plan until it has been realized.[27]

PHILIP Nobody's perfect, as they say.

ANNE You're being overly flippant, once again. The problem with your ideal of an autonomous self who determines her own private conception of the good is that one's social world provides more than, as you said, 'trivial things like table manners and pronunciation norms'; it also provides some sort of orientation in *moral* space, if you will. That is, before the issue of 'choosing one's conception of the good' even arises, we already have a learned sense of the good, a framework which defines the shape of lives worth leading.[28] But we'll have to wait a little while before I can pursue this point . . .

[*Waiter arrives*]

WAITER [*unable to refrain from directing a disapproving glance at Philip's untidy* soupe à l'oignon gratinée *remnants*] C'est fini?

PHILIP [*timidly*] Oui, monsieur.

[*Waiter clears away the soup bowl, and leaves the stage*]

PHILIP I'm sorry—I realize now that I should have offered you some of my soup.

ANNE That's OK—while it's true that I wanted to sample your *soupe à l'oignon gratinée*, this goal was nothing more than a *de facto* commitment to a specific desire, having no more claim on me now that I've ceased desiring it.

PHILIP But you ceased desiring my soup because I finished it—so I'm to blame for your unrealized goal.

ANNE That's true, but I was trying to apply a distinction I invoke in my thesis between what's good merely in the sense of satisfying an existing preference and higher goods crucial to one's self-understanding as a healthy, moral human being.

PHILIP Please elaborate.

ANNE OK. I was saying before that one's social world supplies more than trivial norm-governed practices—it also sets the authoritative moral horizons within which we determine, as you said, 'what's worth doing, achieving, or being'. We cannot make sense of our moral experience unless we situate ourselves within this 'given' moral space . . .

PHILIP [*interrupting*] What do you mean by 'the moral'?

ANNE That's what I was getting to. Moral issues involve what Charles Taylor calls 'strong evaluation', by which he means discriminations of right and wrong, better or worse, higher or lower, discriminations which are not rendered valid by our desires, inclinations, or choices, but rather stand independent of them and offer standards by which they can be judged.[29] Strongly evaluated goods are those higher goods which we ought to acknowledge, regardless of our *de facto* preferences; they command authority irrespective of the particular life we happen to be leading . . . Now we can see the difference between my *de facto* commitment to the specific desire of wanting to taste your *soupe à l'oignon* and, say, a commitment to the good of my family. Only the latter stands independent of my actual tastes and desires, offering a standard according to which the life I'm living can be evaluated—I can be condemned, say, for failing to take care of my mother if she suddenly fell ill in my presence; it would be morally perverse of me to pursue my life as if nothing had happened.

PHILIP [*alarmed*] Oh my God! You just reminded me that I have to call my mother to let her know I'm in Paris.

ANNE So much for leading an autonomous life.

PHILIP I can still lead an autonomous life. But my mother somehow thinks she has control over me if she knows where I am.

ANNE I'll wait if you want to phone her.

PHILIP The problem here is the fancy phone card system, which I don't understand.

ANNE Of course, by 'understand' you're not referring to something which goes on inside your head, a mental process of some sort; one should think of understanding and knowing as capacities, as something we have a practical ability to do . . .

PHILIP [*interrupting*] Fine, fine, I haven't been taught the everyday coping skill which specifies how to use phone cards. Are you satisfied?

ANNE Phone cards are very easy to use. You just buy one at a 'tabac', and follow the instructions on the phone.

PHILIP Don't overestimate my technical competence. I even have trouble with simple things like hammers.

ANNE [*smiles*] I'll go with you, if you like.

PHILIP No hurry. If I'm too prompt, a bad precedent will have been set.

ANNE [*pause*] Getting back to what I was saying, higher, strongly evaluated goods are those that we should feel committed to, those that generate moral obligations on us, like it or not. It is important to emphasize that these higher goods are not somehow invented by individuals, but rather they're to be seen as located within the social world which happens to have provided one's framework of the higher and the lower. It's a moral orientation which is learned by virtue of having been socialized in a particular time and place, not easily justified to others who happen to have picked up a different moral orientation.

PHILIP You mentioned caring for an ill mother. Don't you think that moral obligation can be justified to anyone?

ANNE No, no. This moral orientation rests on contingent facts about how things work in the social world in which we happen to find ourselves; things could have been different elsewhere, for example, feudal Japan where elderly sick women were expected to direct themselves from the household to the nearest mountain peak so as to end their days. Of course, awareness of this contingency doesn't render these moral obligations any less pressing—you ought to care for your ill mother irrespective of what people were doing in feudal Japan. Nor does this contingency render our moral obligations arbitrary or whimsical in their specification[30]—in fact, they make perfect sense to anyone sharing a certain way of life.

PHILIP [*pause*] You have this tendency of making everything sound so straightforward. It may well be that we pick up a certain moral orientation from our social world, but this doesn't make it any easier when it comes to deciding how to lead a good life. I, for one, encounter all sorts of difficulties when it comes to doing good, not the least of which is my mother's interpretation of the obligations that I owe her.

ANNE If you encounter certain difficulties, if things go wrong, so to speak, you might well have to step back from your immediate preferences, reflect upon which goods should be regarded as more worthwhile, more important, more admirable than others, and then change your life accordingly.

PHILIP Now hold on a minute. Before you were saying that the normal mode is that of unreflectively doing what needs to be done, and now you're suggesting that higher goods need to be reflectively endorsed. I hope you've dealt with this conflict in your thesis.

ANNE There's no conflict. I said that reflection might come into play if there's a breakdown of some sort—if your ordinary way of coping with things proves to be insufficient, your identity might well have to be remoulded in terms of a framework of higher goods located within the social habitat to which you belong. Moreover, I never suggested that higher goods *need* to be reflectively endorsed—if I 'implicitly' commit myself to the good of my family, 'automatically' let myself be guided by the obligations which arise from that commitment, such as caring for my ill mother, can I really be condemned on the grounds that I never paused to reflectively endorse that commitment?[31] . . . [*short pause*] . . . In any case, let me summarize where we've come thus far so as to avoid further confusion. I developed the idea that the normal mode of existence is that of unreflectively acting in a way specified by the practices of one's social world, an idea which shows the impossibility of leading a life largely according to a self-selected life-plan. Then, I suggested that one's social world also provides a certain moral orientation, an unchosen framework of the higher and the lower; if I'm right with respect to this latter claim, I've demonstrated that the liberal ideal of a self who freely invents her own moral outlook,[32] or private conception of the good, cannot do any sort of justice to our actual moral experience.

PHILIP [*pause*] Actually, you may well be right that one's social world provides a framework of the higher and the lower, that we cannot coherently regard our moral outlook as freely invented. Things have worth for us in so far as they are granted significance by one's culture, in so far as they fit into a pattern of activities which is recognized by those sharing a certain form of life as a way of leading a good life. That one's social world provides the range of things worth doing, achieving, or being *does not*, however, undermine the liberal emphasis on autonomy, for there's still substantial room for individual choice from within this set. The best life is still the one where the individual *chooses* what is worth doing, achieving, or being, though it may be that this choice has to be made from within a certain framework which is itself unchosen.[33]

ANNE Just one little thing before you go on. What's so important about choice?

PHILIP [*raises voice*] Don't you think it's important to live a life which embodies one's own normative will and judgement, as opposed to being forced into leading someone else's conception of the good life?

ANNE You're drawing upon a contrast between choice and force, as though an action is either chosen or forced. But it just doesn't follow that if an action is unchosen, it's forced. As I've already said, what one does is normally not chosen, if by that we mean entertaining various possibilities and deciding among them, but neither is it forced—we more often than not simply do what needs to be done in a given situation, and it's only if there's a disturbance of some sort that jolts us out of the normal, everyday mode of existence that we might have to think of ourselves as conscious subjects deciding between various ways of pursuing some goal.

PHILIP You're beginning to sound most repetitive. And I still have trouble believing that you don't see the importance of choice. Ask yourself, in what respect do you value another person's way of life? Respect is typically based on the presupposition that their way of life embodies their own practical judgement and choice of what's worth doing. Where that's not true, look what happens—if we believe that another person's way of life is no embodiment of their moral powers at all, that it doesn't embody their own moral choice and individuality, such a person would have lost that minimal respect which we normally grant to another's way of life.[34] The unexamined life is an unworthy life, to paraphrase a well-known thinker . . .

ANNE I think it's the height of arrogance to say that an unexamined life is an unworthy life, that we should withdraw our respect from those who haven't exercised their normative powers of self-determination. Take my grandmother. She was a simple lady, never, as far as I know, reflecting upon 'the things worth doing, achieving, or being'—she simply did what she had to do, which for her involved leading a life guided by the unquestioned authority of the Catholic Church. In practice, this meant helping newly arrived Vietnamese refugees settle in Paris, giving away her possessions to those in great need, among other altruistic acts—everyone liked her, actually. Do you think that her way of life deserves any less respect than that of someone who has exercised their normative powers of self-determination? It may well be that she didn't decide for herself the types of things worth doing, achieving, or being, but her unexamined life was still a worthy life, and deserving of respect, I believe . . .

PHILIP It would be in bad taste to criticize your dead grandmother's way of life, so I won't pursue this point. I want to get you to admit, though, that there are at least some cases where it's crucial to exercise one's normative powers of self-determination. Think of the choice between occupations—surely it's important to choose a line of work one thinks worthy of pursuit, and to accept responsibility for that choice. Unless, that is, you don't find anything wrong with a society where individuals are forced into certain occupations by a state which distributes work according to certain government officials' conception of the good . . .

ANNE You said before that I'm beginning to sound repetitive, but you persist in drawing that contrast between choice and force, as though those were the only alternatives. There are reasons for doing work, reasons that most of us regard as legitimate, that involve neither choice in any sense that's relevant nor state coercion. I do what I do because that's what my mother did or that's what I was always interested in or I slipped into that field by accident and found out I liked it there. Moreover, I'm still to be held responsible for what I do even if my line of work was unchosen.[35] Do you think my thesis supervisor would accept as an excuse for a lousy thesis that I entered graduate studies mainly because of my mother's support and positive example?

PHILIP He might, if he wants to spare your feelings.

ANNE [*coldly*] My supervisor is a 'she'.

PHILIP Sorry . . . [*pause*] . . . I have to admit I'm not convinced. I still think that it's better to choose important matters in one's life and to accept responsibility for those choices, than to 'slip into things' and act in a largely unreflective manner. Moreover, I think that the ideal of normative self-determination captures our deepest understanding of ourselves as members of democratic societies in the late twentieth century,[36] and that common appreciation of the importance of exercising the capacity to choose for oneself a conception of the good life justifies a structure of society within which people are given the resources to choose what's important to them . . .

ANNE If I can't convince you to give up this ideal, you have to at least recognize that there are competing ideals of personhood in 'liberal-democratic societies', and that should your conception of the person be regarded as the final justification for the way society ought to be structured, this might have intolerable consequences for those who do not make the exercise of the capacity to choose things of worth a supreme value.

PHILIP Do you have in mind, as an example of someone who holds a 'competing ideal of personhood', your ex-grandmother, that 'simple lady' who led her life 'guided by the unquestioned authority of the Catholic church'?

ANNE Yes, but we can discuss Mother Teresa if you're not convinced by the example of my grandmother. Mother Teresa associates herself with God's love for human beings, which she sees as having the power to heal the divisions among humans and take them beyond what they usually recognize as the limits to their love for one another. Her outlook understands human moral transformation in terms of images of healing, such as one sees in the New Testament narratives,[37] as opposed to your ideal that makes the exercise of the capacity to choose things of worth a supreme value.

PHILIP Actually, there's no conflict. I said that it's important to exercise the capacity to choose for oneself things of worth, but the particular conception of the good people choose is inessential. So long as Mother Teresa chose her own conception of the good, it . . .

ANNE [*interrupting*] Mother Teresa didn't *choose* her way of life.

PHILIP [*sighs*] I should have guessed. She 'slipped into it', without thinking about it.

ANNE Not that either. As a young nun, Mother Teresa had taught wealthy children, but she left to work and live, as we know, among the slum dwellers of Calcutta. However, she has always insisted that the choice to move was God's, not her own. She simply received an order from God and obeyed[38] . . . [*short pause*] . . . Is it plausible, let me ask you, to claim that Mother Teresa isn't leading a good life because she herself didn't choose her own conception of a worthy life? Is Mother Teresa leading a worse life than, say, a reflective Harvard graduate who considers his career options, assesses these against a background of preferred outcomes and existing values, and decides to be an investment banker instead of a corporate lawyer?

PHILIP I suppose you want me to answer 'no'.

ANNE Yes, that's right. And once you grant the possibility that there are ideals of personhood besides the ideal of normative self-determination—in this case, the ideal of Judaeo-Christian benevolence that comes to mind when we think of Mother Teresa's life . . .

PHILIP [*interrupting*] Not Judaeo-Christian. I'm Jewish, and Mother Teresa wasn't a role model of mine when I grew up.

ANNE Fine, let's call it 'Christian benevolence', an ideal grounded in God's love for human beings. This ideal, I believe, already informs a whole spectrum of judgements in our society concerning the justice of using public funds to help the needy, shelter the homeless, feed the hungry, provide health care for the infirm,[39] and so on, and it seems arbitrary to favour the ideal of normative self-determination as a final justification for our society's political discourse, argument, and judgement about justice where the two ideals might lead to conflicting stances. Think of the euthanasia issue—adherents of the ideal of normative self-determination tend to think that mature and mentally competent patients should be given control over the dying process, and that they should be legally permitted to request lethal drugs from a co-operating physician, whereas the Christian community rejects an ethic that gives the individual unlimited control over her own life—God has given us life as a trust to be lived out in a fallen world with its pain and suffering, and no one can ever claim the moral right to be killed even if being killed is the only way to avoid a painful dying process . . .[40]

PHILIP Before you go on, can you wait until I return from a little trip to the WC?

ANNE OK, but let me briefly summarize where we've come since we moved on to 'ontology', so that you don't forget what we've been talking about. I began with the assumption that we are, first and mostly, embodied agents 'in the world' engaged in realizing a certain form of life. But I emphasized that the stand one takes on the ontological level does not force one into adopting a certain moral stance; a good ontological thesis can, at best, clear the ground to lay bare the options which it is meaningful to support, or, put negatively, it can show which options it is not meaningful to support. It's for the latter reason that I developed Heidegger's idea that the usual mode of existence is that of unreflectively acting in, as he would say, a world of 'ready-to-hand equipment', and that even meaningful reflection in a state of breakdown presupposes some sort of familiarity with the context within which the breakdown manifests itself—to show the impossibility of leading a life largely according to a self-selected life-plan . . .

PHILIP [*interrupting*] Excuse me, excuse me, did I hear 'Heidegger'?

ANNE Yes. Most of what I was saying while you were eating your *soupe à l'oignon gratinée* was taken from part I of Heidegger's *Being and Time*.

PHILIP [*raises voice, tone of accusation*] Heidegger the Nazi?!⁴¹

ANNE Yes, well, he obviously had a political blind spot.

PHILIP Some blind spot!

ANNE We have to separate his views about the social embeddedness of the self from his politics. *Being and Time* can be read fruitfully, whatever Heidegger's political views may have been, and besides, it was written before the rise to power of the Nazis.

PHILIP So was *Mein Kampf*!⁴²

ANNE [*feeling uncomfortable*] Yes, that's true. More important is that *Being and Time* can be read fruitfully whatever Heidegger's actual political views may have been.

PHILIP So you think we should accept what Heidegger says about the social embeddedness of the self, reserving judgement on his politics?

ANNE Of course I think he was misguided about politics, as you do.⁴³ But, more importantly, I invoked Heidegger principally for critical purposes, i.e. to criticize those justifications for a liberal form of social organization which rest on the ideal of certain highly individualistic life-forms, so you can't attack me for the moral stand I wish to take, which I haven't even begun talking about yet.

PHILIP Before you begin something new, let me just . . . [*stands up*]

ANNE I'll finish my summary. After Heidegger, I went on to Charles Taylor's idea that we live in a moral space mapped by strong evaluations, that one's social world provides an unchosen framework which defines the shape of lives worth leading, this time to criticize the ideal of the self who freely invents her own moral outlook. Finally, to argue against your assertion that the ideal of the individual who exercises her powers of normative self-determination from within an unchosen framework constitutes the deepest value underlying political action in liberal-democratic societies, I pointed to a widely shared, firmly rooted ideal which holds life sacred, and I said that privileging your ideal of normative self-determination might lead to intolerable consequences for those of us who believe that a deliberate act designed to cause a patient's death can never be justified, even when suicide has been chosen as a means of escape from severe suffering.

PHILIP Finished?

ANNE Yes. I'm done with my critique of liberal foundations.

[*Philip runs towards the 'toilettes' sign on the right-hand side of the stage. Lights dim*]

Notes

1. The popularity of Sartre's ideas in post-World War II France can be largely explained by a collective desire of the ashamed post-war French to forget the past and make a fresh start—see Ronald Hayman, *Writing against: A Biography of Sartre* (London: Weidenfeld and Nicolson, 1986), 224–5.

2. Susan Moller Okin also makes this point in her article, 'Humanist Liberalism', in Nancy Rosenblum, ed., *Liberalism and the Moral Life* (Cambridge, Mass.: Harvard University Press, 1989), 46.

3. Ian Shapiro advances a criticism of this sort:

   [Communitarians] should shift [the communitarian/liberal debate] to a lower level of abstraction and seek to supply substantive content to the various communitarian proposals they advocate. They should consider how these are to be implemented in the capitalist economies of the late twentieth century, with their powerfully entrenched centralized bureaucratic states, and their seemingly inevitable participation in an ever more mutually interdependent international political and economic order. (*The Evolution of Rights in Liberal Theory* (Cambridge: Cambridge University Press, 1986), 297.)

   See Will Kymlicka, *Liberalism, Community and Culture* (Oxford: Clarendon Press, 1989), 99 n. 9, for references to other criticisms of the lack of political specifics in 'communitarian' writings. Liberal 'political' thinkers, however, have also been accused of eschewing political specifics. Rawls, for example, is accused by Benjamin Barber of remaining 'a long way from genuine politics' (see his *The Conquest of Politics* (Princeton: Princeton University Press, 1989), ch. 3, esp. 89–90) and by John Wallach of being unable 'to fit our political world' (see his article 'Liberals, Communitarians and the Tasks of Political Theory', *Political Theory* (Nov. 1987), 589).

4. See John Rawls, *A Theory of Justice* (Cambridge, Mass.: The Belknap Press of Harvard University Press, 1971), ch. 3.

5. Interestingly, what had been a black and white film changed to colour at the point that the socially disembodied protagonist chose to 'enter' German society.

6. In the same vein, Michael Walzer argues that 'the pre-original [position] idea of a career goes a long way toward explaining Rawlsian outcomes' ('A Critique of Philosophical Conversation', *Philosophical Forum* (Fall–Winter 1989–90), 194).

7. Michael Sandel first developed the argument that Rawls must admit 'thick intuitions' about identity and the good into the original position if his principles of justice are to be recognized as acceptable ones by the citizens to whom they are to apply (see his book *Liberalism and the Limits of Justice* (Cambridge: Cambridge University Press, 1981), esp. ch. 2; see also Charles Taylor, *Sources of the Self: The Making of the Modern Identity* (Cambridge: Cambridge University Press, 1989), 88–9).

8. Schwartzberg is referring to Rawls's article 'Kantian Constructivism in Moral Theory', *Journal of Philosophy* (Sept. 1980).

9. Stephen Mulhall makes a similar point:

> In order to ignore a critique which thinks of itself as metaphysical i.e. as relating to what it is to be a person per se, the liberal theorist claims to be relying *only* upon a view that citizens take of themselves as members of the political community; but if this contention were in fact correct, the liberal theorist would have no grounds for supporting the enforcement of claims which may be exacted from a person in virtue of his membership of one community (the political one) against any conflicting claims which may be exacted from that person in virtue of his membership of other communities (e.g. his commitments as a miner, a socialist, a Black American). For why should this one community's demands be given priority? ('The Theoretical Foundations of Liberalism', *European Journal of Sociology* 28: 2 (1987), 273; his emphasis.)

10. Rawls, it should be noted, means more than what Schwartzberg's reply strictly implies—citizens at large, he urges, and not merely political legislators, should affirm and act from the same first principles of justice in their everyday lives: see his article, 'The Priority of Right and Ideas of the Good', *Philosophy and Public Affairs* (Fall 1988), 269.

11. Rawls emphasizes that reliance upon 'political' intuitions does not presuppose a commitment to any comprehensive religious, philosophical, or moral doctrine in 'Justice as Fairness: Political not Metaphysical', *Philosophy and Public Affairs* (Summer 1985), sect. 1, a distinction that he reaffirms in his more recent article, 'The Priority of Right and Ideas of the Good', 252–3.

12. Will Kymlicka makes a similar point in his book *Liberalism, Community and Culture* (Oxford: Clarendon Press, 1989), 58.

13. One way out of this dilemma would be to argue that (1) Rawls in fact relies upon a (coherent) theory of the person and an account of the good, *malgré lui*, and (2) this 'latent' theory of the person and account of the good constitutes the core (deepest) value underlying political action and political institutions in liberal-democratic societies.

Gerald Doppelt accepts (1) but denies (2) in the following two articles: 'Is Rawls' Kantian Liberalism Coherent and Defensible?', *Ethics*, 99 (July 1989), 815–51 and 'Rawls' Kantian Ideal and the Viability of Modern Liberalism', *Inquiry* (Dec. 1988), 413–49. Specifically, Doppelt argues that Rawlsian liberalism is best understood and defended on the basis of a Kantian ideal of the person as a rational agent capable of normative self-determination, and that while the Kantian ideal is widely shared in democratic societies so are several other firmly rooted conflicting ideals such as competitive individualism, patriarchal conservatism, and Judaeo-Christian benevolence (George Sher makes a similar point in criticizing the claim that most Americans share a morality whose deepest value is rational autonomy in his article 'Educating Citizens' (a review of Amy Gutmann's book *Democratic Education*), *Philosophy and Public Affairs* (Winter 1989), 79), which deliberators in the original position would be unable to choose between.

Will Kymlicka accepts (1) and (perhaps) assumes (2) in his articles 'Rawls on Teleology and Deontology', *Philosophy and Public Affairs* (Summer 1988), 173–90, and 'Liberalism and Communitarianism', *Canadian Journal of Philosophy*, 18 (1988), 181–203, and in his book *Liberalism, Community and Culture*, esp. ch. 3. Specifically, Kymlicka argues that Rawls's theory of justice in fact rests on a conception of the human being and a particular view of the good life, namely, that one can and should understand and evaluate one's current ends; however, Kymlicka does not explicitly argue in favour of (2), a necessary argument if conflicting ideals are to be ruled out of the original position (i.e. if Rawls's 'Kantian ideal' does not constitute the deepest value underlying political action and political institutions in liberal-democratic societies, other ideals enter in the original position and the original position loses its normative force and rationale as a framework for resolving the basic conflicts concerning social justice).

14. Charles Taylor distinguishes between 'ontological issues' and 'advocacy issues' in his article 'Cross-Purposes: The Liberal–Communitarian Debate' (in Nancy Rosenblum, ed., *Liberalism and the Moral Life* (Cambridge, Mass.: Harvard University Press, 1989), 160–82). That these two have been conflated by participants in the 'liberal–communitarian debate', he argues, has been the source of great confusion, for although the stand one takes on the ontological level can be part of the essential background of the view one advocates, the

two issues are distinct in the sense that taking a position on one does not force your hand on the other (see Patrick Neal and David Paris's article 'Liberalism and the Communitarian Critique: A Guide for the Perplexed', *Canadian Journal of Political Science* (Sept. 1990), 428–9, for a similar point). In fact,

> a cursory look at the gamut of actual philosophical positions shows [that] either stand on the atomism/holism debate [i.e. the 'ontological' debate between 'methodological individualists' who believe that social life can be accounted for in terms of the properties of individuals and 'holists' who point to the social embedding of human agents] can be combined with either stand on the individualist–collectivist question [i.e. the 'moral' debate between those who give primacy to individual rights and freedom and those who give higher priority to community life or the good of collectivities]. There are not only atomist individualists (Nozick) and holist collectivists (Marx), but also holist individualists, like Humboldt—and even atomist collectivists, as in the nightmare, programmed utopia of B. F. Skinner, 'beyond freedom and dignity'. (p. 163)

In the context of Taylor's distinction, De la Patrie should be viewed as a holist (see esp. Act I) collectivist (see esp. Acts III to V) for whom her 'ontological stance' forms the background of the view she advocates.

15. De la Patrie's discussion of this question was greatly influenced, or so I'm told, by Martin Heidegger's *Being and Time*, trans. J. Macquarrie and E. Robinson (New York: Harper and Row, 1962), Hubert Dreyfus's book *Being-in-the-World: A Commentary on Heidegger's Being and Time, Division 1* (Cambridge, Mass.: MIT Press, 1991), John Richardson's book *Existential Epistemology: A Heideggerian Critique of the Cartesian Project* (Oxford: Clarendon Press, 1986), and an informal seminar on *Being and Time* given by Charles Taylor at McGill University, Fall 1988.

16. For a similar point, see Dreyfus, *Being-in-the-World*, 67.

17. See David Bonavia, *The Chinese* (London: Penguin Books, 1989), ch. 4, for other Chinese practices that non-Chinese people may find unusual.

18. Heidegger expresses the idea that traditional intentionality (understood as action which comes about in response to consciously formulated mental states—goals, purposes, choices, etc.—as opposed to intentionality understood as the ability to describe one's actions in retrospect) is introduced at the point where something goes wrong with everyday, successful, on-going coping in the following way:

> Being-in-the-world, according to our interpretation hitherto, amounts to a non-thematic circumspective absorption in references or assignments constitutive for the readiness-to-hand of equipments . . . In this familiarity Dasein can lose itself in what it encounters within the world and be

fascinated with it . . . The presence-at-hand of entities is thrust to the fore by the possible breaks in that referential totality in which circumspection 'operates'. (*Being and Time*, 107.)

19. For a similar point, see Dreyfus, *Being-in-the-World*, 67.

20. No liberal, it should be noted, has explicitly 'picked up this assumption', but the relationship between the liberal emphasis on autonomy and De la Patrie's point about 'traditional intentionality' would seem to be the following—a necessary condition of (mostly, always) 'leading one's life from the inside', or (mostly, always) realizing in the world by means of action one's own life-plan, is that action can (mostly, always) be brought about as a result of consciously formulated, reflected-upon mental states (goals, purposes, choices, etc.); De la Patrie argues, following Heidegger, that the latter is an impossibility.

21. Heidegger expresses the idea that one necessarily stays involved in a certain context and that meaningful reflection (understanding, interpretation, etc.) takes place against this (largely background) context, in the following way:

> Being-in is not a 'property' which Dasein [i.e. a way of being concerned with its own Being] sometimes has and sometimes does not have, and *without* which it could be just as well as it could with it. It is not the case that man 'is' and then has, by way of an extra, a relationship-of-Being towards the 'world'—a world with which he provides himself occasionally. Dasein is never 'proximally' an entity which is, so to speak, free from Being-in, but which sometimes has the inclination to take up a 'relationship' towards the world. Taking up relationships towards the world is possible only *because* Dasein, as Being-in-the-world, is as it is. This stage of Being does not arise just because some other entity is present-at-hand outside of Dasein and meets up with it. Such an entity can 'meet up with' Dasein only in so far as it can, of its own accord, show itself within a world. (*Being and Time*, 84; Heidegger's italics.)

> This everyday way in which things have been interpreted is one which Dasein has grown in the first instance, with never a possibility of extrication. In it, out of it, and against it, all genuine understanding, interpreting and communicating, all rediscovery and appropriating anew, are performed. In no case is a Dasein, untouched and unseduced by this way in which things have been interpreted, set before the open country of a 'world-in-itself' so that it just beholds what it encounters. (*Being and Time*, 213.)

22. In the same vein, Gerald Doppelt argues that 'Rawls' emphasis on a Kantian foundation for his theory of justice is most plausibly interpreted as affirming a conception of value—the supreme value of normative self-determination of persons in political and social life' ('Is Rawls' Kantian Liberalism Coherent

and Defensible?', 821), normative self-determination being defined as the maximal possible development of one's (Kantian) moral powers. These moral powers are '(1) the power of a person to shape, pursue, and revise his or her own conception of the good life and (2) his or her power to recognize and respect the exercise of this same power of self-determination on the part of other persons' (ibid. 820). It will be noted that Schwartzberg's defence of liberal foundations has thus moved on to the first part of the possible response to De la Patrie's critique of the original position suggested in endnote 13.

23. For a clear exposition of a Wittgensteinian approach which shows that the fact/value distinction is not an accurate way of dichotomizing either our utterances or the world on the grounds that 'in reality, each contains a rich plurality of elements among which facts and values are only two', see Hanna Pitkin, *Wittgenstein and Justice* (Berkeley, Calif.: University of California Press, 1972), 219.

24. For a similar point, see Dreyfus, *Being-in-the-World*, 152.

25. Wittgenstein developed the idea that rule- (norm-) governed practices of the community are their own justification, that there is no external justification or grounding for our practices. As he puts it in *On Certainty*: 'Giving grounds [must] come to an end sometime. But the end is not an ungrounded presupposition: it is an ungrounded way of action' ((New York: Harper and Row, 1969), para. 102; see also para. 204). For both Heidegger and Wittgenstein, explanation and justification of a community's way of life come to an end in an ungrounded way of action, i.e. 'at the bottom' lies not shared agreement in beliefs but rather shared agreement in our everyday practices (see Dreyfus, *Being-in-the-World*, 155; see also David Bloor, *Wittgenstein: A Social Theory of Knowledge* (London: MacMillan, 1983), 162).

26. Some thinkers of a liberal persuasion (e.g. Kant), it should be noted, value the exercise of the capacity for choice as an end in itself, whereas other liberals (e.g. Mill) value the exercise of the capacity for choice as a precondition for certain states of affairs which arise as a consequence of its exercise—see Kymlicka, *Liberalism, Community and Culture*, 48–50, and his *Contemporary Political Philosophy* (Oxford: Clarendon Press, 1990), 208–10.

27. Another possibility consistent with Schwartzberg's injunction that we ought to exercise the capacity to choose our conception of the good life is that one's conception of the good life be applied *retrospectively* as a criterion to evaluate past actions. Josef K., the unlucky protagonist of Franz Kafka's novel *The Trial* (trans. D. Scott and C. Waller (London: Picador Classics, 1977)) seems to have this idea in mind when he imagines his defence against charges whose content he ignores:

> In this defense he wanted to present a short account of his life and, when he came to any event which somehow was more important than others, to

explain what reasons had led him to act in such a way, and to say whether or not his course of action was, in his present estimation, to be approved or repudiated, and what grounds he could adduce for his present approval or repudiation. (p. 134)

28. For a discussion of this idea, see Taylor, *Sources of the Self,* pt. 1.

29. See ibid. 4, 14, 20, 42, 122, 332, 333, 336, 337, 383 for a discussion of this idea. For more on 'strongly evaluated, higher goods' see Charles Taylor's 'What is Human Agency?', in *Human Agency and Language: Philosophical Papers, 1* (Cambridge: Cambridge University Press, 1985) and 'The Diversity of Goods', in *Philosophy and the Human Sciences: Philosophical Papers, 2* (Cambridge: Cambridge University Press, 1985).

30. John Dunn also makes this point in his *Interpreting Political Responsibility* (Oxford: Polity Press, 1990), 48.

31. In terms of 'higher, strongly evaluated goods that need not be reflectively endorsed', Charles Taylor points to the example of the warrior and honour ethic that seems to have been dominant among the ruling strata of archaic Greece: while the life of the citizen-soldier was deemed higher than merely private existence, the citizen-soldier would not have been acting and judging on the basis of a reasoned (and reflectively endorsed) account of why that way of life is higher than others; the citizen-soldier would know how to behave without ever being told the rules (see *Sources of the Self,* 20–1). It is a feature of the modern identity, though, that strongly evaluated goods (including obligations to the family, or, more generally, those features of 'ordinary, private life' which have come to be 'strongly valued') would typically need to be reflectively endorsed, according to Taylor (see ibid., esp. pts. 2–5).

32. De la Patrie is probably thinking of Rawls's claim that we are 'self-originating sources of valid claims' (from 'Kantian Constructivism in Moral Theory', 543).

33. One self-professed liberal, Will Kymlicka, explicitly accepts that choices of lives worth pursuing have to be made from within an (unchosen) framework: 'It's of sovereign importance to this argument that the structure is being recognized as a *context for choice*' (see his *Liberalism, Community and Culture*, 166; his italics). (For a similar view, i.e. the idea that a (given) social context gives meaning and moral substance to the choice that an individual (can and should) make as to the kind of life she will lead, from someone who (mistakenly, in my view) considers himself to be outside the liberal camp, see Brian Lee Crowley, *The Self, the Individual, the Community: Liberalism in the Political Thought of F. A. Hayek and Sydney and Beatrice Webb* (Oxford: Clarendon Press, 1987), 214–20.) Kymlicka draws from the premiss that the 'cultural structure' provides the possibilities as to (worthwhile) ways of life the political implication that the existence of the 'cultural structure' itself (but not its 'character') ought to be protected by the state (see p. 169).

However, Kymlicka's insistence that we lead our lives 'from the inside', on the basis of tasks acquired through freely made personal judgements from among the possibilities provided by the cultural structure (see pp. 50–1), suggests that he believes in the possibility of a life led on the whole (usually? always?) on the basis of freely chosen practices, which conflicts with De la Patrie's first thesis that the normal (usual) mode of existence is that of unreflectively acting in a way specified by the practices of one's social world (see n. 20).

34. Gerald Doppelt also makes this point:

> in modern liberal-democratic society, on what basis do I respect the value of another person's way of life? Respect is typically based on the presupposition that their way of life embodies their own practical judgement, moral choice and individuality. Indeed, it is the relationship between a person's way of life and their moral powers which civil and political rights protect; this is a large part of what gives these rights value for us. On the other hand, suppose we believe that another person's way of life is no embodiment of their moral powers at all: it is based on social force, domination, completely irrational forces of personality, etc. . . . Such a person has lost that minimal respect for one's own and/or other's personhood presupposed by our notions of human dignity and political rights. In such cases, our respect is withdrawn. The normative preconditions for a minimally worthwhile or legitimate exercise of one's rights have been broken. (from 'Rawls' Kantian Ideal and the Viability of Modern Liberalism', 424–5)

Doppelt (and Schwartzberg) could make his case stronger by arguing that it isn't *respect* which is typically based on the presupposition that a person's way of life embodies his or her own practical judgement, moral choice, and individuality, but rather that we tend to *value* those lives which embody a person's own practical judgement, moral choice, and individuality—respecting a life is a weaker notion than valuing a person's way of life, as there are many people who lead lives which we may not value but who are none the less entitled to our respect and to the right of exercising civil and political freedoms. Against the claim that we tend to value those lives which embody a person's own practical judgement, moral choice, and individuality, De la Patrie could argue that we should value her grandmother's altruistic way of life (see below) even if she hasn't exercised her powers of normative self-determination.

35. De la Patrie is implying that choice isn't a necessary condition for responsibility. Though the view that people can be held responsible for more than internal acts of willing, i.e. that moral concern is with what is actually done rather than simply with those things done as a result of internal acts of willing, has recently come to be accepted in the philosophical community, things have not always been so:

Philosophers have argued that the only thing a person can be held responsible for is his internal act of willing. With such an impoverished conception of willing, it is hardly surprising that philosophers have had difficulty in accepting ordinary notions of responsibility for action. Similarly, if 'willing' is identified with 'striving' or 'controlling', it will be hard to see what is to be admired in effortless generosity. Finally, the recognition of contingencies, so far from being in necessary conflict with moral resources, often plays a central role in determining them. (from D. Z. Phillips's Introduction to D. Z. Phillips and Peter Winch, eds., *Wittgenstein: Attention to Particulars* (London: MacMillan, 1989), 9; see esp. D. Z. Phillips's contribution to the same volume, 'How Lucky can you Get?'.)

36. It will be noticed that Schwartzberg's defence of liberal foundations will have moved on to the second part of the possible response to De la Patrie's critique of the original position suggested in n. 13.

37. Charles Taylor also makes this point in 'The Diversity of Goods', 234.

38. What De la Patrie says about Mother Teresa is confirmed by the article 'Mother Teresa Stands down after a Lifetime of Labour', by Derek Brown, *Guardian* (12 Apr. 1990), 22.

39. See Gerald Doppelt, 'Is Rawls' Kantian Liberalism Coherent and Defensible?', 843, for a similar point.

40. For a more elaborate argument from a Christian perspective against the morality of assisted suicide committed for the purpose of avoiding personal harm, see Robert Weinberg, *Euthanasia, Suicide, and the Right to Die* (Grand Rapids, Mich.: William B. Eerdman's Publishing Co., 1989), ch. 4 (Weinberg does, however, allow for indirect shortening of life by morphine injection if pain is severe and death is near); additional arguments against the *legalization* of voluntary active euthanasia are presented in ch. 7.

Various articles debating the pros and cons of euthanasia can be found in the following edited collections: Robert Baird and Stuart Rosenbaum, eds., *Euthanasia: The Moral Issues* (Buffalo, NY: Prometheus Books, 1989); A. B. Downing and Barbara Smoker, eds., *Voluntary Euthanasia: Experts Debate the Right to Die* (London: Peter Owen, 1986); and Robert Weir, ed., *Ethical Issues in Death and Dying* (New York: Columbia University Press, 1977).

41. See Victor Farias' book *Heidegger et le Nazisme* (Lagrasse: Verdier, 1987), where it is argued that Heidegger was a lifelong, unrepentant Nazi.

42. *Being and Time* was first published in 1927, *Mein Kampf* in 1923, and the Nazis assumed power in 1933 as a minority government.

43. It should be noted that De la Patrie leaves open the question of where exactly Heidegger erred on his way from ontology to Nazi politics. Mark Blitz argues that the source of the problem lies in the fact that Heidegger made an unargued leap from the (ontological) thesis that we are embodied agents 'in the

world' engaged in realizing a certain form of life to the (ontic) claim that the form of life which we are engaged in realizing is (only) a linguistic one in its particular manifestation:

> . . . although 'public' is meant ontologically, public equipment, the public norms and rules, the 'public' interpretation of possibilities and the destiny of a people are apparently intelligible as the Being of an entity roughly equivalent to the specificity and developing history of a politically organized linguistic community. (*Heidegger's Being and Time and the Possibility of Political Philosophy* (London: Cornell University Press, 1981), 205.)

The post-*Being and Time* Heidegger made explicit his belief that human communal existence was shaped (only) by language, which led him to support such policies as Hitler's annexation of other German-speaking peoples (see Catherine H. Zuckert's article, 'Martin Heidegger: His Philosophy and his Politics', *Political Theory* (Feb. 1990), 51–79).

De la Patrie, it will be seen, thinks that the identity of 'Westerners' is constituted by many communities, each of which ought to be embraced (see Acts III–V).

Act II: Political Theorizing as the Interpretation of a Community's Shared Understandings

SCENE: *the same.*

[*Philip enters the stage, and reappropriates his chair*]

PHILIP You know, Anne, your notion of social practices is making me too self-conscious. I was noticing in the toilet that Frenchmen urinate differently than we do.

ANNE [*interrupting*] I don't think you'd want to include *me* in that *we*. I'm a woman, please remember.

PHILIP Of course. More precisely, then, Frenchmen urinate differently than do Canadian males. They seem, um, it's difficult to express in words—more confident, perhaps . . .

ANNE Please don't feel compelled to go into further detail.

PHILIP As you choose . . . [*assumes a mischievous, almost wicked, grin*] . . . There's something else I was thinking about in the toilet, though . . .

ANNE Oh, oh. I fear the rest, but please go on.

PHILIP Do you agree that for some people being a good lover, literally speaking, is a higher, strongly evaluated good?

ANNE [*feeling uncomfortable*] You have all types, I guess.

PHILIP Yes. For some, being a good lover is crucial to their self-understanding. Without this defining feature they would lose something of their moral personality. It's a good they feel they *ought* to be committed to; it structures what they find significant and what they do in a given situation.[1]

ANNE What you're saying is abstractly conceivable.

PHILIP It's more than that. Some people really do think like that, and besides, what's *wrong* with being committed to such an ideal? What's so bad about being able and willing to grant immense physical pleasure to others?

ANNE I'm not sure how admirable an ideal that is.

PHILIP Let's just assume I'm right about this. But some feel they're not living up to that ideal.

ANNE To the ideal of being a good lover, literally speaking?

PHILIP Yes. So they make a conscious effort to learn new techniques from the stock available in society. This involves reading books on sex, watching porn flicks, and, most importantly, learning from experience with various sex partners.

ANNE [*barely audible*] If you say so.

PHILIP But the application of these new techniques is awkward at first. One is too self-conscious in the act, or, as your friend Heidegger might say, bodily interaction is insufficiently 'ready-to-hand'.

ANNE [*coldly*] I wouldn't know.

PHILIP Take my word for it. So what does one do? New techniques have to be practised until they're perfected, that is, until they're integrated into one's network of shared sexual practices. One does well when these techniques can be applied in an effortless, unselfconscious manner, at which point we have a new, improved, ready-to-hand mode of being in bed . . . [*pause*] . . . You know, Anne, I *really am* starting to like your philosophy.

ANNE [*under her breath*] You're suggesting a novel application.

[*Waiter arrives with a* choucroute garnie, *which he serves to Philip*]

PHILIP [*to waiter*] Une autre assiette, s'il-vous-plaît.

[*Waiter grimaces, then leaves the stage*]

PHILIP This we can share. You ought to be rewarded with something more tangible than conversation with me while I'm keeping you from a meal with your family.

ANNE [*recovering her courage*] Actually, there's a strong cultural bias in France against two or more people eating food from the same plate, even among family members.

PHILIP So you don't want any *choucroute*?

ANNE Well, the damage is done, so I'll join you, for I should respect the 'it's not polite to eat food without offering it to others at one's table' norm that you were unselfconsciously acting upon when you offered me some *choucroute*.

[*Waiter arrives with a plate and utensils for Anne*]

ANNE [*to waiter*] Merci, monsieur, on ne ferait pas ça d'habitude, vous savez . . .

[*Waiter smiles, then leaves the stage*]

ANNE Perhaps we should move on to what I call 'the communitarian moral vision', the moral stand that I advocated in my thesis . . .

PHILIP [*interrupting*] Before we do that, before you become too self-satisfied with your critique of 'liberal foundations', let me suggest another defence for a liberal form of social organization—more specifically, for the distinctively liberal notion of the neutrality of the state—that doesn't rest on the self-determination ideal; this justification for political liberalism, then, can appeal to even those of you for whom the ideal of leading a life which embodies one's own practical judgement and choice of what's worth doing isn't a supreme value. On this view, the ideal of neutrality of the state can best be understood as a response to the generally accepted fact that in modern times reasonable people have competing conceptions of the good life. Neutrality should be seen as nothing more than a *modus vivendi* between persons whose ultimate ends do not coincide,[2] a system of mutual advantage requiring only that (*a*) people be willing to coexist with ways of life different than their own[3] and (*b*) the government doesn't justify its policies by appealing to the presumed superiority of any particular conception of the good life[4] . . .

ANNE [*pause*] It seems that this defence of political liberalism would be founded on the supposed fact of deep and irreconcilable disagreements about how we should lead our lives, or, more generally, about the substantive goods that the state might pursue, which gives rise to a need to formulate neutrally justifiable principles of justice.

PHILIP What do you mean 'supposed fact'? You think that our contemporaries agree about the 'substantive goods that the state might pursue'?

ANNE Well, I think it's too dogmatic to deny, a priori, the possibility of substantial agreement with respect to a community sorting out its political concerns. Michael Walzer, as you might know, wrote a whole book showing that even in the USA, that most litigious of societies where little family squabbles can end up being resolved by batteries of lawyers, there are common, widely shared meanings bearing on the proper distribution of social goods such as health care, jobs, prestigious awards, among others.[5]

PHILIP You're referring to *Spheres of Justice*, which I haven't read, but I remain sceptical—when I look at modern societies, I see endless disagreements about the meaning of social goods within communities.[6]

ANNE I don't think that our dispute can be resolved in the abstract, so I suggest that we turn to actual examples of social meanings bearing on the distribution of resources, and perhaps I can convince you to relax your assumption of ineliminable discord. Let's begin with one of Walzer's most convincing examples, his discussion of the practice of medicine.[7] Americans, Walzer argues, have inherited a conception of the practice of medicine whose distributive logic calls for the distribution of health care according to need, rather than the ability of patients to pay; on this view, it is unfair that *A* gets treated before and/or better than *B* if both suffer from the same illness, simply because *A* has more money than *B*.

PHILIP I happen to agree with that distributive logic for health care, but others don't, and one can't draw any political implications simply by noticing that practitioners of a certain profession satisfy needs. Other professions satisfy needs, not all of which are basic, and it doesn't follow that practitioners of those professions ought to distribute their services according to need, much less that the government should enforce that mode of distribution, if that's what you're getting at.

ANNE Yes, you're right. But in the USA, the need for health care has become so widely and deeply felt that nothing short of a national health service which provides minimally decent care to all those who need it would be morally adequate. It's the common appreciation of the importance of medical care in the USA which would justify the creation of a national health service[8] . . .

PHILIP I'm not convinced that 'the need for health care has become so widely and deeply felt in the USA that nothing short of a national health service would be morally adequate.' Americans seem relatively satisfied with their system of mixed private- and government-financed health insurance.

ANNE Don't be so sure about that. Most Americans are very dissatisfied with their health care system.[9] It's a national embarrassment that you have 37 million Americans who are not covered by any insurance plan, a large proportion of whom are not receiving medical care for financial reasons.[10]

PHILIP How do you know that? How do you know Americans are dissatisfied?

ANNE What I say is revealed by polling data.

PHILIP [*as though surprised*] Polling data! . . . [*short pause*] . . . Let me see if I understand. Your claim that there's substantial agreement with respect to how it is that social goods ought to be distributed, a claim you invoked to criticize the liberal assumption of ineliminable disagreement about the substantive goods that the state should pursue, rests on polling data. Attitudes are compiled by means of polls, and a majority presumably represents what you call 'substantial agreement' bearing on the distribution of a certain good, and this majority opinion justifies a certain political practice.

ANNE Of course it's not so simple. Consistent polling data showing that overwhelming majorities support a certain interpretation of a shared meaning bearing on the political life of the community provides strong evidence for that interpretation, but polling data can only reach so much.[11] We shouldn't expect, say, a truck driver from Mississippi to have worked through Walzer's argument that the distributive logic of the practice of medicine inherited from the ancient Greeks is that care should be proportionate to illness and not to wealth, that this is the appropriate moment for political authorities to enforce that mode of distribution because of the fact that the need for health care has become widely and deeply felt in the USA, and that this entails some form of a national health service which provides minimally decent care to all . . . It is hard to imagine, needless to say, that polling data can do justice to this argument, but that doesn't obviate the fact that Walzer succeeded in articulating the best interpretation of the meaning health care has for Americans, and the political consequence that flows therefrom . . .

PHILIP So why bring up polls at all, if Walzer's argument can't be proved or falsified by polling data?

ANNE I said that polls can lend credibility to a certain interpretation of a shared meaning; more precisely, it is a virtue of Walzer's approach— keeping his nose so close to the ground, or, as he would say, interpreting to his fellow citizens their world of shared meanings[12]—that parts of his argument can be empirically evaluated. That his 'fellow citizens' agree with his claim that this is the appropriate moment for political authorities to enshrine by means of law the distribution of health care according to need, for example, is suggested by the following data: 44 per cent of Americans polled agreed with the statement that it's a top priority for the government to propose laws for national health insurance, and a further 38 per cent said it was important, if not a top priority, to propose such laws.[13]

PHILIP As long as no new taxes are required, of course. Americans have a peculiar outlook—they think they can get governmental services without paying for them.

ANNE That's not true. A separate poll found that half of Americans favour government action to guarantee medical care for all *even if new taxes are required*.[14]

PHILIP I find it peculiar that you remember polling data which happens to serve the purpose of rebutting what I say, but, more pertinently, I suspect that you're making selective use of polls. There's probably a poll somewhere which found that a great many, perhaps most, Americans favour more free enterprise in the 'sphere' of medical care. You presumably omitted such findings on the grounds that this would refute your assumption of 'substantial agreement'.

ANNE Philip, surely you don't take all poll results seriously. If a poll found that Americans believe that it's a top priority for the government to paint all buildings white, would you think that data reflected an authentic shared meaning of Americans?

PHILIP No real poll would come up with that result, but it's not inconceivable to imagine an actual poll which contradicted the idea that there's 'substantial agreement' in American society which supports a system of free medical care for all, and I'm wondering how you'd deal with such 'inconvenient' data.

ANNE Not every poll result bears on a certain interpretation of shared meanings. People may have hazy, half-worked-out ideas about what's being asked, they may lack access to relevant facts, they may have been subjected to misleading propaganda, or whatever; in such cases, they may not answer in ways which we should take seriously. Think of the widespread support in the USA for the bombing raid on Libya. It seems to me that was more of a knee-jerk response to a prolonged anti-Qaddafi media campaign orchestrated by the state department, as opposed to a reflection of a shared meaning of Americans justifying the use of firepower to bomb this week's hated dictator.[15]

PHILIP I get the feeling that there's nothing beneath your particular preference structure, that you would label those preferences 'shared meanings', and that you're ruling out of court those preferences which happen to conflict with yours. It is precisely because of people like you that we need a liberal state which aims for neutrality between conceptions of the good, to prevent you from forcing upon others your own particular ideas about the good. Besides, you still haven't said how you'd deal with a poll result which contradicts your assumption that Americans support more governmental provision of medical care.

ANNE Overlooking that *ad hominem* of yours, let me take up your last point. One can imagine a situation where Americans were temporarily to drop their idea that the government should guarantee medical care for all. In a situation of war, say, a certain poll may show widespread support for a policy of directing resources away from health care to the war effort, even if this means that millions of Americans will lack access to medical services. Should this poll result force us to drop the assumption that Americans favour a restructuring of their current health-care system in the direction of one which provides minimally decent care to all?

PHILIP [*pause*] Well, however widespread the support for a national health service, I don't expect that this prospect will realize itself in the near future. There's a very powerful medical lobby with a vested interest in the current American health-care system, and poll results which show support for a national health service will do little to alter this fact . . .

ANNE I'm more optimistic than you are. If there's a more or less explicit consensus in society that a certain practice should be restructured in a certain way, and the force in favour of the status quo lacks moral legitimacy, it may be reasonable to expect change. Of course, it will often be true that powerful economic interests will successfully impede change that people want, but in this case the proper analogy, I think, is the delegitimization of the tobacco lobby—they can appeal to the rights of smokers all they want, but as it's fairly transparent that they're motivated essentially by naked economic self-interest, it's not difficult for the American government to enact anti-smoking legislation that benefits society as a whole while penalizing the tobacco industry.

PHILIP I'm sorry, I don't think it's an analogous situation with respect to medical care. Even if you have a majority in favour of changing the health-care system, you still have a big bloc in right-wing America that feels committed to a system of free enterprise with applications to medical care, and you can't dismiss their viewpoint merely with the statement that 'it's fairly transparent that they're motivated essentially by naked economic self-interest'.

ANNE [*pause*] You're right, in a sense—a plausible claim can be made that there's not really a consensus in American society which supports communal provision of health care, but I don't think that opposition to this idea is either deeply felt or well thought-out. Were Americans to restructure their health-care system in such a way as to guarantee medical care for all, I don't expect serious opposition to last.

PHILIP But how can you know that? You're very fond of making unsupported assertions.

ANNE I can support my claim by appealing to the case of Canada. I think the situation in the USA now is similar to that of Canada in the early sixties. But soon after the inception of public health insurance in Canada, opposition to the idea of government-administered free health care withered away.

PHILIP Because this policy expressed a deeper, underlying shared meaning that health care should be distributed according to need, and that satisfying the need for good health had become a top priority, or simply because this policy worked?

ANNE For both reasons. Or rather, it worked largely because it expressed a deeper, underlying shared meaning . . .

PHILIP [*interrupting*] There's something deeply conservative about what you're saying. It seems that you can really identify a shared meaning once you have a policy that works; where you have a working policy, you look back to find a shared meaning which in turn justifies that policy, and those who would criticize that policy are somehow outside the realm of legitimate debate.

ANNE Of course, not all working policies express shared meanings, nor does governmental action with the aim of moving towards an emerging consensus always work—think of the US Supreme Court's decision in *Brown* v. *Board of Education*, now accepted by Americans as an authoritative interpretation of their civic principles, but governmental action designed to implement this decision by means of forced busing has on the whole failed[16] . . . In any case, getting back to health care, I wanted to point out that government-administered free health care is now an uncontroversial practice in Canada. Canadians, as you know, refer to the 'sacred trust' between the government and its citizens, an inviolable unwritten pact that it's the government's task to take care of the basic needs of its citizens, such as health care. Criticism is directed at deviations from the principle that the government should guarantee the distribution of health care according to need, not at the principle itself.[17]

PHILIP [*absorbed by his* choucroute] This *choucroute*, as I see it, satisfies a basic need. It's too bad the government doesn't ensure its communal provision . . .

ANNE You may be right there. We're talking too much; let's get back to more concrete matters [*joins Philip in his eating enterprise*].

[*Pause*]

PHILIP [*wiping his mouth*] Well, let me try to recapitulate the discussion we've been having since my return from the toilet. You introduced this idea of there being substantial agreement in modern societies with respect to a community sorting out at least some of its political concerns in order to counter the liberal assumption that there are deep and fundamental differences about ultimate ends, and so about the substantive goods that the state might pursue, differences which entail the need for neutrally justifiable principles of justice. Yet your notion of 'substantial agreement', 'shared meanings', 'consensus', and whatever other words you used remains very mysterious to me. I'm still not at all clear as to what counts as a 'shared meaning', or how 'shared' a certain meaning has to be before that meaning justifies governmental action . . .

ANNE Let me try to spell out what I mean by a 'shared meaning'. As I said before, this doesn't refer to momentary public whim, the sort of fleeting communal agreement that may arise in exceptional circumstances such as wartime. What I have in mind is something like an authoritative interpretation of community morality that bears on the proper character of the community . . .

PHILIP [*interrupting*] Does that interpretation have to capture a meaning which is shared by *everyone* in the community?

ANNE No, no, of course not. We can speak meaningfully of 'shared meanings' without invoking the criterion of unanimity. No reasonable person can deny that slavery has come to be regarded as an unjust practice in American society,[18] and the possibility of a slave-holder's grandson who grudgingly admits to his wife that he 'wishes for the old days' doesn't make opposition to slavery any less of a consensus. You have a similar situation in Canada with respect to the medicare system, where those who wish to have their views taken seriously in the political arena will not question the underlying assumption that the government should do its best to guarantee the distribution of health care according to need; the existence of a small cabal of Ayn Rand disciples in, say, Saskatchewan, does not invalidate the idea that there's a broad consensus in Canada on this issue.

PHILIP So you admit, then, that there can be at least some people who disagree with a certain interpretation of shared meanings.

ANNE Yes, but there are certain interpretations of shared meanings which are so uncontroversial—they are 'shared' by such overwhelming majorities—that the luckiest fate of those who defy those shared meanings in the open is to have their viewpoints laughed out of existence— think of the reaction to a congressman who speaks in favour of slavery, an MP who advocates the dismantling of the medicare system in the House of Commons, a letter to the editor which maintains *à la* John Stuart Mill that educated people should have more than one vote, and so on.

PHILIP [*pause*] Actually, what worries me isn't so much your dubious argument that one can meaningfully speak of consensus, or 'substantial agreement', in modern societies so much as your assumption that it's agreement about the meaning of a certain social good which justifies a communal practice. Does that mean that my moral identity is constituted by my community's consensus bearing on 'the proper character of society'? If so, does that mean that I'm never free to affirm or reject the value of my community's consensus?

ANNE I understand your concern. You believe that detachment from the community's shared meanings bearing on communal practices is a necessary condition of moral freedom, of emancipation from the bondage of the social, economic, and political status quo.[19] According to this perspective, one must be able to abstract oneself from the community's shared meanings in order that one be in a position to appraise those commitments rationally and criticize them if necessary.

PHILIP Thank you for having articulated my previously latent view on moral freedom. I suspect a trap, however.

ANNE I just mean to suggest that one need not uphold a universalist perspective on morality in order to criticize a society's practices. Let me distinguish between two approaches to social criticism, and you'll see what I mean. One is the view you presumably hold—one should protest in the name of some trans-communal reality, an objective and universal standpoint applicable to all humans. On this view, one appeals to principles undeniable by any rational person and independent of all social and cultural particularities. Actual communities are judged by this standard, and criticized if judged to be deficient. The second approach involves protesting in the name of the community itself against those aspects of the community which are unfaithful to its own self-image.[20] On this view, critical standards are drawn from the shared meanings of a particular group of people rather than from an external, impersonal standpoint. The critic points to a shared meaning which condemns a certain societal practice—I've already suggested how this could be done in the case of the American health-care system . . .

PHILIP [*interrupting*] This 'critic' of yours appeals to shared meanings which are 'shared' by 'overwhelming majorities' . . .

ANNE I've already said that 'overwhelming majorities' may not agree with a certain interpretation of shared meanings in exceptional circumstances such as wartime. But even when 'times are normal', so to speak, 'overwhelming majorities', or even simple majorities, may not agree with the critic's interpretation of shared meanings . . .

PHILIP How could that be? Why even claim that one is articulating meanings which are 'shared' if one's interpretation doesn't command widespread support?

ANNE Interpretation of shared meanings is not merely a matter uncovering beliefs or attitudes by such means as polling, although polls can lend credibility to a certain interpretation, as I've already said; rather, one should think of this enterprise as a sort of expertise in the understanding of the moral consciousness of the community, not dependent on the approval of the community at the time in which the interpretation has been formulated. The critic thinks she has succeeded in articulating an interpretation of shared meanings most congruent with the deeper aspirations of the community, an interpretation that the community will, it is hoped, come to accept eventually if it doesn't already. In other words, the critic concedes that a majority of citizens might well misunderstand the logic of their own morality.[21]

PHILIP Thank you for that concession, but that's not quite the concession I was looking for. I want you to concede the point that, as you see it, the rock-bottom justification of the criticizing project is the discrepancy between shared meanings and the practice they condemn. There's no court of appeal beneath and beyond the morality of the community . . .

ANNE Why get so upset about that? If you agree that social criticism is only relevant if it's an aid to effective practice, if you're concerned with *success* in criticism, then you cannot but accept the approach I'm suggesting. A critic who tries to push beyond the limits of community consciousness cannot generate any politically relevant knowledge; only criticism which resonates with the habits and modes of conduct of the intended audiences can do so.[22]

PHILIP I don't deny that criticism can be most effective if critical standards are drawn from the community itself, but you are, so to speak, putting the cart before the horse. Most of us who engage in social criticism do so because we think we have principled grounds to do so, principled grounds which are valid independently of whether or not they happen to be affirmed in 'the principles of the community'. Moreover, I can't imagine there being any other motivation for being concerned with success in criticism; surely one wants one's criticism to be effective only because those principled grounds are thought to be sufficient justification for one's criticism, and if those grounds happen to 'resonate with the habits and mode of conduct of the intended audience', so much the better, 'the principles of the community' can be invoked as additional support for one's criticism, but this would be done for strategic reasons, on grounds of political expediency.

ANNE In terms of motivation, you're the one who's put the cart before the horse. We've all been socialized into a certain morality, and when that morality is weighed against the real world and found not to be actualized, we naturally get a little upset. An average American, for example, would have learned that the medical profession's prime purpose is to care for patients, and that physical health matters greatly, and when the TV news reports that a certain hospital in Florida has turned away a car-accident victim in mortal danger on the grounds that 'he didn't have any insurance', that American is provided with the motivation for criticism of the health-care system.[23] In fact, articulation of one's critique in terms of 'principles', 'rights', or whatever, is generally done after one already has the motivation for the critique . . .

PHILIP [*interrupting*] But . . .

ANNE [*also interrupting*] Before we get stalled on this point, let me compare the two approaches to social criticism, drawing upon what you said about justification. Adherents of the first approach—those of you who would ground their criticism in principles valid independently of the moral consciousness of the community—appeal ultimately to standards of rational justification undeniable by any rational person. One can and should base the criticizing project on activities of critical reflection that aim at knowledge independent of any context . . .

PHILIP [*impatiently*] So what's the problem? So what's the problem?

ANNE The problem, quite simply, is that all knowledge is context-bound—the critic cannot extricate herself from her context so as to be true to principles of rational justification independent of any context, even if she tries. To demonstrate this, I'll have to rehearse a little

Heidegger, focusing more directly on his critique of 'Cartesian epistemology', the idea that knowledge is to be seen as the correct representation of an independent reality . . .

PHILIP [*interrupting*] Do you really have to go into Heidegger again? My preference is shifting to that of eating *choucroute* in silence.

ANNE Please bear with me. Heidegger's analysis of 'being-in-the-world' showed that our condition of forming disengaged representations of reality is that we be already engaged in coping with our world, dealing with things in it. Disengaged description is one special possibility, realizable intermittently in states of breakdown, of a being who is always 'in the world' in another way, that is, as an agent engaged in realizing a certain form of life. Even in this theoretical stance to the world, it should be emphasized, we are still involved in the world as agents coping with things—we couldn't form disinterested representations in any other way. So the whole epistemological tradition which conceives of knowledge as just consisting of inner pictures of outer reality is mistaken, for knowledge itself, our representation of things, is grounded in largely inarticulate dealings with things; our understanding of the world cannot ultimately be based on representations at all, if by this we mean depictions that are separately identifiable from what they are of, but rather must be grounded in our dealings with the world.[24]

PHILIP I don't quite grasp the point of this little discourse of yours.

ANNE Well, once we recognize that our knowledge is context-bound, that there's no 'objective' standpoint from which to evaluate how we think, act, and judge, this should lead us to abandon this project that aims at finding independent rational justification for morality, an external and universal perspective that's to serve as a critical standard from which to evaluate the morality of actual communities.[25] And if there's no trans-communal ground from which to seek independent vindication for the moral standards of communities, this means that standards of justification emerge from and are part of a community's history and tradition in which they are vindicated; those moral standards themselves, understood as accounts of the principles which prevail in actual communities, constitute 'the ground', 'the justification' for one's criticism . . . [*Philip cringes in response to this statement*] . . . I don't see why you should be so upset about this conclusion—Rawls himself has disavowed the idea of a trans-historical 'absolutely valid' set of standards which would serve as 'philosophical foundations' for his theory of justice. He explicitly argues that what would justify his theory of justice is its being true to the prevailing moral beliefs and intuitions of people in modern liberal democratic societies.[26]

PHILIP Yes, well, I just can't believe that Rawls believes that that's all which justifies his project. Surely there are times when the 'prevailing moral beliefs and intuitions' themselves are wrong, in which case they can legitimately be criticized from a standpoint outside the community . . .

ANNE What standpoint, if not the view from nowhere, a disembodied universalism which I've shown to be an impossible ideal to attain?

PHILIP There is another possibility. This is the view that there's a universality rooted not in transcendental metaphysics, but in certain empirical commonalities, namely, the kinds of beings we are, 'facts' about the human condition. On this view, there are certain basic goods which are necessary conditions for well-being, goods whose specification does not depend on the approval of 'the community' . . .

ANNE Could you offer some examples of such 'basic goods'?

PHILIP Well, let's speak of needs. No one can deny that there are at least some needs that human beings have in common, whatever their cultural differences—uncontroversial needs include those for food, good health, shelter, and protection from death and gratuitous injury. Any decent social system must, at minimum, satisfy these needs, and it is from this standpoint, from the standpoint of needs applicable to all human beings, that one can criticize actual communities for failing to satisfy these needs . . . So when we turn to the way that health care is distributed in the USA, the free-enterprise system can be criticized simply on the grounds that it fails to provide for the need that Americans have *qua* human beings for physical health, physical health being conceived as one of the necessary conditions for well-being. Thus, one protests neither in the name of some objective, trans-communal reality, nor in the name of 'the prevailing moral beliefs and intuitions' of the particular community that's being criticized; rather, one appeals to basic needs which are not being satisfied, needs which all humans have in common. Isn't this approach to social criticism more promising than your unconvincing appeal to a 'shared meaning' of Americans that there's a deeply felt need for health care and that this implies a national health service? On my view, one is justified in calling for a restructuring of the American health-care system whether or not Americans agree; one can point to a 'shared meaning' in the USA if there is one, but this would be done for strategic reasons, on grounds of political expediency.

ANNE [*pause*] I personally don't find this approach more promising. You're still working with the assumption that one is first and foremost a human being separate from one's context, that particular individuals enter into society armed with pre-existing needs, wants, and desires, and that society is to be criticized if it fails to satisfy those needs. As I see it, what counts as a need, which needs are pressing for satisfaction, and so on, will itself depend upon the way of life of particular societies[27] . . .

PHILIP Do you deny that all humans have an interest in being healthy, regardless of the particular circumstances in which they find themselves? Is this supposed to be a controversial assumption?

ANNE One can conceive of a basic set of needs applicable to all societies, but this would be done at such a high level of abstraction as to be of little use for actual societies. In some societies, 'being healthy' means having one's soul cleansed by the witch doctor, so a call for communal provision of medical care would make little sense in that context. And even in those societies which have inherited the idea of a medical profession that's to treat patients in proportion to their physical illness, it's only recently that the chance for a long and healthy life has become a socially recognized need, with the concomitant development of communal interest in medical care[28] . . . It's possible, then, to posit a set of basic needs applicable to all known societies, but such a set would have to be conceived in terms so abstract as to be of little use in thinking about the problems of actual societies. Criticism which appeals to needs which humans have simply by virtue of being human only has a point in so far as it draws upon those very shared meanings, those prevailing moral beliefs and intuitions which for you have only strategic value.

PHILIP [*pause*] If I understand your position correctly, you would accept as legitimate only that criticism whose justification lies in its faithfulness to the 'prevailing moral beliefs and intuitions' of actual societies; criticism which appeals to universal, impersonal standards of morality is either incoherent, as Heidegger would have it, or irrelevant, if drawn from an abstractly conceived set of needs which doesn't turn out to be a disguised interpretation of the intended audience's already shared conception of needs.

ANNE As you would say, 'so what's the problem?'

PHILIP Your critic, I venture, may on occasion be out of a job. If criticism is justified only by an appeal to 'prevailing moral beliefs and intuitions', and if a certain society fully expresses the 'prevailing moral beliefs and intuitions' of a people in its practices and institutions, that society would be immune to criticism of its communal practices—your 'critic' would be completely mute, no matter what kind of society we're talking about!

ANNE I wouldn't expect that hypothetical scenario to occur. The organization of the political life of a society requires the acquisition and concentration of power and wealth, which inevitably corrupts in practice that society's prevailing moral beliefs and intuitions.[29] No society will ever be immune from the type of criticism I have in mind.

PHILIP You may be right that there will never be a society where there's a perfect match between, let's say, morality and practice. But surely we can conceive of some practices expressive of 'prevailing moral beliefs and intuitions' that deserve to be criticized . . .

ANNE You must have something in mind. Tell me what you have in mind.

PHILIP [*pause*] OK. When I began my studies at McGill, the burning issue at the time among progressive students such as myself was that of saving the achievements of the Nicaraguan revolution from the ravages of the US-backed Contras. Acting on my principles, I joined an international coffee pickers' brigade in Nicaragua. It didn't work too well, I have to admit—they said I was too slow at picking coffee, that my labour input didn't match the resources I consumed, and consequently I had to return home earlier than planned. What I saw in Nicaragua, though, *deeply* disturbed me—I saw hospitals burned, agricultural co-operatives destroyed, peasants killed, all by those 'freedom-fighters' known as the Contras . . .

ANNE I know. Those Contras were really horrible people.

PHILIP I was about to ask you—how would you have criticized the policy of aid to the Contras, given that there was substantial support in American society for this policy?

ANNE First of all, I'm not American, so I shouldn't feel bound by the American perspective in this issue . . .

PHILIP [*interrupting*] What? I thought you said that the justification of the criticizing project derives from the 'prevailing moral beliefs and intuitions' of the intended audience, and now you're implying that you'd be willing to criticize an American practice even if that practice derives its justification from the principles of the American people!

ANNE I'm afraid that you've been under the spell of a great misunderstanding, which I should immediately undertake to dispel. The practice of social criticism I'm defending is criticism by a social thinker directed to fellow members of a community, drawing upon a world of shared meanings—not, let me emphasize, the strange idea of someone who would criticize an outsider's practices by appealing to the outsider's morality, in which case it would indeed be transparent to the 'intended audience' that the critic is drawing up 'shared meanings' for merely strategic reasons. Besides no one has ever argued that one has a special obligation to endorse, or even respect, every stomach-turning practice encountered in faraway lands . . .

PHILIP Now hold on a minute! Your own Michael Walzer argues that justice involves respecting the shared meanings of other societies—we do in fact have a special obligation to respect the cultural creations of others, he would say.

ANNE Mmmh, I'm beginning to suspect that you know more about this stuff than you've let on thus far . . . With respect to Walzer's work, he does give the example of a visitor to an Indian village who engages in the 'entirely respectable activity' of trying to convince the villagers that shared meanings which support the caste system are false—clearly this critic isn't 'respecting' the shared meanings of another society.[30]

PHILIP So you deny that Walzer has said that justice consists in respecting the cultural creations of others?

ANNE Well, perhaps he shouldn't have said that, cast in universalistic terms[31] . . .

PHILIP But you yourself condemned me earlier for failing to respect the French practice of having a coffee after one's meal!

ANNE Yes, it's a shared principle of *ours* that we should respect, on the whole, the cultural creations of others—this is uncontroversially true in the case of shared meanings bearing on mealtime practices.[32] It is absolutely inexcusable that you should have expected the French to bend to your conception of mealtime practices in France . . . But I deny that it's a shared principle of ours that we should respect the cultural creations of others, no matter what they are—if a certain practice, and its underlying justification, is so repugnant to our community's conception of morality, then we might well engage in the 'entirely respectable critical activity' of Walzer's visitor to a hypothetical Indian village. More thought, however, has to be given to this matter.

PHILIP I completely agree that you have to give more thought to this matter.

ANNE The truth is that I didn't deal with this issue of justifiable criticism
of outsiders' practices in my thesis. If you want to evaluate a claim of
mine, I suggest that you stick to this idea of the 'internal' critic who
protests in the name of her *own* community against those aspects of the
community which are unfaithful to its own self-image.

PHILIP Fine, that idea is more than sufficiently problematic. So let's get
back to this issue of the Contras, framing the question slightly differently—how would you, assuming you were an American, have criticized the policy of aid to the Contras, given that Americans endorsed
this policy?

ANNE Actually, polling data shows that Americans consistently opposed
the policy of aid to the Contras.[33]

PHILIP Not polls again! Look, let's just assume that Americans as a whole
supported aid to the Contras—how then could you have criticized this
policy without resorting to an external and universal moral standpoint?

ANNE You want me to imagine (*a*) that I'm American and (*b*) that
Americans supported the policy of aid to the Contras, and then suggest
how I would have criticized this policy?

PHILIP Yes!

ANNE Well, that's not so difficult. If we interpret American political culture, we find that one of its central shared meanings is a commitment
to freedom and democracy abroad. As a critic, I would have been arguing that, by supporting those awful Contras, 'fellow citizens' wouldn't
have been consistently applying 'our' own professed commitment to
freedom and democracy abroad.[34]

PHILIP But that doesn't help! Ronald Reagan appealed to that same value
in order to *justify* aid to the Contras—the Contras, in his view, *promoted* freedom.

ANNE Either he was lying, or he didn't look closely at what it is the
Contras were doing when they were active,[35] which can be specified in
a relatively uncontroversial way. As you said, they attacked hospitals
and agricultural co-operatives, murdering many peasants along the
way, with what seemed to be the general aims of destroying the economic infrastructure and sowing terror in the countryside. This cannot
be rendered consistent with the shared meaning of Americans that freedom should be promoted abroad, which helps to explain, by the way,
why in actual fact Americans found criticism of this policy compelling
and persuasive, notwithstanding the best attempts of the state
department to sell this nasty policy.

PHILIP [*pause*] I still don't think you've addressed this crucial point I've been trying to make—is it not the case that 'shared meanings', or 'prevailing moral beliefs and intuitions', can themselves be wrong? Wouldn't aid to the Contras still be a 'nasty policy' even if Americans thought that this policy was expressive of a shared meaning of theirs? If Americans had a core value that terrorism should be promoted abroad, should an American would-be critic have refrained from criticizing aid to the Contras?

ANNE You have a funny way of arguing—'if this' and 'if that' . . . I don't mind playing these mind games if it entertains you, but counterfactual history won't force me to drop my favoured approach to social criticism.

PHILIP [*raises voice*] Fine, let's stay in the real world, then. Think of South Africa until recently—I don't know of any progressive South Africans who criticized state-sanctioned racism in South Africa on the grounds that there was an inconsistency between the policies of the government and the 'prevailing moral beliefs and intuitions' of South Africans. Surely there's something wrong with racism itself, irrespective of whatever the 'prevailing moral beliefs and intuitions' of South Africans happen to be . . .

ANNE Actually, there have been 'progressive South Africans' who've criticized apartheid on the grounds of its not being true to the South African people's world of shared meanings,[36] and if you don't find this approach plausible, you have to accept that 'racism' cannot be said to constitute a 'prevailing moral belief' of the South African people if we include South African blacks . . .

PHILIP [*hostile tone*] What about Nazi Germany? Nazi Germany can be seen as the realization of the previously latent anti-semitism and authoritarianism of German culture; the Nazis, in other words, expressed the 'prevailing moral beliefs and intuitions' of the German people, and they justified what they did by appealing to those beliefs— the genetic superiority of the Aryan race, the need for a strong leader, and so on. A German who accepts your 'internal' approach to social criticism could do nothing but applaud this regime—what a morally perverse view!

ANNE I'd like to question your presentation of the facts. It's widely accepted that the rise to power of the Nazis was due primarily to the economic and political crisis of the Weimar Republic, which threw the German people into a panic and allowed their good sense to be swept aside by a ruthless tyrant.[37] 'Times were not normal', and in those circumstances, as I've already suggested, a great many people may lose touch with their deepest moral beliefs and intuitions.

PHILIP [*more angrily still*] Don't tell me the Nazis didn't strike deep chords in the consciousness of Germans![38] The German people wanted the Nazis; they supported them throughout their reign.

ANNE How could we know? It's true that the Nazis won more votes than any other party in 1933, but they were still a minority party; after that, of course, the Nazis ruthlessly squelched critical voices, and abolished all procedures by means of which citizens could have made their wishes known. There were no elections, no polls, and no town halls in Nazi Germany.

PHILIP And there was no opposition, no resistance inside Germany.[39] This implies, at minimum, passive acquiescence.

ANNE Acquiescence grounded in fear, but not the realization of the prevailing moral beliefs and intuitions of the German people. The Nazis, it's interesting to note, never publicized what we would consider to be their worst deeds, presumably because they feared a probable backlash if they did; the Nazis, it seems, were afraid of their own people.

PHILIP The German people feared the Nazis, and the Nazis feared their '*volk*'! How absurd! You don't need polls, town halls, and massive publicity to figure out that the Nazis commanded overwhelming and enthusiastic support among Germans—have you ever seen all those smiling faces at the Nuremburg rallies!

ANNE Well, even if it was true that a majority of Germans supported the Nazis at some point, that wouldn't prove the Nazis successfully tapped the 'prevailing moral beliefs and intuitions' of the German people—even in normal times, let me repeat, majorities can get their own morality wrong. This is, of course, usually recognized after the fact, as when Chinese intellectuals shake their heads in disbelief at what happened during the cultural revolution, those awful ten years when conscious attempts were made, no doubt with the overwhelming support of the Chinese people at the beginning, to stamp out their own 'feudal' history in favour of the greater good of equality. Many of those same intellectuals were enthusiastic red guards at the time[40] . . . I think something similar happened in Nazi Germany, and the collective shame that seized the German people after the defeat of the Nazis, along with the fact that post-Nazi Germany adopted democratic institutions so quickly and painlessly, suggests that I'm right. The Nazis didn't correctly interpret the 'prevailing moral beliefs and intuitions' of the German people[41]—if in fact that's what they tried to do; it seems more like a standard case of Machiavellians seizing power and 'strategically' justifying their rule by whatever means lay at their disposal—and a German need not have relied on objective, trans-communal standards of morality to condemn the Nazis.

PHILIP [*pause*] You must know, deep down, that there's something wrong with the view that the critic should rely solely on 'prevailing moral beliefs and intuitions' to condemn his community's practices. I just can't believe that you think a German should depend upon the outcome of a historical investigation into the 'prevailing moral beliefs and intuitions' of the German people before he decides whether or not to condemn Nazi Germany . . . So I want you to forget about actual history for a moment; let's simply assume that Nazi Germany expressed the deepest shared meanings, the prevailing moral beliefs and intuitions of the German people . . .

ANNE [*interrupting*] To be honest, I'm getting tired of your imaginary scenarios—I'm more interested in the interpretation of the relation between shared meanings and Nazi practices that best suits the facts of the case. I've already told you what I think about counterfactual history.

PHILIP [*raises voice*] Well, I'm more interested in counterfactual history than in your tendentious interpretation of 'the facts of the case'. And I'm willing to discuss your thesis, so you do me the favour of hearing me out on this one.

ANNE Please go ahead.

PHILIP Thank you. Let's assume that the Nazis succeeded in articulating and applying the best interpretation of the 'moral beliefs and intuitions' of the German people, and that part of this 'tradition' includes a shared commitment to gross cruelty against Jews. Next, we'll invent a young man, a student of Heidegger's, who learns from his master a philosophy which purports to show the impossibility of extrication from one's context. It makes little sense to appeal to trans-communal standards of morality to criticize one's society, so one must stick to internal moral principles, understood as accounts of the principles which prevail in actual societies. So our student friend, true to his philosophy, 'respects' this particular cultural creation of the German people, a shared commitment to gross cruelty against Jews, along with its practical implication, the extermination of Jews. Isn't there something deeply perverse about this scenario? Wouldn't our student friend have had a moral obligation to oppose the Holocaust whatever most Germans thought about this 'practice'?

ANNE [*pause*] You're looking for a universal moral standpoint which could have served as 'the ground' for an 'internal' critic of Nazi morality . . .

PHILIP Nazi morality! That sounds like an oxymoron to me!

ANNE Please, Philip, I'm trying to help you here. While I don't think one can appeal to 'objective' standards of morality, standards not dependent on the actual historical processes of societies, there's another possibility—a universalism rooted in the convergence of people's understanding of certain core moral propositions. Every society, it seems, has come to accept a bare set of prohibitions—on murder, deception, betrayal, and gross cruelty—prohibitions which constitute a kind of minimal and universal moral code[42] . . . Governments have to pay at least lip-service to, most obviously, the idea that torture is bad. So here's some ammunition for an 'internal' critic who would criticize what her 'fellow Germans' did to the Jews.

PHILIP You're begging the question. I asked you to imagine a society which favours gross cruelty, and you answer with the idea that all societies agree at least in principle that gross cruelty is bad. Besides, even if you're right that there happens to be a sort of trans-communal agreement now that gross cruelty is bad, it's not inconceivable that there'll be a society in the future which doesn't partake of that consensus, so my question is still relevant.[43] My question, let me repeat, is the following—isn't there some ground beneath and beyond 'prevailing moral beliefs and intuitions' which someone born and bred in a fully developed Nazi culture could and should appeal to in order to criticize the 'practice' of exterminating Jews?

ANNE [*pause*] Well, since you're really pushing me on this point, there might well be something which saves the 'communitarian critic' from lapsing into total relativism, without arguing that morality can be grounded in some trans-communal, objective order. I have in mind 'transition arguments', ones that compare systems of thought and/or morality with one another. On this view, there can be progress from position X to position Y if the transition from X to Y can be shown to represent a gain in understanding, whereas a similarly plausible narrative of a possible transition from Y to X couldn't be constructed. So, for example, one can show from the position of a Heideggerian account of the conditions of intentionality where it is the Cartesian construal of knowledge went wrong—we tend to notice the 'un-ready to hand' mode of being occasioned by a breakdown from the normal, everyday mode of ongoing coping in the world, and mistakenly define this 'breakdown' mode as the most primordial, which leads to a search for an impossible foundational justification for knowledge, fruitless hopes to achieve total reflexive clarity about the bases of our beliefs, implausible scepticism about the existence of an 'external' world,[44] radical doctrines of nonsituated freedom, and so on—but we couldn't construct a similarly plausible, error-reducing narrative of a transition from a Heideggerian account of the conditions of intentionality to a Cartesian construal of knowledge. That's why we can say that the Heideggerian critique of epistemology, which shows that we are first and foremost embodied agents already 'in the world', engaged in realizing a certain form of life, can be said to represent a gain in reason, a better understanding of what we are as knowing agents than the Cartesian construal of knowledge as the correct representation of an independent reality[45] . . .

PHILIP I'm not too clear as to how 'the Heideggerian critique of epistemology' bears on the question I was asking you . . .

ANNE I was just giving an example of successful 'immanent critique'. In terms of your question, I imagine that a plausible narrative can be constructed to show that a transition from the Nazi morality you have in mind to a morality which prohibits gross cruelty represents moral growth, whereas this couldn't be done the other way around. So even a German brought up in a culture whose 'prevailing moral beliefs and intuitions' supported acts of gross cruelty against Jews, if she demonstrated this asymmetrical relationship between the 'prevailing moral beliefs and intuitions' of her community and another morality which prohibits gross cruelty, might well condemn that part of her community's morality which favours gross cruelty without appealing to an acontextual moral truth.

PHILIP [*raises voice*] Such tortuous reasoning, and so distasteful! Why not simply accept that certain deeds can be wrong, *objectively* speaking, whatever the morality of actual communities? . . . [*barely concealed anger*] . . . How can this not be true of the Nazi Holocaust, the extermination of six million Jews!?

ANNE Look, I gave you what I could. I can't provide you with any transcommunal criteria of morality that would grant special status to the

Nazi Holocaust in the catalogue of man's historical injustices, if that's what you're looking for.

PHILIP [*his face reddening*] Are you denying that the Holocaust represents a whole new ball game in the history of man's misdeeds?[46] That the Holocaust was the worst thing ever done by one group of people to another?

ANNE I understand why you think that way, being Jewish.

PHILIP [*banging on the table*] Answer my point, God damn it!!

ANNE [*unfazed*] I did, indirectly. It's just not true that the Holocaust is the worst evil ever committed from *anyone's perspective*. Try convincing the Guatemalan indigenous woman who's had half her linguistic group massacred by the military, her own children having been tortured to death in her presence . . .

[*At this point, Philip storms off to the 'toilettes' on the right-hand side of the stage. Lights dim*]

Notes

1. For an example of someone to whom this seems to apply, see Xaviera Hollander's account of her life *The Happy Hooker* (London: Sphere Books, 1972).

2. Charles Larmore develops this idea of '*modus-vivendi* liberalism' in his *Patterns of Moral Complexity* (Cambridge: Cambridge University Press, 1987).

3. This condition is similar to what Charles Larmore calls the value of 'equal respect' (see ibid. 125). Larmore, however, writes that our adherence to his proposed 'system of mutual advantage' also requires that 'everyone' shares the value of rational conversation, which involves abstracting from ideas of what makes life worth living, ideas so close to us 'that we would be unwilling to accept in imagination our lives without [them]' (ibid. 74), for the particular purpose of devising neutrally justifiable principles of political co-operation, but going along this route brings us back to criticisms of the original position which De la Patrie rehearsed in Act I—few are likely to feel bound by obligations which arise in the political domain were there to be a conflict between these and action which flows from 'ideas so close to us that we would be unwilling to accept in imagination our lives without them'.

   Stephen Lukes alludes to another problem arising from the priority Charles Larmore gives to neutrally justifiable principles of justice:

   > Nor can I discuss his interesting, but I suspect mistaken, suggestion that in a liberal political order neutrally justifiable principles of justice, whether consequentialist or deontological, must always rank higher than

the principle of partiality [which underlies particularist duties] (how else could the foreign aid budget be limited?). ('Making Sense of Moral Conflict', in Nancy Rosenblum, ed., *Liberalism and the Moral Life* (Cambridge, Mass.: Harvard University Press, 1989), 132.)

If neutrally justifiable principles of justice—equality of resources, opportunities, capacities, results, or whatever—have ultimate priority, why not make those principles world-wide imperatives? At the very least a special commitment to the particular community within which political decisions are made must count as an underlying justification for those decisions, unless liberals want to deny what all known political communities have taken for granted, namely, that the government ought to concern itself first and foremost with meeting the needs and interests of the community over which it governs.

4. Charles Larmore similarly argues that a government acts neutrally when its political decisions 'can be justified without appealing to the presumed intrinsic superiority of any particular conception of the good life' (*Patterns of Moral Complexity*, 44). For an argument that Rawls has to be interpreted as endorsing this sort of neutrality (i.e. that the state should not justify its policies on the grounds that certain ways of life are more worth living than others, as opposed to advocating that government action should have neutral consequences), see Will Kymlicka, 'Liberal Individualism and Liberal Neutrality', *Ethics* (July 1989), 883–6.

5. See Michael Walzer, *Spheres of Justice* (Oxford: Basil Blackwell, 1983).

6. Ronald Dworkin also makes this point in his review of *Spheres of Justice, New York Review of Books* (14 Apr. 1983). Interestingly, Alasdair MacIntyre, in his book *After Virtue*, 2nd edn. (Notre-Dame, Ind.: University of Notre-Dame Press, 1984), shares this belief about there being no shared meanings in liberal societies bearing on the just way of distributing social goods, but whereas for Dworkin this alleged lack of shared meanings doesn't bear on the issue of justice (which doesn't depend on the character of any particular society), MacIntyre thinks that this alleged lack of shared meanings rules out the possibility of justice (he defines justice as an idea rooted in 'a community whose primary bond is a shared understanding both of the good for man and the good of that community'—see *After Virtue*, 232–3), and leads in practice to interminable conflicts over the most basic moral and political issues, with only force winning out in the end.

De la Patrie, it will be recalled, points to competing views (at the end of Act I) bearing on the euthanasia issue, so her position must be that there are some shared meanings (latent or realized) bearing on practices, and other cases where there are competing meanings bearing on certain practices—where the latter applies, the communitarian involved in the political process should admit that she's taking sides, defending one aspect of the culture against another (see Act II n. 41).

7. See Walzer, *Spheres of Justice*, 86–91.

8. Walzer responds in a similar way to an objection Robert Nozick made to Bernard Williams's claim that the only proper criterion for the distribution of medical care is medical need:

> Robert Nozick asks why it doesn't follow 'that the only proper criterion for the distribution of barbering services is barbering need'? Perhaps it does follow if one attends only to the 'internal goal' of the activity, conceived in universal terms. But it doesn't follow if one attends to the social meaning of the activity, the place of the good it distributes in the life of a particular group of people. One can conceive of a society in which haircuts took on such central cultural significance that communal provision would be morally required, but it is something more than an interesting fact that no such society has ever existed. (Ibid. 88.)

9. A survey of attitudes towards medical care in the USA, Canada, and Great Britain found Americans to be the most dissatisfied, with 89% saying that their health-care system needs 'fundamental change or complete rebuilding'. Furthermore, 61% of Americans polled said they would favour a system like that in Canada, which was described as one in which the government pays the cost of health for everyone out of taxes, and sets fees charged by hospitals and doctors (see 'Canadian Medicare Attracts Americans', *Toronto Globe and Mail* (14 Feb. 1989), pp. A1, A5).

10. Eighteen million Americans are not receiving medical care for financial reasons (see ibid. A5).

11. For an argument that intensive, qualitative interviews with a small set of people can fill in gaps left by opinion polls and even generate (accurate) findings which survey research cannot reach, see Jennifer L. Hochschild, *What's Fair* (Cambridge, Mass.: Harvard University Press, 1981), 21, 24–5. Hochschild found that the Americans she interviewed, both rich and poor, support more equality than they realize (and that could have been noticed by means of polling)—see e.g. p. 280.

12. See Walzer, *Spheres of Justice*, p. xiv.

13. See *New York Times* (27 Nov. 1988), p. E15.

14. The exact figure is 51% (from 'The Week in Review Section', *New York Times* (2 Nov. 1988), p. 31).

15. See Noam Chomsky and Edward Herman, *Manufacturing Consent* (Boston: South End Press, 1988), for an overall explanation, backed by a litany of compelling examples of why the State Department and the mainstream press try to shape opinions the way they do.

16. For a vivid account of the problems caused by the implementation of the forced busing policy in the Boston context, see Anthony J. Lukas, *Common Ground: A Turbulent Decade in the Lives of 3 American Families* (New York: Knopf, 1975).

17. Canada's system of government-administered free health care was briefly challenged by medical extra-billing and hospital patient fees, but these were eliminated by the 1984 Canada Health Act. While this law was controversial in political circles before it was enacted, Cabinet resistance was weakened when the health ministry commissioned a survey which showed that 70–80% of Canadians in all ten provinces opposed user fees and extra-billing (it is probable that this percentage would have been higher had there been actual cases of people being refused medical care on financial grounds). See Monique Bégin (Canada's Minister of Health and Welfare at the time), *Medicine: Canada's Right to Health*, trans. David Hamel and Lucille Nelson (Toronto: Optimum Publishing International, 1988).

18. De la Patrie's statement implies that there could have been a time when slaves and masters inhabited a world of shared meanings where slavery would have been regarded as a just practice, but the historical record of slavery rules out this possibility:

> 'There is absolutely no evidence from the long and dismal annals of slavery', writes Patterson, 'to suggest that any group of slaves ever internalized the conception of degradation held by their master.' Slaves and masters do not inhabit a world of shared meanings. The two groups are simply at war
> . . . (Walzer, *Spheres of Justice*, 250, quoting Orlando Patterson, *Slavery and Social Death: a Comparative Study* (Cambridge, Mass.: Harvard University Press, 1982), 97.)

19. See Alasdair MacIntyre, 'Is Patriotism a Virtue?', *Lindley Lecture*, University of Kansas, 1984, pt. 4, where this view of moral freedom is presented and criticized.

20. This view is similar to Michael Walzer's defence of 'internal criticism' presented in his *Interpretation and Social Criticism* (Cambridge, Mass.: Harvard University Press, 1987), a view which is developed through a series of examples in his subsequent book, *The Company of Critics* (New York: Basic Books, 1988).

    In the same vein, Richard Rorty argues that the 'heroes of liberal society' are the strong poet and the utopian revolutionary who 'protest in the name of the society itself against those aspects of the society which are unfaithful to its own self-image' as opposed to 'protesting in the name of humanity against arbitrary and inhuman social restrictions' (see his *Contingency, Irony and Solidarity* (Cambridge: Cambridge University Press, 1989), 60).

21. Walzer makes a similar 'concession' in *Spheres of Justice*, 99. William Galston comments that, notwithstanding Walzer's extended animadversions against the expansion of judicial powers in a democracy, the logic of his argument that majorities can be wrong on occasion in terms of applying 'the principles they professed to uphold' forces him into (also) conceding that 'judicial review can be legitimate and even on occasion necessary' (from 'Community,

Democracy, Philosophy: The Political Thought of Michael Walzer', *Political Theory* (Feb. 1989), 129). *Contra* Galston, however, it does not follow from the fact that 'experts' at interpreting the community's morality can (on occasion) do a better job of this than majorities that those experts are entitled to enforce by means of law the practices that flow from that interpretation (as opposed to trying to persuade the majority of their interpretation, with political change coming about as a result of the democratic process). When Walzer argues that a shared commitment to democratic decision-making includes commitment to democratic decision-making within the workplace, with the implication that 'workers' control of companies and factories' (*Spheres of Justice*, 318) should be regarded as the appropriate arrangement in the 'sphere' of work, he would probably admit that this is not a majority view, and it seems highly unlikely that Walzer would think that judges should be empowered to enforce by means of law workers' control of companies and factories.

22. It is a recurrent theme of Michael Walzer's work that criticism can be most effective from within an existing morality and a shared tradition—see e.g. *The Company of Critics*, pp. x, 19, 233–5.

23. One recent case particularly outraged many Americans, providing them 'with the motivation for criticism of the health-care system'—a woman named Charlesetta Brown arrived at New York's Harlem Hospital in the final stages of labour, but the hospital said it was full and refused to admit her. She gave birth on a stretcher in the admissions office, assisted only by two ambulance technicians, while doctors and other hospital employees watched. When an administrator ordered the doctor to help, he refused (see 'Bouquets and Brickbats', *Montreal Gazette* (28 Sept. 1991), p. B2).

24. For a similar recapitulation of Heidegger's idea of being-in-the-world focusing on the critique of traditional epistemology, see Charles Taylor, 'Overcoming Epistemology', in Kenneth Baynes, James Bohman, and Thomas McCarthy, eds., *After Philosophy: End or Transformation?* (Cambridge, Mass.: MIT Press, 1987), 459–88). Taylor draws from Heidegger's critique the implication that 'the task of reason has to be conceived quite differently [than the ideal of total disengagement]: as that of articulating this background [of non-explicit engagement with the world], "disclosing" what it involves' (pp. 477–8).

25. Richard Rorty, although drawing principally from the works of the late Wittgenstein (as opposed to De la Patrie's reliance on Heidegger), similarly argues that there is no standpoint outside what Rorty calls 'the particular historically conditioned and temporary vocabulary we are presently using' from which to judge this 'vocabulary' (see *Contingency, Irony and Solidarity*, 48, and ch. 3 generally).

For an argument critical of Habermas's attempt to assess moral and political projects in terms of a transcendental standard of 'rightness', also drawing from the works of the late Wittgenstein, see James Tully, 'Wittgenstein and

Political Philosophy: Understanding Practices of Critical Reflection', *Political Theory* (May 1989), esp. 174–92. Tully notes that

> Habermas's justificational activity does not transcend habitual practices but, rather, rests on the unreflected acceptance of juridical ways of thought and action . . . The practice itself [of thinking about, reflecting on, and acting in politics in juridical ways] mistakenly appears to be universal as a consequence of the special role the claim of universality plays *within* the practice of trumping other forms of argument. (p. 189; Tully's emphasis.)

26. In his Dewey Lectures, Rawls says:

> What justifies a conception of justice is not its being true to an order antecedent and given to us, but its congruence with our deeper understanding of ourselves and our aspirations, and our realization that, given our history and the traditions embedded in our public life, it is the most reasonable doctrine for us. ('Kantian Constructivism in Moral Theory', *Journal of Philosophy*, 77 (1980), 519; see also Chandran Kukathas and Philip Pettit, *Rawls: A Theory of Justice and its Critics* (Cambridge: Polity Press, 1990), 107, where the Dewey Lectures are invoked to counter the Walzerian accusation that Rawls embarked upon 'transcendental philosophy'.)

Both Rawls and Walzer, then, conceive of their project as cultural interpretation, and their dispute will turn on who did a better job of it. Against Rawls is the idea that individuals are to view their natural talents as assets of the whole community, an idea which may fit the Japanese context where 'talented individuals are supposed to let the rewards of talent flow back through them anonymously for the benefit of their group, company, or family' (Ellen Frost, *For Richer, For Poorer* (New York: Council on Foreign Relations, 1987), 68–9), but few people in Western liberal democracies think of their natural talents in such a manner.

27. Raymond Plant similarly advances an argument 'that there can be no specification of human needs outside of this or that society or form of life' (*Community and Ideology: An Essay in Applied Social Philosophy* (London: Routledge and Kegan Paul, 1974), 81) on the grounds that

> what counts as a need, or any other human attribute, capacity or power depends on the kind of social and ideological context involved . . . Instead of seeing a person, as it were approaching the social world with already determinate and identifiable needs and desires which demand fulfilment in the social world, the ability to identify aspects of one's own experience such as a nexus of needs or desires or wants was taken by Wittgenstein, and those who follow him here to *depend* upon a public language, with

public rules, set in a background of social convention, habits and tradition. (Ibid. 79, 80; Plant's emphasis.)

28. In medieval Europe, Walzer notes, the 'cure of souls' mattered more than the 'cure of bodies':

> Among medieval Christians, eternity was a socially recognized need; and every effort was made to see that it was widely and equally distributed, that every Christian had an equal chance at salvation and eternal life: hence, a church in every parish, regular services, catechism for the young, compulsory communion and so on. (*Spheres of Justice*, 87.)

29. Walzer draws from this phenomenon the implication that 'Morality is always potentially subversive of class and power' (*Interpretation and Social Criticism*, 22). For similar arguments that point to the inevitable gap between 'the morality' of social institutions and shared meanings, hence of the possibility that the latter can be invoked to criticize the former, see Hanna Pitkin, *Wittgenstein and Justice* (Berkeley, Calif.: University of California Press, 1972), 187–90 and Mark Blitz, *Heidegger's Being and Time and the Possibility of Political Philosophy* (London: Cornell University Press, 1981), 256–7.

30. De la Patrie is referring to the following passage:

> Assume now that the Indian villagers really do accept the doctrines that support the caste system. A visitor to the village might still try to convince them—it is an entirely respectable activity—that those doctrines are false. (*Spheres of Justice*, 314.)

Given Walzer's (and De la Patrie's) other claim that criticism is most effective if it draws upon an existing morality, however, this 'visitor' would in all likelihood be wasting her time.

31. William Galston points out that Walzer's premiss that social worlds cannot be ranked and ordered with regard to their understanding of social goods is inconsistent with his other premiss that justice consists in respecting the cultural creations of others—the latter implies that a society which respects the cultural creations of others is superior to one which does not (according to some trans-communal standard), i.e. the latter implies that social worlds can be ranked ('Community, Democracy, Philosophy', 123).

32. Given what De la Patrie has said earlier about mealtime practices in Act I, however, there should not be any 'shared meaning' beneath and beyond the practice itself justifying that practice—why we eat as we do is explained (and justified) simply by the fact that that is what we in fact do. Some practices, then, would seem to be supported (and justified) by a certain morality (e.g. the practices of the caste system), and others are not (e.g. eating practices).

33. See Noam Chomsky, *Turning the Tide: U.S. Intervention in Central America and the Struggle for Peace* (Boston: South End Press, 1985) for a compelling

explanation of why the US government provided aid to the Contras notwithstanding widespread opposition to this policy among the American public—
Chomsky's basic point is that the American government could not admit that
the goal of its Contra policy was to support a group which would sow enough
terror and destruction in Nicaragua to avert the danger that the 'virus' of successful, independent development might 'infect' the region (hence limit
access to the raw materials of the region). On Chomsky's terms, the US government's Contra policy succeeded, i.e. Nicaragua did not prove to be a
showcase of successful, independent development, and as a special bonus its
war-weary, demoralized population eventually voted in a government more
friendly to US big business interests.

34. For a particularly devastating report by a Pulitzer-Prize-winning journalist
who spent over five years covering the Contras and their CIA handlers which
shows how the American presence in Nicaragua betrayed American ideals, see
Sam Dillon, *Commandos: The CIA and Nicaragua's Contra Rebels* (New York:
Henry Holt and Co., 1991).

35. Another possibility, which is consistent with De la Patrie's second alternative,
is that Reagan brainwashed himself into believing his own pronouncements
that aid to the Contras promotes freedom. This would have been analogous to
the process by means of which top military men came to accept the 'window
of vulnerability' idea in the late 1980s, as discussed by Steven Kull, who interviewed 84 current and former US defence policy-makers (who spoke on condition that their identities would not be revealed) for his book, *Minds at War:
Nuclear Reality and the Inner Conflicts of Defense Policymakers* (New York:
Basic Books, 1988). The excerpt below is from a chapter entitled,
'Maintaining the Perception of Balance' (quoted in *Harper's Magazine* (Sept.
1988), 27):

> Another respondent who was involved in developing the window of vul-
> nerability concept described the process with remarkable lucidity. Early in
> the interview he had dismissed military rationales for weapons deploy-
> ments, emphasizing instead the concern for perceptions. When he
> described how he had become involved in the window of vulnerability
> idea, he told of gradually accepting a belief that he had not taken seriously
> at first. Speaking of a call for a strategic buildup in the late 1970s, he said,
>
> A: It did make sense then . . . Those were the good old days of the win-
>   dow of vulnerability. Until we wished it out of existence with the
>   Scowcroft Commission . . .
> Q: Did you buy the window of vulnerability idea?
> A: No, not entirely. It was invented in part of my office. [We] discovered
>   it in 1975. I distinctly remember it . . .
> Q: You don't seem to think the problem they focused on was a real prob-
>   lem.

A: [*Nods affirmatively.*]

Q: Do you think most of the people involved with that thinking also recognize that it wasn't really a problem?

A: I think for a while I did believe it. I think for a while a lot of us believed it . . . I think we probably ended up scaring ourselves a bit. Sort of like the tales children tell themselves—'Hey, let's get really scared.' And then you do your old 'Geez, it's terrible.'

Q: Did you know you were doing that?

A: [*Under his breath*] Did we know we were doing that? In part, probably, yes. The trouble with intellectuals is that they get seized by the power of their ideas and then say, 'Gee, this is fun.' Or you play, 'what if' and then . . . you forget at a certain point that you're playing what if.

36. The Afrikaner poet, Breyten Breytenbach is one example—the South African nation, in his view, can only come into being when apartheid is overcome, for it is apartheid that curbs 'the forming of a South African nation— politically, economically, culturally and therefore also racially—which should be one of the most normal things on earth given our interdependence and mutually hybrid origins' (quoted in Walzer, *The Company of Critics*, 217).

37. It is an interesting question to what extent this explanation of the rise to power of the Nazis can be generalized, i.e. is it generally true that tyrants with little concern for the shared meanings of their subjects are most likely to manifest themselves in periods of economic and political instability? For this view, one can point to the large majority of underdeveloped nations, where opportunists, crooks, and mentally unstable tyrants more often than not take advantage of frequent crises to assume power. (It is a separate, though crucial, question whether or not the economic and political crises of underdeveloped nations are importantly due to the activities of the economic and political structures of the developed world.) Against this view, one can point to stable, self-reproducing dynastic tyrannies in history—the 4,000-year cycle of dynasties in China comes to mind as a paradigm case. What is distinctive about the tyrannical behaviour of ancient Chinese rulers, however, is that it had very little to do with the ordinary lives—local, communal arrangements, family affairs, and so on—of the vast majority of the common people. In other words, it is this policy of benign neglect which helps to explain the stability of the dynastic system in China. That the Chinese Communist Party broke this unwritten, golden rule of long-term political power in China—i.e. the Chinese will tolerate a government so long as it does not interfere too much with their ordinary lives—by organizing recurrent waves of terror invasive of the lives of common people prompts Simon Leys to comment that the Communists 'betrayed a strange incapacity to understand their own people'. (*New York Review of Books* (11 Oct. 1990), 10.)

38. What Schwartzberg says coincides with the view of John Lukacs, who in a review article of Goebbels's diaries ('In Love with Hitler', *New York Review of Books* (21 July 1988), 14–16) argues that the Nazis' rise to power was due in part to the fact that National Socialist propaganda 'struck deep chords in the consciousness of increasing numbers of Germans' without, however, explaining what he means by this. He goes on to say that this alleged fact suggests the need to revise 'the accepted view that the sudden rise in Nazi votes was a result of the economic crisis that befell Germany soon after the New York stock market crash in 1929'. Though Lukacs points out that the appeal of the Nazis had already begun to grow in 1929, a prosperous time in the history of the Weimar Republic, he seems to base his claim that Hitler and Goebbels had deep insight into the consciousness of the German people primarily on the absolute confidence of these two men that it was just a matter of time before they would be in power, a confidence they possessed long before the economic and political crisis of the Weimar Republic. I find it difficult to share Lukacs's opinion that this confidence *per se* is 'astonishing'—a visit to the nearest mental hospital will uncover, I'm sure, two men who have the same level of confidence that it's just a matter of time before they rule their country.

39. This is confirmed by Michael Balfour's recent book, *Withstanding Hitler in Germany: 1933–1945* (London: Routledge, 1988).

40. Jung Chang tells her story in *Wild Swans: Three Daughters of China* (New York: Simon and Schuster, 1991).

41. Another possibility is that the 'prevailing moral beliefs and intuitions' of the German people harbour inconsistencies, and that a 'pro-democratic' German would be defending that aspect of German culture against its 'authoritarian' aspect—more generally it can be argued that 'internal criticism' involves (on occasion) taking sides, drawing upon one aspect of a culture to criticize another. Schwartzberg, it should be noted, would not have been appeased had De la Patrie raised this point, for the 'internal critic' who admits to taking sides, as opposed to claiming that her interpretation captures the 'deepest', 'most authentic' morality of her people, would still be restricting herself to the morality of her people.

42. In his *Interpretation and Social Criticism*, Walzer develops the idea of transcommunally shared prohibitions, which he sees as 'products of many people talking, of real if always tentative, intermittent and unfinished conversations. We might best think of them not as discovered or invented but rather as emergent prohibitions, the work of many years, of trial and error, of failed, partial and insecure understandings' (p. 24). Galston endorses this sort of 'nontranscendent universality' which supposes 'that the denizens of the various caves, though divided on many issues, converge on their understanding of core social and moral propositions' ('Community, Democracy, Philosophy', 126).

43. It is presumably the possibility of a society which does not recognize Walzer's
     interpretation of 'a kind of minimal and universal moral code' that led
     Walzer to shift his justification for this code from the fact of it having arisen
     from 'the actual historical processes of societies' (*Interpretation and Social
     Criticism*, 24) to the (acontextual) proposition that these prohibitions are
     necessary if humans are to realize their potential as culture-creating creatures
     (in a discussion held following the 'Tanner Lectures' he gave at Oxford in
     Trinity Term, 1989). Notwithstanding his claim that this code belongs to the
     realm of 'absolute justice', whereas his (relativist) idea of spheres of justice
     with shared meanings underlying the distribution of social goods applies to
     (how we should think about) 'distributive justice', this concession to advo-
     cates of a (transcendental) universalism not dependent on 'the actual histori-
     cal process of societies' undermines his 'spheres of justice' project—why
     shouldn't there be basic goods other than 'mere prohibitions' which human
     beings need (as 'transcendental liberals' would have it) to realize their poten-
     tial as culture-creating creatures, with implications for distributive justice?

44. Barry Stroud has canvassed and found wanting various attempts at offsetting
     the slide into scepticism (the view that one could never know anything about
     the world around us, or even if there is such a world) by those (e.g. Kant,
     G. E. Moore, Quine) who remain within the Cartesian epistemological tradi-
     tion—see his *The Significance of Philosophical Scepticism* (Oxford: Clarendon
     Press, 1984).

45. In his article 'Overcoming Epistemology', Charles Taylor similarly argues
     that the Heideggerian account of the conditions of intentionality should be
     seen as a gain in reason, a better understanding of 'our deep or authentic
     nature as selves' (p. 483). Taylor develops the idea of 'transition arguments',
     that there can be intellectual and moral growth from position X to position Y
     if the transition from X to Y can be shown to represent a gain in understand-
     ing, whereas a similarly plausible narrative of a possible transition from Y to X
     could not be constructed, in 'Explanation and Practical Reason', Wider
     Working Paper WP72, World Institute for Development Economics
     Research (Helsinki, 1989).

     In the same vein, Alasdair MacIntyre, in his recent book *Whose Justice?
     Which Rationality?* (London: Duckworth, 1988), argues that there can be
     progress within a tradition if that tradition responds successfully to a stage of
     dissolution of historically founded certitudes which MacIntyre terms an 'epis-
     temological crisis'. The solution to an epistemological crisis requires the
     invention or discovery of new concepts and the framing of new types of the-
     ory which meet three requirements:

     > First, this in some ways radically new and conceptually enriched scheme,
     > if it is to put an end to epistemological crisis, must furnish a solution to
     > the problems which had proved intractable in a systematic and coherent

way. Second, it must also provide an explanation of just what it was which rendered the tradition, before it had acquired these new resources, sterile or incoherent or both. And third, these first two tasks must be carried out in a way which exhibits some fundamental continuity of the new conceptual and theoretical structures with the shared beliefs in terms of which the tradition of enquiry had been defined up to this point. (p. 362)

46. Heidegger infamously discounted the uniqueness of the Holocaust in terms of 'the history of man's misdeeds' by comparing 'the manufacture of corpses in the gas chambers and the death camp' to mechanized agriculture in a lecture he gave at Bremen in 1949 (see Catherine H. Zuckert, 'Martin Heidegger: His Philosophy and his Politics', *Political Theory* (Feb. 1990), 71). Heidegger thought that both should be regarded as embodiments of the 'same technological frenzy' (ibid. 71), which, if left unchecked, would lead to a world-wide ecological catastrophe (see Peter Kemp, 'Heidegger's Greatness and his Blindness', *Philosophy and Social Criticism* (Apr. 1989), 121).

Act III: A Communitarian Moral Vision and Some Political Consequences

SCENE: *the same.*

[*Waiter rushes over*]

WAITER [*to Anne*] Ça va, Madame? Il y avait du bruit.

ANNE Oui, ça va.

WAITER Et votre compagnon? Ça va bien, dans sa tête?

ANNE [*hesitates*] Euh, oui, je pense.

[*Waiter leaves; Philip comes back, and reappropriates his chair*]

ANNE It's nice to see you. I wasn't sure if you were coming back. I thought you might have exited by means of the bathroom window, existentialist anti-hero style.

PHILIP No, I just needed some time alone to think. In any case, the bathroom is located in the basement.

ANNE Please, tell me what you've been thinking about.

PHILIP OK. Have you heard of the idea of *Volksgemeinschaft*, or the community of the racial people? This idea was central to Nazi ideology, which depended heavily upon ideas of blood relationships and the rootedness of the organically given soil and landscape.[1]

ANNE [*bored*] Yes, I've heard of this idea.

PHILIP My point is significant. I believe that this idea stems from a lament for *Gemeinschaft*, the intimate, reciprocating local community with little if any physical and social mobility. In *Gemeinschaft*, something which one is born into and grows within, the individual fails to differentiate between his interests and those of the local community. The *Gemeinschaft* ideal is that of the static, orderly, rooted conception of community, where people simply assume and fulfil socially given roles. Members of the community are tied to fixed modes and hierarchies of status and power; their behaviour is regulated by an instinctive, unqualified attachment to the local community.[2]

ANNE Notwithstanding your dry academic tone, I detect a certain hostility to this notion.

PHILIP [*raises voice*] You're certainly right about that—you'll excuse me if I have a prejudice against anything Nazis have found congenial . . . Fortunately, the *Gemeinschaft* ideal is unrealizable in the modern world—the size and concentration of capitalist societies have meant the breaking up of older, small-scale communities and of long-standing ties between people,[3] such that even if you wanted to re-implement *Gemeinschaft* now, your attempts would be futile. Communitarianism, in short, is both dangerous and backwards-looking.

ANNE Now hold on a minute, Philip. I never said that modern-day communitarians uphold the *Gemeinschaft* ideal.[4] Moreover, I'm not so sure that such a community has ever existed. I do not know off hand of any society where members have subordinated *all* their commitments to the good of *one* community.[5] Plato recognized as much when he abolished, in his ideal Republic, the family for his philosopher-king guardian class so as to enable these to preoccupy themselves solely with affairs of state.[6]

PHILIP Oh? So what's your ideal, then? Is it *Gesellschaft*, modern large-scale society composed of atomistic individuals who associate only on instrumental grounds and whose relationships are governed by legal, rational notions of consent, volition, and contract?[7]

ANNE Why this dichotomy? In the modern world, at least, we think of ourselves neither as undifferentiated *Gemeinschaft* subjects living in small, self-sufficient villages, nor as alienated, free-floating *Gesellschaft* people. Rather, we find that we do in fact have communal attachments, but that our loyalties stretch to more than one community— home-town, nation, family, and so on[8] . . . So when you ask about the communitarian ideal, or the moral stand that one should adopt with respect to a communal life most appropriate for those of us living in the modern world, we must begin with a recognition of the fact that most of us identify with *many* communities.

PHILIP That, I presume, is what you did in your thesis.

ANNE [*excitedly*] Yes! Communitarians, you see, have been criticized for failing to develop a theory of community[9]—everyone knows that communitarians place special emphasis upon communal life, but few have a clear grasp of what sort of community we are to value. So what I did— and this represents my most original contribution to scholarship—is to distinguish between several types of communities to which we feel deeply attached. In fact, my discussion of the various types of communities that have come to characterize the identity of 'Westerners' constitutes the main body of my thesis!

PHILIP Are you saying that we haven't even reached the main body of your thesis yet? I think we should order some wine . . .

ANNE Why, are you bored?

PHILIP No, of course not—the wine can only add to my joy. Besides, we'd be abiding by the French custom of deliberating while sharing good wine.

ANNE Mmh, you may have a point there. You can choose the wine, so long as you choose from within the category of wines compatible with *choucroute*.

PHILIP [*calls waiter*] *Garçon!*

ANNE [*alarmed*] Don't say 'garçon', which is thought to be a demeaning appellation. Say 'monsieur' instead.

PHILIP Sorry . . . *Monsieur!*

[*Waiter comes to Philip's table*]

PHILIP [*to waiter*] Nous voulons un vin pour accompagner cette choucroute, s'il-vous-plaît.

WAITER [*looking at the now-empty platter of* choucroute] C'est un peu tard, monsieur.

PHILIP [*determined to pursue his request*] Quel vin pouvez-vous suggérer?

WAITER [*confidently*] Le vin blanc accompagne la choucroute. Vous pouvez choisir entre un Riesling et un Gewurztraminer d'Alsace. Le Riesling est un vin sec tandis que le Gewurztraminer est plutôt fruité.

PHILIP Le sec, s'il-vous-plaît.

[*Waiter leaves*]

PHILIP That was an easy choice, as I only understood one of the alternatives. 'Sec', I know, means dry, but I didn't quite grasp the other one.

ANNE He said 'fruité', which means 'fruity', or wine which tastes of the grape.

PHILIP Whatever. As long as it's not alcohol-free, I'll drink the wine [*Anne cringes in response to this statement*].

[*Waiter arrives with a Riesling, which he serves to Anne and Philip, without bothering to ask Philip to sample the wine.*]

PHILIP Cheers, as we say in England.

ANNE A la vôtre, as we say in formal French.

[*Both drink some wine*]

PHILIP You were saying something about the communitarian ideal . . .

ANNE Yes. I said that an argument in favour of communal life for those of us living in the modern world must begin with a recognition of the fact that most of us identify with many communities. So in my thesis I drew attention to the particular communities that have come, for whatever concatenation of historical reasons, to constitute our identity. Given deeply felt attachments to those communities, I then drew certain 'communitarian' political implications, by which I mean, stated in general terms, a palatable and feasible politics that allows people to experience their life as bound up with the good of the communities which constitute their identity, as opposed to a liberal politics concerned primarily with securing the conditions for individuals to lead autonomous lives . . .

PHILIP [*interrupting*] One thing at a time, one thing at a time! Before you go any further, let me ask you a simple question—why even begin with an argument that seeks to promote communal life? Is there more than your particular preference for giving priority to the good of collectivities?

ANNE The justification for the communitarian ideal, which emphasizes this need to experience our lives as bound up with the good of the particular communities out of which our identity has been constituted, is twofold. Firstly, the communitarian ideal is consistent with, but not derivable from, communitarian ontology. I already said that communitarian ontology—the idea that we are first and foremost social beings, embodied agents 'in-the-world' engaged in realizing a certain form of life—represents a gain in understanding over those ontologies/epistemologies which give priority to a disengaged subject standing over against an external world, so a moral stance, as I see it, must be at least consistent with communitarian ontology. But while one's ontological stance can form the essential background for one's moral stance, I granted that the two are distinct in the sense that ontology can do no more than structure the field of possibilities in a more perspicuous way, or define the options which it is meaningful to support by advocacy, so another argument is required to explain why one has adopted a particular moral stance. That argument, quite simply, is the congruence of the communitarian ideal with a deeper understanding of ourselves and our aspirations. If you ask yourself what matters most in your life, I think that the answer will involve a commitment to the good of the communities out of which your identity has been constituted, a need to experience your life as bound up with that of what we can call 'constitutive communities' . . .

PHILIP That doesn't sound like much of an argument to me, if only because I don't quite understand what you're talking about. What does this mean, a 'constitutive community'? How does one distinguish those communities out of which our identity has been constituted from other forms of association?

ANNE Good question. In my thesis, I proposed three criteria for distinguishing *constitutive* communities from other forms of association, contingent attachments, fleeting 'facts' about oneself, and so on. That is, there are three ways of answering the question 'how can constitutive communities be identified?' The first, and perhaps most obvious, is how people answer the question 'who are you?' If you are asked about your identity, you wouldn't answer 'I am a member of the neighbourhood committee campaigning for better garbage service.' Rather, you'd answer 'I'm Canadian, a member of the Schwartzberg family . . .'[10]

PHILIP [*interrupting*] I'd also answer 'I'm Jewish.'

ANNE Yes. So the first step for those concerned with identifying constitutive communities, in distinguishing those from contingent facts about one's identity, is to focus on how it is that people themselves define their sense of who they are.

PHILIP Why do you say 'the first step'? Isn't people's sense of who they are a sufficient step?

ANNE It's not sufficient for the reason that people can be confused about their identity, certain features of their identity can be repressed, or whatever. It's a psychological truism that people can go wrong in terms of their self-understanding, so someone's conscious belief about which community or communities matters most to them can't be the final say in this matter. We implicitly recognize this when we say things like 'He's so American', a statement whose truth value does not depend on the American's recognizing that 'being American' strongly influences his way of being in the world. In fact, we would often say this of people attempting to escape or deny their 'Americanness' . . . But before you interrupt me, as you've done so often in this discussion of ours, let me go on to the second way of distinguishing constitutive communities from other forms of association—constitutive communities provide a largely background way of meaningful thinking, acting, and judging, a way of being in the world which is much deeper and more many-sided than any possible articulation of it. If someone asks you what it means to be a Jew, for example, you can say a few things, but deep down you know that this sort of question can't be properly answered. That's not true of the voluntary association I mentioned earlier, which is nothing more than what you think of it, i.e. a gathering of individuals from your neighbourhood campaigning for better garbage service.

PHILIP I don't like this implication of yours that my own self-interpretation of 'what it means to be a Jew' only scratches the surface. If most of 'what it means to be a Jew' lies in the background at any one time, if I can never bring to consciousness much of 'what it means to be a Jew', does that mean that this feature of my identity is exempt from evaluation and possible rejection?[11]

ANNE [*excitedly*] Precisely! If constitutive communities provide a largely background way of being in the world, it follows that those communities can't be shed like membership of a voluntary association. You can walk out of the neighbourhood committee I've been talking about and at that point no one can plausibly claim that you're still a member of that committee; but even if you try to strip yourself of your Jewishness, this will in all likelihood prove to be self-defeating. It will be apparent to any outsider that you're still a Jew.

PHILIP [*raises voice*] That sounds both wrong and potentially dangerous. How can you say that I'm locked into a so-called 'Jewish way of being' no matter what I do, that being Jewish is a permanent, non-revisable feature of my identity? There's a whole, tragic history of 'Jews' being defined as Jews by outsiders, you know.

ANNE We don't have to talk about Jews if you would prefer not to—let's take my case. I was brought up in a Catholic home and culture, practised religious rites as a child, most of my friends are Catholic, and I feel personally harmed by an attack on the Catholic religion. Do you think it makes sense to say that I can stop being Catholic and become something else?

PHILIP I don't know about your case, but I think I could substantially reforge my religious identity if I really had to. I have a friend who did just that—he adopted Buddhism. I admit that he's a little, um, how shall I say—mentally unstable. But it sure can't be denied that he changed.

ANNE Your interpretation of your friend's mental condition bears significantly on our discussion. Let's say you go to a stimulating lecture on
Buddhism. That evening, while sitting back comfortably in our Oxford
armchair, you reflect upon your existing commitments, and decide that
Buddhism sounds more interesting than Judaism. So you 'choose' to
adopt Buddhism, phoning your mother the next day to announce that
you've become a Buddhist. Now, I don't know your mother, but I'm
fairly certain she would think you'd fallen mentally ill . . .

PHILIP Not just that. She'd send an assassination squad over to
England—I too was brought up in a very religious household. But to
take a more serious example, let's say that I gave up Jewish religious
practices, my Jewish friends, and so on, and then adopted and practised Buddhism for a period of twenty years. At that point, I think, it
would be accurate to say 'I am a Buddhist.'

ANNE It would be more accurate to say 'I am a Jew turned Buddhist, still
fundamentally different from someone for whom Buddhism has been
constitutive of her identity since birth, i.e. who was born and bred in a
Buddhist household and culture.'

PHILIP Maybe I'd still be different from 'someone for whom Buddhism
has been constitutive of her identity since birth', but I wouldn't be a
Jew in any meaningful sense of the word once I abandoned Jewish religious teachings, Jewish friends, and all the other Jewish things we can
name.

ANNE My point is that even the best interpreter of the Jewish religion can
name only a few 'Jewish things'. Much of what it means to be a Jew, or
to be a Canadian, or to be a member of the Schwartzberg family, lies in
the background. Our identity, as I said, is much deeper than any possible articulation of it. How can you subject something to willed change
if it can't be rendered meaningfully explicit?

PHILIP Even if you're right that much of 'what it means to be a Jew'
resists articulation, it doesn't follow that ceasing to be something
requires knowing in detail what it means to be that thing. Does an
atheist have to know in detail what it means to be an atheist in order to
forsake his atheism for religion?

ANNE Atheism isn't much more than a particular belief reducible to
propositional form, namely, the belief that there's no God—this belief
can be brought to consciousness, reflected upon, and subjected to
willed change, although of course forsaking atheism for religion would
normally have more to do with revelation than reflection . . . If you've

been brought up in a Jewish household, by contrast, then 'being Jewish' would be much more than a belief system—you, for example, probably don't even notice your Jewish accent . . .

PHILIP [*interrupting*] Jewish accent? What does that mean?

ANNE For example, the rising intonation at the end of your questions, heavily suggestive of sarcasm. But there's much more than that—the Woody Allenesque way in which you move those thick eyebrows of yours is another distinctively Jewish trait. I'm only scratching the surface, of course.

PHILIP That's crazy! One is only a Jew in so far as one manifests distinctly Jewish behaviour!

ANNE No, of course the Jewish identity is normally experienced as a religious belief system, special concern for the fate of Israel, knowledge of Jewish history, and so on. But the relative unimportance of beliefs can be brought out in the following, rather morbid example that I'm borrowing from my thesis. Suppose you have two women, *A* and *B*. *A* is Catholic, *B* is Jewish, but both marry Jewish men. *A*, to please her Jewish husband's family, converts to Judaism, and ends up learning more about Jewish religion and history than *B* knows about her own religion and history. Five years after the couples are happily married, an unfortunate event occurs—both Jewish men die in separate car accidents. *A* and *B* are of course shattered by this event, and both choose the same route as a means of escaping the psychological pain caused by the death of their husbands—they seek to shed their Judaism, as this religion reminds them of time spent with their ex-husbands. Now, consult your intuitions here—who will have an easier time of it? *B*, brought up as a Jew, or *A*, who although better versed in Jewish religious teachings and history than *B*, only recently converted to Judaism? I think that the attempt to escape Judaism will likely prove to be self-defeating for *B*, but not for *A*, who can fall back on the Catholicism of her youth, a religion which she never really left behind in the first place. In other words, it makes more sense to say of *A* that she can 'stop being Jewish', even though she may have had more conscious knowledge of Jewish religious teachings and history than *B* who merely adopted her Jewish identity by being reared in a Jewish household . . . My point then, is that we're principally connected with those 'constitutive' features of our identity in a way which resists articulation, and that this explains why it's not possible to stand apart from those features so as to subject them to evaluation and possible rejection.

PHILIP I don't know about this idea that one is inextricably bound up with one's 'constitutive communities', but you may have a point that the question of identity doesn't turn on the issue of knowledge about the particular community with which one identifies. A Chinaman who reads a good book about Canadian history will probably have a better grasp of that subject than I do, and perhaps he will surpass me in his ability to articulate 'what it means to be a Canadian', but that doesn't mean he's more Canadian than me.

ANNE If I were 'in your shoes', so to speak, I wouldn't be so anxious to reveal my ignorance of Canadian history.

PHILIP Well, I've been away from Canada for a few years, you know. In any case I have a very important question to ask you. Let's assume that, in answer to the question 'who are you?', I answer, among other things, 'I'm Jewish.' Next, let's also assume that the Jewish community constitutes my identity in a largely background way. I can try to articulate 'what it means to be a Jew', but I can't really get to the essence, with the consequence that this aspect of my identity isn't amenable to willed rejection. And now let me remind you of your 'communitarian ideal', this idea of experiencing our lives as bound up with the good of the particular communities out of which our identity has been constituted—this idea, I venture, simply doesn't follow from the fact of a certain community or communities constituting one's identity. Why should I want to experience my life as bound up with the good of these 'constitutive communities'? It may be *descriptively* true that I'm Jewish, and even that this is a permanent feature of my identity, but so what? Why should I *value* the Jewish community?

ANNE You have a very uncommon perspective on this issue. If you define yourself as a Jew, this would normally be interpreted as something more than a descriptive fact about yourself—you'd be saying that you experience a sense of shared fate with that of the Jewish community as a whole, that you have a special bond of solidarity with other Jews, and that this bond gives meaning to your life. Defining yourself as a Jew, then, would normally entail *valuing* the Jewish community in a way that's not true of other religious communities.

PHILIP All I can say is that in my case the 'fact' of being Jewish doesn't entail 'valuing' the Jewish community. When I read about Israel's treatment of Palestinians, I feel very alienated from what you called my 'Jewish way of being', to the point that I seek to reject that part of myself. Have you never heard of the phenomenon of the 'self-hating Jew'?

ANNE Is that really how you think of yourself, as a self-hating Jew? Isn't that appellation normally employed as a term of opprobrium, meant to impugn the motives of the person who's being targeted for attack?

PHILIP You may have a point there. I don't think of myself as a self-hating Jew, but you still haven't answered my point about it not following from the fact of defining myself as a Jew that I ought to 'value' the Jewish community, or to experience my life as bound up with the good of the Jewish community.

ANNE Let me clear up two possible misunderstandings about what it means to 'value' a constitutive community, and this may cause you to overcome your reluctance to admit that Jews have a special place in your heart.[12] The first is perhaps the most obvious: that you experience your life as bound up with the good of a certain community does not entail adopting a stance of indifference, much less hostility, to 'outsiders'.[13] You may feel part of the Canadian community, but that doesn't mean that you should be indifferent to, say, the plight of starving Ethiopians. The second possible misunderstanding is the following: 'valuing' a community doesn't mean that you have a special obligation to endorse every particular belief or deed of that community. Some beliefs may not cohere with people's deepest sense of how they ought to live, and some practices can be condemned by shared meanings, as I've already said. That you experience a sense of shared fate with the Jewish community as a whole, then, does not necessarily rule out the possibility of criticizing Israel's activities in the occupied territories. In fact, this sense of shared fate, this concern for the Jewish community as a whole, would largely explain why your attention is drawn to this issue in the first place—you detect an inconsistency between what you've learned about 'what it means to be a Jew' and what 'we' are doing in the occupied territories,[14] you're concerned about the effect of this policy on the character of the Israeli people in the long run . . .

PHILIP Actually, I'm more concerned about the effect of Israel's activities in the occupied territories on the Palestinian people than I am about the effect of this policy on 'the character of Israelis', and there's something morally perverse about the suggestion that it's the latter which would justify my opposition to what 'we' are doing in the occupied territories . . .

ANNE I'd rather not get into this question of justification again. I just meant to suggest that your experience of shared fate with the Jewish community might itself lead you to direct critical energies at your own community—why do you care more about Israeli repression in the occupied territories than about Chinese repression in Tibet?—in the context of the argument that 'valuing' a community doesn't imply endorsement of every particular belief or deed of that community . . . So having cleared up the second possible misunderstanding about what it means to 'value' a constitutive community, do you still want to maintain your separation between 'the fact' of being Jewish and the 'value' that you'd be committed to the overall good of the Jewish community in a way that's not true of other religious groupings? Do you still deny that with your self-definition as a Jew comes the experience of being bound up with the good of the Jewish community?

PHILIP Let's leave my case alone. I still haven't heard any arguments from you that would satisfy someone who (*a*) recognizes that his identity is constituted by a certain community and (*b*) far from experiencing his life as bound up with the good of that community, feels alienated from that community, doing what he can to escape from its grip.

ANNE This imaginary person of yours would be seriously disturbed, and perhaps that's what should motivate him to accept the idea that constitutive communities should be 'valued'.

PHILIP You're going to have to explain yourself.

ANNE Well, I've already said that a constitutive community provides a largely background way of meaningful thinking, acting, and judging, but I want to emphasize that applying effort to 'escape from its grip', trying to flee this setting which gives meaning to your life, is not merely self-defeating in the sense that one has adopted a project which cannot be significantly realized. It's much more serious than that— those who seek to cast aside a constitutive community will suffer from an acute form of disorientation, their world will come to be seen as deprived of sense, as emptied of meaningful possibilities.[15] This painful and frightening state will take different forms in different places— excessive brooding in trendy cafés for the French, the Swedes will toy with suicidal thoughts, Americans will visit their neighbourhood psychiatrist, and so on—so it is difficult to be more precise without turning to a detailed look at particular examples . . .

PHILIP Essentially, though, you're saying that I'm mentally ill if I feel alienated from one of my 'constitutive communities' . . .

ANNE That's one way of putting it. I wouldn't say that.

PHILIP What do you say in your thesis?

ANNE I use the term 'damaged human personhood'.

PHILIP 'Damaged human personhood'? So yours is a thesis about human nature—if someone seeks to escape a 'constitutive community', this, to use your words, 'setting which gives meaning to one's life', that person will suffer from an acute form of disorientation which calls for remedy. All humans have this need for experiencing their life as bound up with the good of the particular communities which constitute their identity, and when they turn their backs on this need, their 'personhood' is damaged in some deep way.

ANNE Since you like using my words, I'll make more use of yours—'so what's the problem?'

PHILIP Well, I don't see how you can accommodate the 'damaged human personhood' thesis with your earlier claim that you were against the idea of proposing needs which are the property of human beings as such, outside of the particular context which determines what's to count as a need. If communitarian ontology rules out the possibility of conceiving of asocial human beings who enter society with a basic set of needs which demand fulfilment, and central to the communitarian ideal is this idea that one's 'personhood' is damaged if this need for communal identification goes unfulfilled, you have to admit that 'communitarian ontology' and 'the communitarian ideal' are inconsistent. So you should retract what you said earlier about the consistence of the communitarian ideal with communitarian ontology helping to justify that ideal . . .

ANNE Look, I never denied that there were psychological or anthropological universals, but everything important in terms of one's conception of personal goals and communal recognition of certain problems which call for political solutions will indeed depend on how these 'universals' are interpreted in particular contexts . . . You have spiritual outlooks such as Buddhism which want us to transcend or escape particularist attachments—in the Buddhist view, attachment to all physical and mental aspects of our environment is suffering, and suffering is only overcome with the liberation from particularist attachments.[16] The ultimate goal of Buddhism is the attainment of nirvana, that state where all particularist attachments have been uprooted—a 'Buddhist mother' would treat a total stranger no differently than she treats her only child[17]. . .

PHILIP [*interrupting*] Were this a Buddhist world, I pity the 'total strangers' who would be smothered by the love my mother shows for me.

ANNE [*ignoring Philip's comment*] It is interesting to note that Buddhists agree on the whole with my diagnosis of the prospects for those who come to lose their commitment to particularist attachments—it's a state where life's possibilities become levelled, without any sensations, where the good and bad become indistinguishable.[18] But whereas the Buddhist calls this state 'nirvana', we in the modern world would find something deeply pathological about someone for whom the good and the bad, the trivial and the meaningful, have become indistinguishable, about a person unable or unwilling to take a stand on the many things which have significance for us. Someone who has 'overcome suffering' would, in our view, be damaged in some deep way. Given that others may differ in their interpretation of this state, however, I'll reserve use of the term 'damaged human personhood' to those of us in the modern world, 'Westerners', if you will, who lose their commitment to the particular, constitutive groupings that previously filled their lives with meaning . . .

PHILIP [*pause*] Let me ask you something, Anne. I'm Jewish, as you know by now. In terms of my relationship with the Jewish community, it would seem that you offer only the choices of experiencing my life as bound up with the good of the Jewish community or striving in vain to escape from the grip of that community, which you seem to associate with some form of mental illness. Is it not possible, though, to feel indifferent with respect to one's religion? That someone neither defines themselves by their religion nor embarks on a painful, self-defeating enterprise to rid themselves of their religion, but merely stands in a more or less neutral relationship with respect to their religion?

ANNE I don't think it's possible for those of us who've had a very religious upbringing, but it's certainly true that religion no longer plays the dominant role of filling most people's lives with meaning that it used to. Religion, that is, no longer constitutes most people's identity, which helps to explain why I didn't dwell on this subject in my thesis . . .

PHILIP [*interrupting*] Before you go any further, you're going to have to say a little bit about which 'people' you're talking about. It's typical of your approach thus far that you invoke a mysterious community's way of life to support your claims, but this tactic leaves me more confused than enlightened . . .

ANNE I've already said that I sought to provide an account of a communal life most appropriate for those of us living in the modern world, 'Westerners', if you will, describing and distinguishing between the various sorts of communal attachments that we, 'inhabitants of late twentieth-century democracies', currently have . . . And perhaps this is, finally, the appropriate moment to turn to a detailed look at those communities, but I should say at the outset that I did nothing more than provide a 'snapshot view' of the particular communities that have come to constitute the identity of Westerners, providing neither a historical explanation of why it is that we've come to define our identity in terms of certain communities and not others, nor a metaphysical account *à la* Hegel which bears on the importance of certain communal forms of life . . .

PHILIP So how did you go about identifying 'our' constitutive communities?

ANNE I've already told you the three criteria I employed to distinguish 'constitutive communities' from contingent attachments. I said that one should start with how it is that people in fact define themselves, i.e. how they answer the question 'who are you?' Next, I said that a constitutive community provides a largely background way of meaningful thinking, acting, and judging. The last criterion will have emerged from our discussion of the last few minutes—one loses a commitment to a constitutive community at the price of being thrown into a state of severe disorientation where one is unable to take a stand on many things of significance.

PHILIP And how did you go about applying these criteria? You said that one should start with how it is that people in fact define themselves— did you begin by distributing a poll to 'Westerners', to inhabitants of Canada, Germany, Iceland, Australia, and so on, asking them to answer the question 'who are you?'

ANNE Please, Philip, make an effort to contain your scepticism. That I identified certain communities as constitutive rests ultimately on the intuitive obviousness of these as constitutive communities, but that's not necessarily a disadvantage if I succeeded in capturing our intuitions about identity . . .

PHILIP Not too fast. Let's begin with my intuitions, and see if you can capture these . . .

ANNE There are, so I've argued in my thesis, three sorts of communities out of which the identity of 'Westerners' is constituted, communities which are clearly demarcated, though they may overlap somewhat. The first type I call a 'community of place', and by this term I mean nothing more than the most common meaning associated with the word

'community'. In ordinary language, we think of community as linked
to locality, in the physical, geographical sense of a community that's
located somewhere. And when we say 'my community', we generally
mean 'my neighbourhood', the place where I live, have friends, go
shopping, join clubs, and so on. Community of place, then, refers to
the place we call home, the place where we're born and bred and often
the place where we'd like to end our days even if home is left for some
time as an adult.[19]

PHILIP What if I was born in, say, Miami, while my parents were vaca-
tioning there? Is Miami then constitutive of my identity, even if I was
brought up in Montreal? Surely being born somewhere is not a sufficient condition for that place to be constitutive of one's identity. Is it a
necessary condition?

ANNE Were you born in Miami?

PHILIP Yes, unfortunately. I came a bit earlier than planned, however,
and my mother never lets me forget how I ruined a good vacation. But
I have no personal recollection of this event.

ANNE Well, if you have no recollection of your time spent in Miami,
then of course Miami cannot be said to be constitutive of your identity. It makes no sense to begin constructing a personal narrative history from a time and place of which you have no memory.

PHILIP Oh? Why did you mention birth, then?

ANNE I don't mean to be too rigid about this. I just mentioned birth
because the place where we're born also happens to be the place where
we normally spend the crucial childhood years when social meanings
are imbued, and consequently the place that's laden with formative
memories.[20]

PHILIP It's kind of ironic that we're talking about the importance of
home here in a Paris café . . .

ANNE Although sometimes we only become aware of the profound
attachments to our home when we're abroad. If I'm in a far-flung
tourist spot, say, and I unexpectedly meet someone from my home
town, I feel a closeness to that person which I don't experience with
others I meet abroad.[21]

PHILIP [*pours more wine in Anne's glass*] And I feel close to you, Anne.

ANNE I was making a theoretical point from chapter 3 of my thesis. The
point is that after a period of feeling ill at ease, whether consciously or
not, while interacting with people and things, it feels good suddenly to
meet someone with an overlapping personal history—no longer having

to control for different points of cultural reference, one can be natural once again. Of course, this sense can be recovered also upon one's return, which helps explain the expression 'there's no place as good as home', an expression that's uttered after other places have been seen.

PHILIP When I feel good, infrequently though that may be, this feeling is not due to the fact that I may find myself in Montreal. I would have been much the same person had I been born and bred somewhere else.

ANNE Do you honestly believe that 'home' doesn't significantly contribute to one's make-up, that the answer to 'who am I?' shouldn't include where I'm from? That those who are born and bred in different places don't necessarily pick up different ways of life?

PHILIP [*pause*] I agree to a certain extent with your emphasis on 'home'. Rural farming folk have a sentimental tie to the soil and people who live in a small, homogenous village have deep attachments to their home. But in modern society, most people live in urban areas with a high rate of mobility, they work in a different neighbourhood than the one they live in, the character of their city changes quite rapidly, they don't know their neighbours, etc. Need I go on?

ANNE Yes. This picture of 'modern society' seems to be a product of your imagination.

PHILIP [*raises voice*] Have you never heard of the United States? Americans are notorious for their mobility, changing homes almost as frequently as they change marriage partners. How can you say that this majority has a home that's constitutive of their identity?

ANNE Actually, the fact is that over 50 per cent of Americans live within 50 miles of the place where they grew up.[22] We have a case here of an atomist belief system that skews your interpretation of reality.[23]

PHILIP Fifty miles?

ANNE Yes, over half live within 50 miles of their home.

PHILIP So the circumference of one's community of place, according to your thesis, is the boundary created by the points at the tip of a 50-mile radius from the place where one has grown up?

ANNE Quite seriously, Philip, I'd rather you not make fun of what I say unless you have a constructive purpose in doing so.

PHILIP I'm sorry. My serious point is that people are less determined by, and attached to, their home if they're from the large cities of contemporary society than if they were born and bred in the small communities of the past. It simply isn't true that people from large cities think of their home as being 'constitutive of their identity'.

ANNE Have you seen any Woody Allen films? Do you not think that New York is constitutive of Woody Allen's identity?

PHILIP You may have a point there. One could barely imagine Woody Allen without his 'New-Yorkness'.

ANNE Yes. Another example of a big city being constitutive of one's identity comes from the film *My Dinner with André*, also set in New York. Have you seen this film?

PHILIP No, but I've seen many other films.

ANNE Are you feeling OK?

PHILIP The more wine I drink, the better I'll feel.

ANNE I'll go on, assuming you're still capable of meaningful conversation. *My Dinner with André* is set in a restaurant, and the film consists essentially of a dinner table conversation between a playwright and a director turned spiritualist named André. The playwright, who had not been leading his life in accordance with his deepest aspirations, is confronted with André's critique of modern society as one where few are in touch with 'what's fundamentally important to them'. As a consequence of this encounter with André, the playwright is made to reconsider 'what really matters' in his own life. In the final scene, the playwright, having left the restaurant, looks outside his taxi window and the city seems to have assumed previously latent meanings, particular buildings being associated with particular memories from his childhood. The playwright has recognized, and reaffirmed, his home . . .

PHILIP [*pours himself more wine*] I'm sorry I missed that movie. It sounds very moving.

ANNE I was trying to answer your objection that few urban dwellers feel that their city is constitutive of their identity—even in large cities one gets to know people and places in one's neighbourhood, one makes one's way about the city without thinking about it too much, the city's diversions and cultural opportunities are made use of, to the point that the city becomes inseparable from one's identity. And you don't just have to take my word for this—try asking the Parisians in this café how they feel about their city.

PHILIP That won't be easy. You seem to have more tourists than Parisians frequenting *La Coupole*; besides, Parisians are not exactly known as a people receptive to the queries of non-tribe members.

ANNE I think you'll find Parisians very helpful if you show some interest in, and acquaintance with, their form of life. This involves reasonable familiarity with their language, with distinctions between types of food and wine, and with the latest intellectual debates. Their largely unde-served reputation of hostility to visitors has been pinned upon them by tourists who provoke negative reactions because they expect Parisians to sympathize with their not having made the effort to acquaint them-selves with local practices . . .

PHILIP . . . such as knowing that coffee is served after one's meal.

ANNE For example.

PHILIP You're tapping my Jewish tendency of feeling guilty in response to minor lapses from perfection.

ANNE That wasn't my intention; but let's not digress from the subject at hand. We were discussing the importance of home, whether this be a small village or a large city.

PHILIP [*pause*] OK. Maybe it's true that some individuals have a home that, as you say, is 'constitutive of their identity'. However, not every-one has a home—someone who's father has worked in diplomacy, for example, would have moved from place to place as a child and would most likely not have developed a deep attachment to a home.

ANNE Maybe so, but such persons as you describe—this can also apply to someone who's father is a career military man—are likely to grow up damaged in some way. I mean it doesn't follow from the fact that there are 'home-less' persons that it wouldn't have been better for those people to have developed deep attachments to a home.

PHILIP Oh, oh. More of this 'damaged human personhood' stuff.

ANNE That's not something to be scoffed at. People who lack a place they can call 'home' almost always recognize that there's something missing in their life, a hole in their soul, if you will. Sometimes they suffer severe psychological damage as a result, moving from place to place as an adult because they lack emotional bonds tying them down some-where.[24] As soon as they can better satisfy their so-called economic needs elsewhere, they move. Finding a place to live is reduced to a mar-ket choice. Even worse, as a result of not having stayed somewhere long enough to experience deep, long-term friendships in their youth, such people develop a defence mechanism that protects them against intense emotional involvement with others so as to avoid the pain caused by the loss of a friend when the relationship must, as they feel deep down, inevitably end . . . [*her eyes misty with sadness*] . . . They can't experi-ence true love . . .

PHILIP It sounds like you have someone in mind.

ANNE [*shifting in her chair*] You might remember, from a few years back, my boyfriend Jean-Guy. His father worked for the Canadian military, and he never spent more than a year or two in one place during his childhood. Consequently, he never felt very attached to Montreal—when he's asked where he's from he says 'where am I not from' or 'I don't have a home.' When it came time to go to university, he left Montreal—even though I was there—and went to the University of Toronto simply because he wanted, as he would say, 'something different'. And when he got there, he was perpetually dissatisfied, changing programmes three or four times . . .

PHILIP What a monster!

ANNE I expect you to be more sensitive when I'm telling you about someone very close to me who left Montreal for studies elsewhere without a good reason for doing so.

PHILIP Are you implying that there's something wrong with leaving one's home town for university studies elsewhere?

ANNE No, of course not, not if you have good reasons for leaving. I'm sure you had your good reasons for going to Oxford.

PHILIP And what if I didn't? Do you have something against those who leave home just to experience something new? What if I just hop in a car and go 'on the road' indefinitely, Jack Kerouac style? What's *wrong* with that?

ANNE Such aimless excursions betray a profound immaturity, meaning lack of touch with one's deepest self-understandings, and will inevitably backfire from a psychological point of view. It's not a coincidence that Jack Kerouac died a few years after he went 'on the road', a broken-down, overweight alcoholic completely dependent on his mother . . .

PHILIP Another 'damaged human personhood'.

ANNE Do you not agree with the proposition that home should not be left indefinitely without some very good reasons for leaving?

PHILIP And what counts as a good reason to leave?

ANNE There's no general answer to that question. In my thesis, I discuss two such reasons: economic pressure, such as a mine that closes down and forces the workers to move elsewhere in order to find a job; and political pressure, such as being forced into exile by a nasty government.[25] What's interesting is that once these reasons for leaving home no longer apply—the mine reopens or democracy returns to one's country—most tend to return home,[26] at least to end their days . . . By the way, Philip, do you plan to return to Montreal eventually?

PHILIP Well, yes, but not for the reason that you suspect, i.e. that Montreal is constitutive of my identity and I have no compelling reason to leave it. There are sufficient grounds to want to be in Montreal independent of the fact that I happen to have been born and bred there. Speaking as a detached observer, Montreal embodies the best of Europe and the best of North America—the world-weary sophistication of Europe and the growth and dynamism of North America harmoniously interweave.[27] So when the Montreal-born novelist Mordecai Richler returns home after a twenty-year stint in London and writes a book entitled *Home Sweet Home*,[28] I think that he mistakes his rational attachment to Montreal's distinctive characteristics for an irrational attachment to home. I would go further to speculate that the same is true of communitarians, i.e. that they mistakenly interpret their attachment to home as a need to be rooted somewhere instead of a feeling that's due to their coming from cities with desirable characteristics. I don't know of any communitarians from Leeds, Detroit, or Hamilton.

ANNE Maybe a dim-witted social scientist with time on his hands can investigate your hypothesis. Meanwhile, let me just point out that Richler's best works deal with his childhood in Montreal, works which were created while he lived in London. We know that novelists sometimes feel they must leave the place where their novels are to be situated for the reason that it is often in confronting another way of life that one's own assumptions and practices are thrown into relief and thus come to critical self-consciousness, hence allowing the articulation and manipulation of one's memories from familiar surroundings for purposes of literature. Once this reason for having left his home no longer applied, Richler moved back to Montreal, as you just pointed out.

PHILIP But the Montreal he moved back to was very different from the Montreal of twenty years ago, which means that he was merely attached to the city *per se*, irrespective of its character, an attitude which I find quite irrational.[29]

ANNE If it was true that the Montreal he came back to was completely overhauled, such that the buildings, streets, cultural institutions, and people that constitute his early memories of Montreal had been replaced by an unrecognizable urban landscape, then Richler's return would indeed have been pointless. Fortunately, there has been sufficient continuity for Richler to link the contemporary character of

Montreal with his early associations; hence, Richler's return was rational.[30]

PHILIP I'm sure Richler would be glad to hear that—have you informed him of your opinion?

ANNE More sarcasm. This is getting tedious.

PHILIP You have to admit, though, that your argument sounds a bit funny. Each one of us has a deep need to be rooted somewhere and if someone lacks a fixed home, we have a case of a 'damaged human personhood' . . . Have there not been, however, nomadic tribes? Are they all 'damaged human personhoods'?[31]

ANNE I've already said that I restricted the scope of my interpretation of constitutive communities to those of us living in 'the modern world', and it would seem that we've evolved into sedentary creatures, into the kinds of beings with a deep need for identification with a community whose face can be recognized, and that fulfilment of this need is a condition of psychological stability.

PHILIP So I'm mentally unstable if I lack this identification with 'home'.

ANNE Why do you find that proposition so absurd? Look what happens when you have rapid change in the character of the community—people come to feel uprooted, community identification is replaced by alienation, and you have an increase of antisocial behaviour such as crime, vandalism, and excessive drinking. This was documented by Jane Jacobs in her critique of the once fashionable policy of razing, instead of renovating, run-down tenements to be replaced by functionally adequate but characterless low-income housing blocs.[32] It is now widely recognized that such projects rapidly deteriorate into a no-man's-land unfit for human habitation.[33]

PHILIP Mmh, it makes more sense now. What you're saying is that since people have an interest in identifying with familiar surroundings, political authorities ought to consider the existent character of the local community when, for example, considering plans for development.

ANNE [*happily*] Yes, yes, finally you're making an effort to understand! One concrete political implication might be granting community councils veto power over building projects that fail to respect existent architectural styles. Were this a possibility here, I doubt that the local population would have authorized that monstrosity outside known as the Tour Montparnasse.

PHILIP I don't much like that skyscraper myself.

ANNE It should never have gone up. It's a real tragedy, given what we know of Montparnasse in its heyday—what used to be a run-down area favoured by local artists and international literary figures has been turned, under the presiding aegis of the Tour Montparnasse, into a commercial wasteland of fast-food franchises, tacky boutiques, and sterile office buildings.[34] It's no wonder that few Parisians frequent this area anymore.

PHILIP Luckily for Montparnasse, tourists such as ourselves still come here.

ANNE But a place cannot live on its reputation alone.

PHILIP [*pause*] I've just thought of a counter-example to your claim that people would favour, were this a possibility, stability and continuity in the look of their community. Think of the western part of the United States, where people seem drawn to that area precisely by the promise of rapid change.

ANNE Don't be so sure about that. It's true that you've had a lot of uncontrolled development in the western part of the United States— and of Canada, by the way—but residents there are counting up the costs and not liking it one bit. The tide is turning in favour of continuity . . .

PHILIP How do you know this?

ANNE I've been following this issue quite closely in the news. I've read recently that residents in Seattle are reacting against a downtown building boom that has remade their city's skyline—they've just forced a five-month moratorium on all construction while considering permanent steps to curb skyscrapers, such as a measure to limit construction to the equivalent of one 40-storey building per year.[35] One can only hope that this trend will continue, that more will realize that their interest lies in a local community whose face they can recognize, and that political authorities will feel the pressure to maintain continuity in the character of the places where people live.

PHILIP Not to mention the survival of local communities. In Romania, for example, whole communities used to get wiped out by governmental dicta.

ANNE But more insidious in Western societies is that whole communities get annihilated in response to economic, rather than strictly political, pressures. This is true especially of single-industry communities such as mining towns or fishing villages which suffer substantial out-migration when the industry goes bust.

PHILIP So what do you recommend?

ANNE I don't know, perhaps job re-training schemes could be implemented when it appears a certain industry is about to enter a period of decline. And as a stop-gap measure, the state can implement laws regulating plant closures so as to protect local communities from the disruptive effects of capital mobility and sudden industrial change.[36]

PHILIP Even if I agree in principle with the latter policy, I don't think it's compatible with a successful economy, assuming an overall capitalist structure. After all, one of the central characteristics of modern economies is the free movement of capital, which necessarily destabilizes communities.[37]

ANNE That's not completely true. Do you agree that Japan's economy has been faring very well since World War Two?

PHILIP [*hesitates, but answers honestly*] Yes.

ANNE Well, in Japan we have a case of a successful economy that coexists with an emphasis on stable communities. Whereas in the USA and most other capitalist countries the consumer is sovereign, in the sense that lower prices are favoured regardless of the costs which include lay-offs, job changes, shifts into new businesses, and rapid change in the character of local communities, the Japanese economy is structured in such a way that the producer's interest comes first; that is, the desire to preserve every person's place in the Japanese productive system is paramount, even if it means penalizing consumers through higher prices.[38] So, for example, Japanese government directives have made it difficult to open discount stores, supermarkets, and other low-cost outlets that would improve the consumer's standard of living but would threaten smaller, family-owned stores.[39] As a consequence, the retail system in Japan remains that of the tiny greengrocer down the block,[40] whereas in the USA the fragmented, diverse Mom and Pop stores were bulldozed under by large-scale, low-cost operations such as Sears and K-Mart.[41]

PHILIP In other words, the average Japanese has to pay more for his bowl of rice than the American has to pay for his hamburger. I'm not convinced as to the superiority of the Japanese system . . .

ANNE The point is that there's a trade-off between preserving the existing order in the form of stable communities, predictable jobs, and freedom from foreign interference, and a lower cost of living. And for the Japanese, preserving the existing order matters more than a lower cost of living.[42]

PHILIP If you're correct about the Japanese case, you've shown that there's nothing inherently incompatible between a successful capitalist economy and relatively stable communities. However, it is probable that the Japanese state has proven successful in enacting laws that protect local communities largely because, as you said, preserving the existing order matters more to the Japanese than a lower cost of living. Since Americans seem to prefer cheaper prices, I doubt that the American state could prove nearly as successful in enacting laws that protect local communities . . .

ANNE My intuition is that social peace, predictable jobs, and stable, evolutionary change in the character of their communities matter more to Americans than a cheap hamburger, but that most Americans, unlike the Japanese, are simply not aware of the trade-off between preserving the existing order and consumer welfare.[43] If you want to rebut this claim, however, you'll have to wait a while, as it's my turn to divest myself of superfluous fluids.

[*Anne gets up and proceeds to the 'toilettes' sign on the left-hand side of the stage. Lights dim*]

Notes

1. Raymond Plant also makes this point in his essay 'Community', in *The Blackwell Encyclopedia of Political Thought*, ed. David Miller (Oxford: Basil Blackwell, 1987), 90.

2. The nineteenth-century sociologist, Ferdinand Tönnies, lamented what he thought to be the loss of *Gemeinschaft* in the modern world—see his book *Community and Association*, trans. C. Loomis (New York: Harper and Row, 1963).

3. Charles Taylor expresses this idea in his essay 'Legitimation Crisis', in *Philosophy and the Human Sciences: Philosophical Papers, 2* (Cambridge: Cambridge University Press, 1985), 248–88.

4. Raymond Plant develops the view that the *Gemeinschaft* ideal is incompatible with a modern world which has seen the decline of the local community and the development of specialist functional groups, arguing instead for developing a sense of community by attempting to develop a sense of functional interest (see his *Community and Ideology: An Essay in Applied Social Philosophy* (London: Routledge and Kegan Paul, 1974)).

    Christopher Lasch, in his essay 'The Communitarian Critique of Liberalism' (in Charles Reynolds and Ralph Norman, eds., *Community in America* (Berkeley: University of California Press, 1988), 174–84) argues that communitarians do not favour the *Gemeinschaft* ideal for the reason that people have a diversity of commitments in the modern world.

5. The possibility that small peasant communities in feudal Japan approximated to the *Gemeinschaft* conception of community is challenged in the Kurosawa film *The Seven Samurai*. In this film, leaders of a peasant village in feudal Japan had to deal with a recalcitrant subset of families who initially refused to allow their houses to be abandoned and left vulnerable to attack by bandits, a sacrifice which was necessary from the village leaders' point of view in order to save the village as a whole. In other words, the families asked to sacrifice their houses faced a conflict between commitments to their families' houses and the good of the village, which is inconsistent with the (perhaps vulgarized) *Gemeinschaft* notion that members of a village feel only committed, and act according, to the good of the village (i.e. *Gemeinschaft* rules out the possibility that one can have many commitments which may conflict).

6. Such a counter-intuitive and unrealistic idea (given what we know about the ruling classes in known human societies, with none ever having dispensed with the family) leads one to take seriously the Straussian political philosophers, who have interpreted Plato in an ironic way, speculating that Plato's intention was to expose the foolishness and impossibility of undoing the dictates of nature.

7. *Gesellschaft* was contrasted with *Gemeinschaft* by Ferdinand Tönnies, the former being meant to characterize modern society, and the latter small, long-lost communities of the past. I know of no modern-day communitarian who (1) accepts this dichotomy and/or (2) wishes to re-implement *Gemeinschaft* in modern society (on the grounds that abandoning this ideal leads inescapably to *Gesellschaft*).

8. One communitarian, Michael Sandel, can be interpreted in a way that suggests he thinks that only one community constitutes the identity of the members of a society:

> [Members of a society] conceive their identity—the subject and not just the object of their feelings and aspirations— as defined to some extent by *the* community of which they are a part. (*Liberalism and the Limits of Justice* (Cambridge: Cambridge University Press, 1981), 150, my italics.)

However, Sandel elsewhere allows for the possibility that someone's identity may be constituted by more than one community:

> Intrasubjective conceptions . . . allow that for certain purposes the appropriate description of the moral subject may refer to a plurality of selves within a single, individual human being, as when we account for inner deliberation in terms of the pull of competing identities . . . (ibid. 63)

9. See e.g. John Dunn, *Interpreting Political Responsibility* (Oxford: Polity Press, 1990), ch. 11; Nancy Rosenblum, 'Pluralism and Self-Defense', in Nancy

Rosenblum, ed., *Liberalism and the Moral Life* (Cambridge, Mass.: Harvard University Press, 1989), 215 and Stephen Holmes, 'The Permanent Structure of Anti-liberal Thought', ibid. 229; and Nancy Rosenblum, 'Moral Membership in a Post-liberal State', *World Politics* (July 1984), 586.

10. Needless to say, people may answer this question differently in different contexts, but if people are pressed and asked to articulate only those things that define their sense of who they are, one can assume that they will come up with certain consistent answers: nation, religion, family, and other examples of 'constitutive communities' that De la Patrie discusses below.

11. If a constitutive community is 'exempt from evaluation and possible rejection', as De la Patrie would have it, this presents a second problem for those liberals who would found political liberalism on the idea that one can and should understand and evaluate one's current ends (the first, it will be recalled, is that the normal mode of existence is that of unreflectively acting in a way specified by the practices of one's social world, which shows that one cannot (normally) lead a life 'from the inside'—see Act I n. 33). A necessary condition of 'leading one's life from the inside' is that no single end, goal, practice, task, project, commitment, role, or attachment be beyond individual evaluation and possible rejection (see Will Kymlicka, *Liberalism, Community and Culture* (Oxford: Clarendon Press, 1989), 50–60, and his article, 'Liberalism and Communitarianism', *Canadian Journal of Philosophy*, 18 (1988), 190–1), but a constitutive community, because it provides a largely background way of meaningful thinking, acting, and judging, would seem to be exempt from evaluation and possible rejection.

12. Interestingly, (the Jewish) Rosa Luxemburg explicitly denied this very thing—she wrote in a letter to her friend Mathilde Wurm that she has no special place in her heart for the sorrows of Jews (from Michael Walzer, *The Company of Critics* (New York: Basic Books, 1988), 226).

13. Obvious though this point may seem to De la Patrie, Brian Barry criticizes Walzer for (allegedly) holding the thesis that 'Caring about a society [means] wishing its good at the expense of injustice to others' (from Barry's review of Walzer's books, *Interpretation and Social Criticism* and *The Company of Critics*, in *Philosophy and Public Affairs* (Fall 1990), 368). Though Walzer (and other communitarians) may well hold the thesis that identification with a group means favouring one's own group simply because it is one's own group (a thesis Barry disparagingly calls 'collective selfishness', ibid. 367), one can favour one's group—by, say, disproportionately directing one's personal effort and the resources of the community at satisfying the agreed-upon needs of one's own group—without wishing that this be done *at the expense of injustice to others* (moreover, aggressive forms of communal self-assertion tend to occur after aspirations to cultural self-determination have been suppressed, often in the name of the Enlightenment ideals of unity, universality, and

liberal rationalism—see the Nathan Gardels interview with Isaiah Berlin, 'Two Concepts of Nationalism', *New York Review of Books* (21 Nov. 1991), esp. 19–20).

14. See George Steiner, 'A Jew's Grief', for an example of someone who criticizes Israel's activities in the occupied territories on the basis of what he's learned about the ideals embedded in the Jewish religion (reprinted in *Harper's Magazine* (Oct. 1988), 18–20).

15. Charles Taylor similarly diagnoses those who would lose a commitment to a particular religion, nation, or tradition which partly defines their identity:

> were they to lose this commitment or identification, they would be at sea, as it were; they wouldn't know any more, for an important range of questions, what the significance of things was for them.
>
> And this situation does, of course, arise for some people. It's what we call an 'identity crisis'. It is an acute form of disorientation, which people often express in terms of not knowing who they are, but which can also be seen as a radical uncertainty of where they stand. They lack a frame or horizon within which things can take on stable significance, within which some life possibilities can be seen as good or meaningful, others as bad or trivial. The meaning of all these possibilities is unfixed, labile, or undetermined. This is a painful and frightening experience. (*Sources of the Self: The Making of the Modern Identity* (Cambridge: Cambridge University Press, 1989), 26–7.)

16. The Buddha said:

> Monks, birth is suffering, ageing is suffering, illness is suffering, death is suffering, union with the hateful is suffering, separation from the beloved is suffering, failing to obtain the desired is suffering. In short, attachment to all physical and mental aspects of our environment is suffering. This is the Noble Truth pertaining to suffering . . .
>
> Monks, total elimination and abandonment of such craving and liberation from all attachments are the ideal goal. This is the Noble Truth concerning the elimination of suffering. (Quoted in Kogen Mizuno, *Basic Buddhist Concepts*, trans. Charles Terry and Richard Gaye (Tokyo: Kosei Publishing Co., 1987), 110.)

17. De la Patrie is referring to the ideal of extending unlimited, universal love and goodwill to all living beings without any kind of discrimination, one of the 'Sublime States' characteristic of those who have reached nirvana. In the Buddha's words: 'Just as a mother would protect her only child even at the risk of her own life, even so let one cultivate a boundless heart towards all beings' (quoted in Walpola Sri Rahula, *What the Buddha Taught*, 2nd edn. (London: Gordon Fraser, 1967), 97; see also p. 75). It should be noted, how-

ever, that the Buddha never expected more than a tiny minority of monks to strive for this ideal, and the Buddha prescribed a set of particularist duties for (the majority) not inclined to retire from the hurly-burly of ordinary life, including duties bearing on family life (ibid. 78–9).

18. Referring to nirvana, the Buddha says:

> Here the four elements of solidarity, fluidity, heat and motion have no place; the notions of length and breadth, the subtle and the gross, good and evil, name and form are altogether destroyed; neither this world nor the other, nor coming, going or standing, neither death nor birth, nor sense-objects are to be found. (ibid. 37)

(It is not obvious, however, how someone who has reached nirvana can be both acting according to certain ideals, e.g. the ideal of universal love, and yet somehow be 'beyond good (and evil)'.)

19. The novelist John Updike describes his constitution by, and attachment to, his Pennsylvania home town, Shillington, in this moving account of his return there one spring evening:

> Toward the end of Philadelphia Avenue, beside the park that surrounds the town hall, I turned and looked back up the straight sidewalk in the soft evening gloom, looking for what the superstitious old people of the country used to call a 'sign'. The pavement squares, the housefronts, the remaining trees receded in silence and shadow. I loved this plain street, where for 13 years no great harm had been allowed to befall me. I loved Shillington not as one loves Capri or New York, because they are special, but as one loves one's own body and consciousness, because they are synonymous with being. It was exciting for me to be in Shillington, as if my life, like the expanding universe when projected backwards, gained heat and intensity. If there was meaning to existence, I was closest to it here. (*Self-Consciousness: Memoirs* (London: André Deutsch, 1989), 27.)

If De la Patrie is right about there being a plurality of constitutive communities, however, the last line quoted above is an exaggeration. This view is borne out by subsequent parts of Updike's memoirs, where he reveals his deep attachments to his family, the Catholic religion, and the USA.

20. Proust, in describing his relation to the flowers he encountered on his childhood walks, expresses how deeply touched he was by the landscape of his childhood:

> The flowers that people show me nowadays for the first time never seem to me to be true flowers. The Méséglise Way with its lilacs, its hawthorns, its cornflowers, its poppies, the Guermantes Way with its river full of tadpoles, its water-lilies, and its buttercups have constituted for me for all

time the picture of the land in which I would fain pass all my life . . . the
cornflower, the hawthorns, the apple-trees, which I happen, when I go
out walking, to encounter in the fields, *because* at the same depth, on the
level of my past life, at once established contact with my heart. (Quoted
in Bruce Chatwin, *The Songlines* (London: Picador, 1987), 303–4.)

21. What De la Patrie says here does not apply merely to Westerners—according
to a shared belief of the Chinese, meeting someone from one's home town by
chance outside of one's home town is one of the four happiest possible events
in one's life.

22. The exact figure is 54% (from 'Harper's Index' in *Harper's Magazine* (June
1988), 17).

23. De la Patrie's rejoinder fits into what Michael Walzer calls 'the second communitarian critique of liberalism', which 'holds that liberal theory radically
misrepresents real life . . . Liberal theory distorts . . . reality and, insofar as we
adopt this theory, deprives us of any ready access to our own experience of
communal embeddedness' ('The Communitarian Critique of Liberalism',
Political Theory (Feb. 1990), 9, 10). The 'second critique' was developed most
fully in the American context by the authors (Robert Bellah, *et al.*) of *Habits
of the Heart* (Berkeley, Calif.: University of California Press, 1985), who argue
that often the habits (social practices) of the American people are better than
they can say, i.e. that the (liberal) language dominant in American society
distorts people's self-understanding by leading them to misdescribe their
communal experiences in individualistic terms. The 'first communitarian critique of liberalism' according to Walzer, holds that liberal political theory
accurately represents (fragmented, decomposed) liberal social practice (see pp.
7–9 of the article mentioned above). However, the only communitarian
whom Walzer places in this camp, Alasdair MacIntyre, explicitly rejects the
idea that actual individuals in liberal society, completely separated from their
community, act solely according to their private interest (an idea which
Walzer attributes to the 'first communitarian critique'—see p. 8): '[Our con-
temporaries] tend to live betwixt and between [the tradition-less liberal self
and the tradition-constituted self], accepting usually unquestioningly the
assumptions of the dominant liberal individualist forms of public life, but
drawing in different areas of their lives upon a variety of tradition-generated
resources of thought and action, transmitted from a variety of familial, religious, educational, and other social and cultural sources' (MacIntyre, *Whose
Justice? Which Rationality?* (London: Duckworth, 1988), 397; my brackets).
This passage places MacIntyre squarely within the 'second communitarian
critique of liberalism'.

24. It should be noted, however, that a 'home-less childhood' need not produce
the unlucky outcome that De la Patrie describes. The biographer Michael
Holroyd, whose latest project Anthony Burgess predicts will be, when com-

pleted, 'one of the three great literary biographies of this century' (review of
Bernard Shaw 1856–1898: The Search for Love, *Atlantic Monthly* (Oct. 1988),
91), says of his childhood:

> My father was half Irish and my mother Swedish, and I grew up every-
> where, including London . . . My parents remarried again and again, and
> I'd spend time with my father and my stepmother and my mother and
> my stepfather in different places. One stepparent was Hungarian, another
> French. I was all over the place. The closest I got to a proper English life
> was when I stayed with my grandparents, my father's parents in the coun-
> try here. When I came to London, finally, I felt I didn't know anyone. I
> still feel I don't, really. (Quoted in D. Plante, 'In The Heart of Literary
> London', *New York Times Magazine* (11 Oct. 1988), 80.)

Instead of reacting to his 'home-less childhood' by 'moving from place to
place as an adult', Holroyd filled the 'hole in his soul' by 'travelling' into the
minds of other persons—he spent seven years on Augustus John, eight on
Lytton Strachey, and fifteen thus far on George Bernard Shaw. Holroyd himself compares biography to foreign travel: 'You go to a country quite unlike
your own and you pick up something of that way of life, that language and
your life is changed by the experience' (quoted in the *New York Times Book
Review* (30 Oct. 1988), 43).

25. Of course, 'being forced into exile by a nasty government' may involve leaving one's country as well as removal from the community of place of one's
childhood. However, De la Patrie could claim that 'unhealthy psychological
consequences' result primarily from the latter aspect of exile, for 'internal
exile' (e.g. a Russian exiled to Siberia, or a Chilean exiled to the South) can
be just as bad as 'external exile'.

26. Argentina's premier folk-singer, Mercedes Sosa, exemplifies the tendency that
De la Patrie describes. Forced into exile in 1979 by the military dictatorship
that ruled her country, she returned to Buenos Aires in 1982 with the restora-
tion of civilian rule in Argentina. Interestingly Sosa found that she couldn't
sing while in exile. She explains the reason why:

> It was a mental problem, a problem of morale. It wasn't my throat, or
> anything physical. When you are in exile, you take your suitcase, but
> there are things that don't fit. There are things in your mind, like colours
> and smells and childhood attitudes, and there is also the pain and death
> you saw. You shouldn't deny those things, because to do so can make you
> ill. (Quoted in 'Mercedes Sosa: A Voice of Hope', *New York Times* (9
> Oct. 1988), H21.)

However, Sosa's experience in exile had some beneficial consequences. She
says it made her grow and mature as an artist because it opened her horizons:

By distancing me from my homeland and ripping me out by my roots, it forced my repertory to become more international. Before, I was always tied to our rhythms and songs. I wouldn't be able to do the things I am doing now recording with jazz groups and orchestras, if I had not made a path for myself outside of Argentina. (ibid.)

It is unfortunate that De la Patrie and Schwartzberg do not discuss this phenomenon of the opening of new possibilities that often occurs when other ways of life are encountered. The interested reader will find that this phenomenon is addressed in Hans-Georg Gadamer's essay 'The Universality of the Hermeneutical Problem', in *Philosophical Hermeneutics*, trans. and ed. David E. Linge (Berkeley, Calif.: University of California Press, 1976), 3–17.

27. See the pamphlet, 'Montreal: International Finance Centre', prepared by the International Financial Centres Organization of Montreal in co-operation with the Ville de Montréal, for a similar description of the virtues of Montreal.

28. In actual fact, as is clear from the full title of Richler's book, *Home Sweet Home: My Canadian Album* (Toronto: McClelland and Stewart, 1984), the title refers to things Canadian rather than things connected with Montreal *per se*. To make matters more complicated, Richler has recently launched a polemical attack on what he perceives to be Quebec's anglo-bashing and anti-Semitic tradition, all the while affirming his attachment to the province of Quebec as his home (see e.g. 'The New Yorker, Quebec, and Me', *Saturday Night* (May 1992), 17–20, 87–8).

29. Schwartzberg's position that it would be irrational to remain attached to a community radically transformed from what one knew it to be conflicts with Will Kymlicka's position that what matters (for individuals and for politics) is the *existence* of a community, even if its character is completely modified (although each is referring to a different type of community, this need not concern us here). Kymlicka justifies his position by appealing to the example of the 'Quiet Revolution' in Quebec, a community which underwent substantial change in the 1960s but to which most of its members none the less remained attached (see his *Liberalism, Community and Culture*, 166–7). This example, however, cannot serve his case as he wants it to, for while the French community in Quebec undeniably underwent substantial change in the 1960s, it is misleading to refer to the end product of that transformation as 'the end of a "culture" in the first instance [i.e. the sense of understanding the term "cultural community" as referring to the character of a historical community]' (p. 167)—most Québécois still spoke French, many (but fewer) still went to church, ate dishes made with maple syrup, wished that the French had won the 'War of 1759', listened to Québécois folk-songs, just to name a few of the continuities in the character of the French community in

Quebec, and it remains an open question whether or not the Québécois would have retained their allegiance to a community completely transformed from what it used to be.

30. In the last part of *Zuckerman Unbound* (London: Cape, 1981) Philip Roth's fictional *alter ego*, Nathan Zuckerman, briefly returns to his home town of Newark, New Jersey, only to find the lower-middle-class Jewish neighbourhood of his youth transformed into an impoverished Black ghetto. Following De la Patrie's logic, it would presumably have been irrational had Zuckerman returned to live in Newark.

31. See Bruce Chatwin's book, *The Songlines*, for an engaging look at the 'nomadic' Australian Aborigines and their travels along 'songlines', or tracts of land transmitted from generation to generation by means of songs which correspond to the particularities of the land. Chatwin, however, makes the leap from the idea that the Australian Aborigines' way of life makes sense given their history and the conditions in which they currently live to the idea that the Aborigines are more 'truly human' than the rest of us, and that 'everyone' ought to emulate their way of life: '. . . Man, originally, was a "wanderer in the scorching and barren wilderness of this world"—the words are those of Dostoevsky's Grand Inquisitor—and that to rediscover his humanity, he must slough off attachments and take to the road' (p. 181).

There are two problems with Chatwin's view: (1) he doesn't take into account the possibility that 'Man' may have evolved differently in different times and places, and (2) it is difficult to conceive of a workable economic and social system that would allow for 5 billion such truly human 'Men', were Chatwin's proposal that 'Man' ought to 'slough off attachments and take to the road' put into practice by today's world population.

32. De la Patrie is referring to Jane Jacobs' book, *The Death and Life of American Cities* (New York: Random House, 1965).

33. If De la Patrie is right that collective decisions in favour of rapid change in the character of the community and the consequent loss of attachment to the community by its members lead to an increase in crime, it can be assumed that collective decisions to restore the community to what it used to be, and the consequent increase in attachment to the community by its members, would lead to a decrease in crime. Evidence for this assumption is presented in the article by James Q. Wilson and George L. Kelling, 'Making Neighbourhoods Safe', *Atlantic Monthly* (Feb. 1989), 46–52—e.g. when trash was carted away, abandoned cars removed, potholes filled in, and the streets swept, the burglary rate of a formerly run-down crime-ridden housing project in Newport News, Virginia, dropped by 35%.

34. See Paul Webster, 'Last Tango in La Coupole', *Guardian* (6 Jan. 1988), 6.

35. See *The New York Times* article, 'Seattle Finds High Cost to its Boom Seeks to Limit Skyscrapers', repr. in *Montreal Gazette* (5 Dec. 1988). For more on

Seattle's efforts to preserve its atmosphere and character, see Ellen Posner's article 'A City that Likes itself', *Atlantic Monthly* (July 1991), 94–100.

36. Michael Sandel and Michael Walzer also make this suggestion in 'Morality and the Liberal Ideal', *New Republic* (7 May 1984), 17, and 'The Communitarian Critique of Liberalism', 18, respectively.

37. Christopher Lasch also makes this point in his review of John Kenneth White's book *The New Politics of Old Values*, *New York Review of Books* (21 July 1988), p. 7.

38. The case of Japan, with its economy structured in such a way that the producer's interest comes first, suggests a way out of Thomas Nagel's self-confessed doubts whether the constellation of motives necessary for a (desirable) strong egalitarianism is compatible with a modern productive economy (see his 'Locke Lectures' delivered at Oxford University, Hilary Term, 1990—published as *Equality and Partiality* by Oxford University Press in 1991). Nagel expressed the belief that an acquisitive motive, or a desire to accumulate consumer goods, is a necessary component of one's psychological make-up if one is to work hard in the context of a modern economy, but Japanese workers seem motivated to work hard more from a felt obligation to their company and the pride they take in turning out a good product. Moreover, American workers employed in Japanese-owned firms in the USA seem to share these 'Japanese' traits (see Andrew Hacker's critical review of James Fallows's book *More Like Us: Making America Great Again*, *New York Review of Books* (30 Mar. 1989), 6–8), which suggests that the 'American' consumer ethic may be a response to the way that work is structured in the USA, i.e. a worker will accept the cost of an alienating workplace if she is promised a reward of (great) enjoyment of consumer goods, an unnecessary reward if the worker identifies with her employer and takes pride in her product.

39. One such law passed in the 1970s required that a firm wanting to open a store of more than 500 square metres must first get the approval of all the local shopkeepers (see Tim Jackson's article 'Nothing Succeeds like 7-Eleven in Japan's Bizarre Retail System', repr. in *The Straits Times* (30 Oct. 1991), 27).

40. The Bush administration, however, did its best to alter Japan's retail landscape—Bush's 'Structural Impediments Initiative', or 'Store Wars', was aimed at forcing the Japanese to scrap the 'Large-Scale Retail Store Law', thus allowing more large supermarkets, the natural outlets for imported goods (see Peter McGill's article 'Japanese fear "Store Wars" threat from US', *Observer* (4 Mar. 1990), 15).

41. De la Patrie is exaggerating here. In San Francisco, for example, neighbourhoods are banding together to preserve their colourful, small, owner-run shops by keeping homogenizing fast-food franchises and large chain stores out of their shopping districts. Undesirable ventures are pressured out of business by such means as consumer boycotts, lawsuits by preservation soci-

eties, and even arson! See the Katherine Bishop article, 'Haight-Ashbury Rejects Change in Struggle to Retain "60s" Heritage', repr. in *Montreal Gazette* (22 Oct. 1988), 14.

42. James Fallows makes this point in 'Japan: Playing by Different Rules', *Atlantic Monthly* (Sept. 1987), 22–32. Although it is not clear from this article whether Fallows favours the Japanese 'pro-producer' system or the American 'pro-consumer' system, Fallows makes explicit his preference for the latter in subsequent articles (to the surprise of this reader, it has to be admitted). In one of these articles, for example, he pleads the case in favour of Japanese consumers, claiming that if the Japanese state lowered trade barriers, Japanese citizens would choose to buy cheaper imported goods and thus raise their standard of living (even, presumably, at the cost of less predictable jobs, more foreign interference, and less stable communities).

43. De la Patrie may well be right here—one poll found that 65% of Americans agreed with the suggestion that, in order to address the foreign trade deficit, the USA should impose higher taxes on imports, and nearly all said that they would hold this position even if it increased prices for some goods (see 'Deficit Should be Priority: Poll', *Montreal Gazette* (28 Nov. 1988), 18). It is plausible to assume that Americans would be even more likely to accept increased prices for some goods if they thought that this would lead to social peace, predictable jobs, and stable communities, benefits that Americans would in all likelihood agree are more crucial than lowering the foreign trade deficit *per se*.

Act IV: On the Importance of the Nation

SCENE: *the same.*

[*Anne enters the stage and unselfconsciously eases her being into the seat she had vacated*]

PHILIP [*refills their wine glasses*] I hope you feel better.

ANNE For the moment, I do. It's unfortunate that we have to be distracted by animal necessities.

PHILIP [*pause*] I think I have a fairly good idea by now of what you mean by 'community of place'. What's next on your agenda?

ANNE I don't think agenda is the right word—our meeting here is unplanned. However, we might want to discuss the second type of constitutive community that I elaborated upon in my thesis, which I called 'communities of memory'.

PHILIP Let me ask you, then, a question that probably won't throw you off. What's a community of memory?

ANNE Well, I borrowed the term from the authors of *Habits of the Heart*,[1] a best-selling book that criticizes individualism in favour of the republican and biblical traditions that Americans use to make sense of themselves and their society . . .

PHILIP Ummh, yes, I've heard of that book. Wasn't it written by, for, and about the community of white middle-class Americans?

ANNE If you're implying that the authors of *Habits of the Heart* left out many of the experiences of non-white Americans by limiting themselves to the language and practices of white middle-class Americans, that would be an accurate observation.

PHILIP It's more than an 'observation'. It's a criticism that cuts deeply into the book's methodology—answering the question of what it means to be an American on exclusively white grounds is both backward and dangerous.[2] I believe that it's typical of communitarians to sweep under the carpet the ways of life of minority cultures.

ANNE [*patiently*] Let's limit our discussion to the book for the moment. I don't think the authors can be blamed for having focused on the culture of the white middle class—with a limited budget and a small research team, it was best to concern themselves with the group that dominates the cultural institutions and sets standards that no member of the American nation, the community under study, could have escaped.[3] The book is a useful beginning, and there's nothing stopping others from applying the authors' methods to minority cultures in America.[4]

PHILIP So there's nothing wrong with excluding minorities from a study of what it means to be an American?

ANNE [*losing patience*] As a beginning, no; as a purported final say on the matter, yes. But in any case, the book's importance cannot be denied—that the book succeeded in articulating a deep, previously dormant strain in American culture is borne out by the extent to which the book captured the imagination of the American public.[5]

PHILIP To what extent was that? I was in England at the time, where the American *zeitgeist* makes less impact than in the nominally independent country of Canada.

ANNE Are you saying that you haven't even read *Habits of the Heart*?

PHILIP I've read a nasty review, which is enough for me. So perhaps you should say what was meant by 'communities of memory'.

ANNE Communities of memory, as the authors of *Habits of the Heart* see it, have a history in the sense of being constituted by their past—a shared history going back several generations is the most salient characteristic of a community of memory. Besides tying us to the past, such communities turn us towards the future as communities of hope—we strive to realize the ideals and aspirations embedded in the past experience of those communities, seeing our efforts as being, in part, contributions to a common good.[6]

PHILIP Please go on. I'm still not at all clear as to what you mean by 'community of memory'.

ANNE Don't be surprised—it's hard to get clear about important things . . . What I mean, put colloquially, is something like a group of strangers who share a history that's expressed in their everyday life and ideas.[7] It's hard to be more precise while discussing this notion in the abstract.

PHILIP I recommend, then, that we go on to examples of 'communities of memory'.

ANNE As you choose, Philip. But before we do that, I'd like to emphasize the importance of communities of memory. Such communities carry a moral tradition that helps to provide the narrative unity of our lives, which entails an obligation to sustain and promote the ideals and aspirations embedded in their history through memory and hope, linking our destiny to that of our ancestors, contemporaries, and descendants. If individuals fail to nurture their communities of memory, they lose a source of meaning and hope in their lives, and very serious harm is done to their self-esteem and sense of personal competence, not to mention the consequences for future generations when a moral tradition is lost.

PHILIP If what you say is right, this may explain my lack of self-esteem. So please be more concrete—what are *my* communities of memory, and how can I nurture them?

ANNE Well, for one thing, you're a member of the Canadian community of memory, notwithstanding your previous attempt to diminish its importance *vis-à-vis* the American nation. In fact, had you been in Canada during the last election, you would have participated in the nation-wide conversation about what it means to be a Canadian, given our tradition. The practical implication of this process would have been to formulate a historically informed answer about whether or not the Free Trade Pact with the United States helps to promote the Canadian way of life, and you would have cast your vote accordingly.

PHILIP [*defensively*] I did vote, by the way—one can vote from abroad . . . But perhaps I didn't vote in the way you would have liked me to— thinking about the Canadian identity that our tradition has bequeathed to us, and voting in such a way as to sustain it. It sounds like you're advocating blind worship of tradition.

ANNE Let me introduce a distinction that should serve to clarify my position. I defend tradition, not traditionalism.[8] Traditionalists contrast non-rational tradition, or what Edmund Burke called 'wisdom without reflection',[9] with abstract reason that breeds conflict, but this often turns out to mean nothing more than dogmatic assertions of right and wrong that express the interests of a stronger party in a relationship. The tradition I defend, on the other hand, is based on the understanding that moral principles and virtuous exemplars from history must be interpreted to be applied, to be useful in particular situations with novel features. What I have in mind is a historically extended, socially embedded argument about the good of the community whose identity it seeks to define.[10]

PHILIP If I understand you correctly, we should argue until we arrive at an uncontroversial interpretation of the good of the community. To test the effectiveness of the procedure, let's see if we can agree on the good of the Canadian nation.

ANNE [*ignoring Philip's request*] I never said anything about 'uncontroversial'. Our task as constituent members of communities of memory is to find meaning in the morass of history from which one can draw moral lessons,[11] though it's true that vital traditions may embody continuities of conflict,[12] with people differing as to the meaning of tradition in particular cases.

PHILIP If different interpretations of a particular tradition are permissible and available, I can just pick and choose which interpretation suits me best.

ANNE It's not an arbitrary process, as I'm sure you know deep down. I think we can agree that not all interpretations are equally valid, that a better interpretation is one that fits better with what are recognized as the historical facts and that tells a more plausible and compelling story about which values ought to be fundamental in the tradition.[13] An interpretation of the Canadian tradition that focuses on heroic displays of leadership on the world stage will not convince 'fellow Canadians', who take an almost perverse pride in their comparative insignificance.

PHILIP I agree with that aside about how Canadians view themselves in relation to the major powers, but this doesn't represent a 'plausible and compelling story' about the good of the Canadian nation. In fact, given what you said earlier about constitutive communities providing a largely background way of meaningful thinking, acting, and judging, it would seem that such a story can't even be told—if my 'Canadian way of being' is much deeper than any possible articulation of it, why should I even bother joining an argument about the good of the Canadian nation?

ANNE That it's impossible to provide a full and definite statement about 'what it means to be a Canadian' doesn't mean that relevant aspects of the Canadian tradition can't be brought to light for the situation at hand. Moreover, there are times of collective decision-making when it would seem especially crucial for those concerned with the good of their nation to join the argument about its tradition[14]—the national debate during the last federal election about which distinctively Canadian practices and institutions would be undermined by the Free

Trade Pact with the USA was one such case, but you were in England at the time . . .

PHILIP I'm still not at all clear as to how I could have joined this argument even if I'd been in Canada at the time. What are the institutional mechanisms for such arguments?

ANNE There's no general answer to that question, as the particular form of the mechanism for conversation and argument would depend on the type of community of memory. For a national community of memory such as Canada, the mechanisms include national political institutions, citizens groups, neighbourhood assemblies, and the media. For religious communities of memory, you'd have churches, temples, synagogues, and the like . . . The truth is, I have no special insight into the matter over and above common sense.

PHILIP [*pause*] Let me see if I understand. To each community of memory, there corresponds a tradition whose good its constituent members ought to seek, arguing over details as the situation calls for it. The way in which constituent members will argue over the good of the community varies according to the type of community.

ANNE [*excitedly*] Yes, yes! You see, you can be helpful if you want to.

PHILIP Don't be so sure. It's still much too vague for my taste, and it's still not obvious to me what counts as a community of memory. Why don't you spell out for me, in point form if possible, the defining features of a community of memory?

ANNE Now you're back to your old unhelpful self. I can't give you necessary and sufficient conditions if that's what you're looking for. What I can do, however, is to offer more examples from my thesis, which should give you a better idea of what it is that counts as a community of memory. I considered two types in my thesis—national communities of memory and linguistic communities of memory, the latter being a less obvious, more controversial example.

PHILIP Why do you assume that the nation is an obvious example of a community of memory?

ANNE It's just a fact that the nation has become a very important focus of identity in the modern world, that most people feel deeply bound up with the history and destiny of their nation.

PHILIP Perhaps 'most people' would come to question their national loyalties if nations were exposed as the cultural artefacts that they are.

ANNE What do you mean?

PHILIP Nations did not evolve from historical communities as communitarians might have wanted them to. Rather, nations came into historical being primarily thanks to the conscious policies of various commanders-in-chief[15]—Vietnam, for example, was scornfully invented by a nineteenth-century Manchu dynast.[16]

ANNE That doesn't seem very relevant. Do you think that the Vietnamese would withdraw their special commitment to the good of the Vietnamese nation if they were made conscious of its historical origin?

PHILIP It depends on how rational the Vietnamese are.[17]

ANNE My point is the following—whatever the origins of nations, they have undeniably evolved into entities which command a profound emotional legitimacy—at least this is true of the Western nations I dealt with in my thesis.[18] Moreover, we feel a certain moral responsibility for our nation's deeds, both good and bad, throughout history— we can say intelligibly, for example, 'Canadians should own up to the injustices the Canadian nation committed against its Japanese citizens in World War Two.'[19]

PHILIP Although one should be wary of ascribing too much responsibility to 'the nation'. A lot of what's done in the name of 'the nation' in fact serves the interests of a certain dominant class.

ANNE That could be, but at the moment identification with the nation matters much more than identification with an economic class, and consequently most citizens tend to feel at least partly responsible for their nation's deeds. It's an obvious point that, say, working-class people in the USA identify much more with fellow Americans than with the Canadian proletariat.

PHILIP Wouldn't you say that that phenomenon arose as a result of an early twentieth-century compromise that ensured raising living standards and labour peace by balancing the competing interests of labour and capital? Had it not been for the terms of this compromise, you can be sure that class conflicts would have been more evident.

ANNE Yes, possibly, although class conflict in developed nations may have been muted more by extraction of material resources from the Third World and exploitation of its cheap labour pool. But my concern here is less with explanation than with description, and it cannot be denied that this sense of being part of a living national community colours the meaning of our lives, and it seems like this will remain true in the foreseeable future. We feel a special concern for the fate of our compatriots, which entails a commitment to the good of our nation in a way that's not true of other nations.[20]

PHILIP Once again, what you say is starting to sound dangerous. It's true that I'm Canadian, but nothing at all seems to follow about the kind of person I am, or about the relation I must or should have with other Canadians. If I feel special ties to the Canadian nation, it's because Canada has realized in its institutions and practices the rule of law, individual rights, and some principle of fairness and equal treatment. In other words, I'm moved less by ties of blood and soil than by something like Rawls's two principles of justice.

ANNE [*raises voice*] You can't seriously believe that! If Rawls's two principles of justice count as your test of patriotic allegiance, why don't you move to Sweden, where those principles are probably realized to a greater degree than in Canada?

PHILIP [*smiles*] Actually, I've given some thought about moving to Sweden, but not for the reason you suggest. The women there have a special reputation, as you might know.

ANNE [*coldly*] I'll assume you're attempting a joke. The serious point I was making is that you must feel an allegiance to Canada that cannot be explained primarily in terms of the realization of certain universal principles of justice there—patriotism involves allegiance to a particular historical community, to a distinct way of life.[21] That is to say, citizens think of themselves primarily as bearers of a national history from which certain moral lessons have been drawn . . . [*thinking of examples Philip might relate to*] . . . Americans assume collective pride and pleasure in their triumph over the Nazis, French persons share collective humiliation and regret connected with their extensive collaboration with the Nazis during the occupation of France in World War Two, and so on.

PHILIP Of course, there's rarely agreement with respect to these matters. Many Frenchmen are inclined to deny or repress their history of involvement with the Nazis. And let's not talk about Germans . . .

ANNE Historical details will be argued over. None the less, it is this sense of sharing a national history that underlies a commitment to the good of one's nation.

PHILIP OK. Let's grant you this proposition. Would you not agree, however, that there comes a point when this commitment to the good of one's nation has to be put into question? If, say, current institutions and practices depart to a great extent from the 'moral lessons' that one has learned as a member of that national community, it seems to me that allegiance to the basic good of one's nation should be withdrawn.

Think of Stalin's Soviet Union, which systematically disowned its own true history, substituting in its place a largely fictitious history and replacing the moral bonds deriving from its history by the bonds of reciprocal self-interest. Do you not think that allegiance to that sort of nation would be an irrational attitude?[22]

ANNE My answer, put briefly, is 'no'. Let's take the case of Solzhenitsyn, who, as you may know, was forced into exile by the Soviet government. Though you could not find a more severe critic of Stalinist-type institutions and practices, he always maintained his special commitment to the good of the Soviet Union, or at least, to the good of the Russian people, arguing that the imposter Bolsheviks had thwarted the will of the Russian people whose authentic way of life lay in the institutions and practices of nineteenth-century Russia.[23]

PHILIP In other words, Solzhenitsyn draws upon the past to criticize the present. What if I find nothing admirable about my nation's past with which to criticize current institutions and practices? What would you say to the students in Tiananmen Square who looked, perhaps idealistically, to the USA as a source for their demands of democracy and freedom?

ANNE I'll remind you that there's a tradition of student demonstrations for more freedom and democracy in China, dating from the May Fourth, 1919 student movement. Besides, Chinese students made a point of affirming and reaffirming their patriotism, emphasizing that they wanted a Chinese-style democracy that maintains some form of continuity with the past.[24] You see, one cannot be both patriotic and a totalizing critic who finds nothing valuable in one's national history; totalizing critics are vilified as 'anti-nation' by fellow citizens, hence excluded from the national dialogue about the good of one's nation. To be patriotic, in short, means finding *at least something* valuable in one's national history.

PHILIP [*pause*] Let's assume, for the sake of argument, that I find 'at least something' valuable in Canada's national history. What happens if I find something even more valuable in, say, France's national history? Should I then shift my patriotic allegiance to France?

ANNE Please, Philip, don't ask ridiculous questions. You don't choose your patriotic allegiance according to how much you like a nation's history. My point is that the Canadian nation must hold a special place in your heart, that you experience a sense of shared fate with 'fellow Canadians' in a way that's not true of other nations.

PHILIP What would you say to an anarchist friend of mine in Shawinigan who wishes for nothing less than the abolition of the nation-state?

ANNE Look, even the most strident anarchist cheers, if only secretly, for her country's athletes in the Olympics. Special concern for the good of one's nation cannot be extirpated merely by the adoption of a consciously held political doctrine.

PHILIP Mmmh, you may have a point there. A few years back, I tried to strip myself of my attachment to Canada after the Canadian government rejected me for a scholarship. This meant choosing a game from an international ice hockey tournament held in Montreal according to certain objective criteria such as skating ability and scoring potential, rather than attending a game involving the Canadian national team simply because of my subjective feelings for Canada, as I would have done in the past. I finally settled on the game between the Czechs and the Soviets, which, happily, proved to be very successful in fulfilling the criteria which determined my choice of teams . . . The only problem is that I was completely bored, falling asleep on several occasions despite greater than normal doses of coffee and energy-boosting chocolate bars. It occurred to me that my heart, as they say, simply wasn't in the game, a sentiment which I realized could only be invoked if the Canadian team played.

ANNE [*smiling*] Thank you for that frank admission . . . It should be noted, however, that patriotic allegiance is more than identification with national sports teams. We seek the good of and take pride in distinctive national projects, projects conceived in the past and carried on in the future, which can be . . .

PHILIP [*interrupting*] I've no idea what you're referring to. I personally don't see myself as an agent carrying out a distinctive Canadian project . . .

ANNE Projects I have in mind can be unselfconsciously carried out by the citizens involved. Do you think that each Swiss citizen, when sweeping the debris from the public space adjacent to their personal living quarters, is consciously aware of partaking of a national commitment to cleanliness[25] and orderliness?[26] Or that the French are consciously cultivating their love of good food while searching for the best baguette in town?

PHILIP I don't know about the French, but having spent the past few years in England, I can tell you that the English seem aware of their love of bad food. Most notorious, and most unbelievable from the point of view of foreigners, is their attraction to 'marmite', a brown, viscous substance that's often spread on toast. It can be safely said that being English—or perhaps, to be more precise, British—is a necessary condition for liking marmite.

ANNE Yes, well, isolating eating practices is a good way of identifying communities of memory. What's eaten tends to vary enormously according to the cultural context, notwithstanding the homogenizing effects of the global market.

PHILIP [*pause*] Ummmmh, I recommend that we go on to the next course. All this talk about food is having an effect on my appetite.

ANNE Faithfulness to the cultural context requires that we have some cheese, which tends to follow the main course in France.

PHILIP I won't object, even though I don't particularly feel like having cheese at the moment. I suppose we ought to have the type of cheese that 'tends to follow' *choucroute*, whether or not we enjoy that cheese— what's good, according to you, is 'what's done here', wherever 'here' happens to be.

ANNE Now hold on a minute, I never said that. Take the case of cheese— some cheeses are better than others irrespective of the cultural context in which the cheese is consumed.

PHILIP Who determines what counts as a good cheese?

ANNE The 'cheese-eating community', if you will. There seems to be a fairly stable consensus with respect to what counts as a good cheese among cheese *aficionados*.

PHILIP I like velveeta processed cheese best.

ANNE You must be joking!

PHILIP Not at all.

ANNE In that case, I doubt that you've ever made a serious effort to appreciate a good cheese like, say, camembert. If you do, I'm sure you'll come to prefer camembert over velveeta.

PHILIP How do you know this?

ANNE Look, it's just a fact that people, when given the opportunity, come to prefer flavourful cheeses over insipid ones like velveeta. There's a certain asymmetry in the relationship between the two cheeses under discussion—while many graduate from a liking of velveeta to a prefer- ence for camembert, no one has ever moved, as far as I know, from a liking for camembert to a preference for velveeta.

PHILIP [*pause*] So what should we do, then? Have a good cheese or a local cheese?

ANNE Luckily, that's not a decision we have to make. While one can, in
principle, face a conflict between the goods of faithfulness to the cultural context and consumption of quality products, the French have
overcome this problem with respect to cheese by developing a national
preference for good cheese.

PHILIP You seem to have a soft spot for the French, but there's nothing so
special about their 'national preference for good cheese'—the English,
for example, take their stilton and their cheddar very seriously . . .

ANNE Not as seriously as the French take their good cheeses—the French
allow cheese made with non-pasteurized milk to be sold on the market,
as they're prepared to take health risks for the sake of eating good
cheese which the English are not . . . You see, national preferences will
be reflected to a certain extent in a country's legal system, and . . .

PHILIP [*interrupting*] Enough talk . . . *Monsieur!*

[*Waiter arrives*]

WAITER Oui?

PHILIP Un camembert pour deux, s'il-vous-plaît.

[*Waiter leaves, and returns with a camembert which he serves to Philip
and Anne*]

PHILIP Merci, monsieur.

WAITER [*his respect for Philip having increased*] Je vous en prie.

[*Waiter leaves*]

PHILIP [*tastes the camembert*] Very interesting . . .

ANNE Don't worry, you'll get used to it. If you persist, you'll actually
come to enjoy it.

PHILIP [*pause*] One little point, Anne. You may be right that national
identity entails certain preferences in terms of food, sports teams, and
the like—even my anarchist friend need not object so far. But I notice
that you've avoided saying anything about politics so far, a crucial
omission given the subject we've been discussing. Nations, after all, are
political communities.

ANNE Indeed, the bonds of commonality tying us to nations bear on our
political concerns. It is these bonds that explain why we feel politics
should be carried out in such a way as to benefit, first and foremost,
citizens of the nation. I wonder if your anarchist friend would deny
that, say, the French government owed a special obligation to the

French hostages kidnapped in Lebanon, as opposed to working for the release of British or American hostages.

PHILIP My friend wouldn't accept the moral validity of the categories with which you begin your analysis.

ANNE Let's leave her alone then—she has no hope of having her views widely shared.

PHILIP 'He'. My friend is a 'he'.

ANNE The use of personal pronouns in English is a controversial matter since, as I'm sure you know, many English speakers of a feminist orientation feel that the old system of using male pronouns to refer to both sexes is sexist. It is precisely when a cultural practice is thrown into relief in this way that it becomes a matter of personal choice whether or not to maintain this practice. Since I sympathize with feminist concerns, I'll use female personal pronouns to refer to both sexes so as to further undermine the sexist linguistic practice which many, including yourself, choose to maintain.

PHILIP I don't like being lectured to. All I know is that my friend would object if he was referred to as a 'she'.

ANNE Perhaps not if she was informed of my argument. In any case, I suggest that we terminate this digression so as to get back to the substance of our discussion . . . No one can doubt that a nation can claim allegiance to its political purposes, an allegiance which is most clearly summoned in times of war. We care deeply about the fate of our particular nation, and we're willing to risk harm and danger to ourselves *qua* individuals for the sake of the nation if it's necessary to do so in order to preserve its core values.[27]

PHILIP There's a serious problem with your claim that 'a nation can claim allegiance to its political purposes'—this hidden assumption of yours that nations are identical with states. Does a Tibetan care deeply about the fate of the People's Republic of China? Would a Tibetan willingly risk his life in order to preserve 'Chinese values'?

ANNE Well, Tibet seems to be a distinct and separate nation, bound to the People's Republic of China merely by the repressive apparatus of the Chinese state. But I'll remind you that I'm concerned with the communal attachments that 'we', 'Westerners', currently have and will have in the foreseeable future, so I'm restricting my claims here to Western nations.

PHILIP OK, let's take that up. Do nations coincide with *de facto* boundaries between states in the Western world?

ANNE Of course there's no definitional link between nations and states,
but the historical answer, it seems to me, is 'yes', with a few exceptions
such as the Basque region of Spain. France, Italy, the USA,
Switzerland, Sweden, Norway, Australia, and so on are both *de facto*
states and national communities of memory with distinctive purposes.
Though it's a matter of degree of course, France, for example, being
more of a nation-state than most Western countries.

PHILIP [*singing the Quebec separatists' rallying-cry*] Gens du pays, c'est
votre tour, de vous laisser, parler, d'amour . . .

ANNE Your point is well taken, and where there's little overlap between
the nation and the state—if the Québécois don't experience a sense of
shared fate with 'Canadians', if they feel indifferent to or oppressed by
federal political institutions—one would expect movements for some
form of political autonomy[28] . . . But I still think that, generally speaking, politics of the state, as conducted within national political institutions, bears crucially on the bonds of commonality that tie citizens to
nations. Most citizens strongly identify with the historically established
practices and institutions of their state—we have only to think of the
esteem, verging on worship, that Americans have for their constitution.

PHILIP Curious. You are speaking favourably of the large-scale bureaucratic state, suggesting that citizens are deeply attached to the practices
and institutions of their state. Yet I know that communitarians tend to
favour small-scale, local politics[29] . . .

ANNE Yes, but I don't think it should be an either/or choice between politics which involves face to face interaction at the local level and the
politics of the nation-state. The communitarians you're referring to are
responding to a widespread sense that national political institutions
appear too distant from our ordinary concerns, a feeling that we're at
the mercy of the political forces that govern our lives—this idea that
national political institutions suffer to an extent from a 'legitimation
crisis'.[30] Hence political decentralization in some areas, particularly in
social and cultural affairs, is necessary if we're to establish our full
status as citizens who take part in and identify with the political
process.

PHILIP Why stop at social and cultural affairs? What's wrong with complete decentralization?

ANNE Most of us, with the possible exception of your anarchist friend,
recognize the need for national political institutions. This is so not just
because we partake of a national community of memory with distinc-

tive purposes and projects whose good we seek, but also for the practical reason that in modern societies certain tasks cannot feasibly be decentralized—few would favour further democratization of responsibility for nuclear defence,[31] economic planning in modern societies seems to be, if anything, falling under the control of supra-national organizations such as the EEC, it is difficult to imagine how, say, individual states or towns in the USA could, on their own, devise a policy bearing on the large-scale influx of Mexicans across their borders, and so on. An important question for communitarian politics, then, will be 'which tasks of the national government can be decentralized so as to increase identification with the political process without undermining the necessary functions of the state?'

PHILIP [*pause*] Let's assume that we have a fully developed communitarian society, one that's not too implausible given current political realities. I imagine that this society would look something like present-day Switzerland, very decentralized with a lot of political participation at the local level. At the national level, you'd have certain functions left to the state, such as the ones you mentioned. My question is the following—what mechanism would there be to maintain the strong, non-instrumental identification with the institutions of the state you presuppose, other than something similar to the very demanding military conscription you now have in Switzerland? Your interpretation of communitarianism would seem to have militaristic implications . . .

ANNE You're forgetting one function of the state, a function that all Western states currently share to different degrees . . .

PHILIP [*interrupting*] You mean taxation?

ANNE Taxation, yes, but taxation for a specific purpose—to provide for the welfare of citizens by redistributing the state's revenue in accordance with socially recognized needs.[32] One consequence of the bonds of commonality that citizens of nations feel for each other will be an attempt by the national community to organize politically so as to meet the historically agreed-upon needs of citizens; and a successful attempt at doing so, i.e. a reasonably fair redistributive scheme, will in turn reinforce those bonds of commonality.

PHILIP But why should the nation-state be the site of distributive justice? Why can't that task be decentralized with the rest if it's feasible to do so?

ANNE Any effective scheme of distributive justice, as I see it, presupposes a bounded world of people deeply committed to each other's fate—

most of us will not agree to enshrine generous actions in law, and to
live by those laws, if we can't identify in some way with the recipients
of those generous actions[33]—and it just so happens that the nation-
state has emerged, for whatever concatenation of historical reasons, as
the unit within which our sense of solidarity is strongest.

PHILIP [*getting impatient*] You said before that people are greatly attached
to their 'community of place', that people feel a special sense of commitment to the good of their home town, and presumably of its inhabitants. So why couldn't, say, Montreal be the site of distributive justice?
Why does it have to be the nation-state?

ANNE Well, smaller units than the nation-state would seem to be ham-
pered by their limited resource base.[34] Besides, for most people, strong
feelings of solidarity stretch beyond their home town to that of their
nation as a whole—New Yorkers feel just about the same sense of
burning injustice when told of Texans who fail to receive proper medical care because they lack the necessary funds as they do when confronted with the ill-health of their own destitute homeless population.
But this bounded world of people deeply committed to each other's
fate will generally stretch no further than the nation—New Yorkers, it
goes without saying, feel little moral obligation to organize themselves
politically so as to provide for the welfare of poor Mexicans who happen to have been born on the wrong side of the Rio Grande.

PHILIP One little question. If citizens are so committed to the good of
their fellow nationals, why is private interest the motor of politics, with
each interest group fighting for its slice of the pie? Quite simply, it's
empirically false to assert that politics in Western states is driven by
conceptions of the common, national good. Perhaps my acquaintances
constitute an unrepresentative sample of the population at large, but
I've yet to meet any virtuous citizens who abstract from their own personal interest in order to contribute to the purposes of their national
community . . .

ANNE Communitarian politics entails that citizens should be engaged in
politics as members of a nation committed to advancing its common
good rather than as private persons with particular interests to advance,
a vision of politics that I believe expresses our deepest shared understandings. Let's take the United States—supposedly the most selfish of
nations—as a test case for this assertion. National political institutions
in the USA can be traced to constitutional founding fathers such as
James Madison who tried to foster the common good by designing an

elaborate constitutional mechanism to filter and refine popular passions in the hope that individuals of vision and virtue would reach office at the national level. The promise of the American constitutional system was that the virtue of the people would, after this filtering process, lead them to choose for their officials and representatives individuals who would be civic-minded and great-spirited enough to place the national good above their own or their local region's special advantage.[35]

PHILIP Something obviously went wrong somewhere . . .

ANNE No, not really. This political vision still pervades US politics—the public understanding of national figures such as the President, members of the US Senate and the Supreme Court, is that they embody roles as representatives not of factions but of national order and purpose.

PHILIP I'm very moved by this ode to the American political system. Now we know that national political figures ought to seek the good of the nation as a whole, or at least that they must appeal to the common national good in order to legitimize their activities . . .

ANNE That's far from a trivial point, Philip. It's clear that national leaders are more successful at establishing the peace among competing factions if they appear to be acting in the national interest, i.e. according to the common good of the nation as a whole. The King of Belgium is such a figure, which is why he is entrusted with the task of mediating conflicts between the Flemish and the Walloon communities. Where that's not true of national political figures, for example, in the case of Ronald Reagan, whose politics were tied to the good of a wealthy élite rather than the good of the nation as a whole, those leaders should be criticized.[36]

PHILIP Maybe it's true that Belgium has a good King. The objection I was hoping you would address, however, is that there's a pervasive gap between how politics is carried out and how politics ought to be carried out according to ordinary citizens' purported self-understandings. That is, you might want to explain why it is that citizens seem motivated by private interest in the political arena, voting with their pocketbooks and so on, whereas one would expect citizens to be engaged in seeking the common good of the nation if the nation is the powerful locus of identity that you make it out to be.

ANNE The cheap answer is that society is not structured in such a way as to enable citizens to realize in practice their commitment to the good of the nation—too many of our institutions underwrite and legitimize unworthy ambitions such as power and wealth. The interesting part is how to get from here to a properly structured society. Let's go slowly, for the body of society will have to be submitted to a very delicate operation that involves removing a certain idea propagated by liberal theorists, an idea which has 'infected the body politic', if you will . . .

PHILIP [*drinking more wine*] And what idea would that be?

ANNE It's a certain idea which favours a society that provides a wide range of projects and programmes to which a life can be dedicated. Do you accept this idea?

PHILIP I feel like I'm playing the role of the Socratic victim, but I'll still go along—yes, it does seem to me that it's better to live in a society which offers a rich array of qualitatively different meaningful life-plans than one which limits choice as to modes of life[37] . . . What's your point, anyway?

ANNE My point is the following—for the liberal, a criterion of a good political community is that it expands individual choice. This view rests on the liberal premiss that a rational person always prefers to be offered a greater availability of choices, since individuals are not compelled to accept extra options if they do not want to, nor do they suffer from being offered more choice.[38]

PHILIP Let me ask you something, Anne. Do you honestly think that a situation where an individual is offered more choices is not necessarily better than one where that individual has less?

ANNE Yes, I honestly think that, and moreover, I believe that I can get you to agree with me. It's a liberal myth that choice *per se* is good. I shouldn't have the choice of buying a portable bomb at my neighbour-hood grocer . . .

PHILIP [*interrupting, losing patience*] As long as more choice doesn't involve harm or potential harm, choice is beneficial.

ANNE Let me propose an example that refutes the contention that more choice is inevitably good. Actually, it's the philosopher Peter Singer's example. He asks the question 'should a market be allowed in addition to a voluntary blood system?'[39] He answers 'no', the reason being that turning blood into a commodity means that if no one gives it, it can still be bought, which makes altruism unnecessary and so loosens the bonds that otherwise exist between strangers in society.[40] Do you agree with Singer's position, or do you think individuals should have the choice of selling blood on the market?

PHILIP [*hesitatingly*] I'm not sure if I agree with Singer's reasoning, but I have to admit that I do not think it would be a good thing to have the opportunity to sell blood on the market.[41]

ANNE Well, once we agree that more choice can have unwanted costs, it is not preposterous to suggest that some choices currently available to individuals in society have undesirable consequences at the collective level, and that these ought to be curtailed if individuals are to realize what really matters to them. Let me bring this discussion back around to your observation that citizens do not seek the good of their nation as much as one would expect them to in view of the strong ties that they feel for their nation. One reason for this gap may be that citizens have the choice of pursuing their private economic interest as soon as they leave school, a choice that individuals feel they must take up if they're not to fall behind in the rat race, so to speak. If that choice were curtailed by, say, implementing a compulsory period of two years within which 18- and 19-year-olds must serve the national community in some civilian capacity . . .

PHILIP [*interrupting*] What do you have in mind? Being forced to help old ladies cross the street?

ANNE There are more productive uses to which healthy young bodies can be put. You can have them work as nurses' aides, as neighbourhood firepersons, they can help to reintegrate former prison inmates back into society, they can care for mentally ill persons, or whatever.[42] Any of these practices within the scheme of a compulsory service period will strengthen the moral bonds holding the nation together and thus narrow the gap between citizens' latent attachments to their nation and how they manifest those feelings in practice.

PHILIP [*swallows a breath*] I doubt that I would like the society in which your ideas were enforced . . .

ANNE It's not as sinister as it might sound on first hearing. You see, it's not a question of enforcing abstractly thought-out ideas on an unwilling public—the whole point of communitarian politics is to structure society in accordance with people's deepest shared understandings, one means of which may be to persuade people that choice should be limited when the structure is favoured that enables individuals to do what they really want to do without incurring substantial cost.

PHILIP Now hold on a minute. Are you suggesting that 'healthy young bodies' prefer, deep down, to serve their nation in the way you suggest? Think of American youth and their preoccupations—rock music, fast food, fashion, not to mention other sources of bodily gratification.

ANNE That's not true—once again, your atomist belief system skews your interpretation of reality. In fact, there's a deep-seated American commitment to community service[43]—you're probably familiar with New Deal job programmes and the like. A compulsory service scheme would simply tap this presently dormant disposition.

PHILIP Even if you're right about this—which I doubt—why does it have to be compulsory service? Why not simply introduce a service programme and let people join it if they want to?

ANNE Look, the problem isn't simply that people lack the institutional means to express their commitment to the good of the nation. It's also that promises of money and power can tempt young people to lose sight of what's important, an insight that many arrive at late in their life when it suddenly transpires to them that they've been pursuing goals of no intrinsic value. We're familiar with what's known as the 'middle-age crisis' . . . So a compulsory service scheme would make young people do things whose worth they may only come fully to appreciate later on—things they may not have done at the time had they been offered the possibility of doing something else.[44]

PHILIP But you admit that a compulsory service programme would force a very reluctant group of youngsters to do things they wouldn't normally want to do. I wonder how effectively people can help society if they're reluctantly forced to do so . . .

ANNE The policy of compulsory service work can be implemented in such a way that the people affected would not find it too disagreeable—for example, by offering civilian duty as an alternative to compulsory military service in those countries where the latter applies, or by linking government subsidies for higher education and post-secondary job training to service work.[45] And if I'm right that there already exists a deep commitment to community service, those affected by such a policy would come to appreciate and enjoy their work after an initial period of adjustment.

PHILIP And what would you do with those who refuse to join your scheme?

ANNE That is a technical question for policy-makers to decide.

PHILIP [*raises voice, as if threatening Anne*] What would you do as a policy-maker if I refused to join your scheme—would you throw me in jail?

ANNE Look, all I can say is that the matter of how to deal with recalcitrants hasn't been much of a problem in those Western countries that offer a choice of compulsory military service or a more lengthy period of civilian work. If I were a policy-maker, what I would do differently is to favour civilian service by either eliminating military conscription altogether or increasing its time commitment relative to the option of civilian service.[46]

PHILIP Why? What's wrong with military service? I would have thought that you'd favour this policy, as there's no more direct way of serving the nation than that.

[*Waiter arrives on stage, empties the Riesling in Anne and Philip's glasses, then leaves, his presence unacknowledged by the mutually absorbed conversationalists*]

ANNE Two points. Firstly, military conscription appears to be unnecessary in Western countries given the current relaxation of Cold War tensions. And more pertinently, military service, with its emphasis on hierarchy, discipline, and obedience, merely serves the interests of state power, whereas civilian service, which promotes co-operation and commitment, contributes to the moral health of the nation[47] and derivatively of its constituent members. You see, the idea is that by maximizing contributions to the nation's purposes early on, more would come to acknowledge the nation's purposes as their own, and subsequently participate in the political life of the nation as virtuous citizens committed to the nation's well-being.[48]

PHILIP [*pause*] Let me see if I've got your proposal right. It comes down to implementing laws that limit choice so as to help citizens realize that their true interest lies in seeking the good of their nation.

ANNE Please, Philip, it's not so bad. All laws limit choice. I just wanted to point out that it's not too implausible to suppose that certain laws can be implemented on the grounds that they favour the structure that enables citizens to manifest their love of country . . .

PHILIP [*interrupting*] That's bad enough for me. I have problems with your assumption that it's the state which will make us acknowledge, whether we like it or not, our 'love of country' . . .

ANNE You're distorting my position—my point is that the state's policies can either stifle or help to realize our deepest needs, and, given our deep attachment to the nation, I would favour those policies which help us to act on that attachment . . . Besides, let me remind you that I do not hold a unitary view of community—the nation is only one of many constitutive communities, and legislation won't have as important a role to play where there's a problem in terms of recognizing and seeking the good of other constitutive communities. In other cases, deliberation among friends about moral commitments might matter more—if you feel that your life lacks meaning, that you're not leading your life in accordance with your deepest commitments, the solution might well lie in a good friend who can help you grasp something about your identity that had lain dormant.[49]

PHILIP Is this what we're doing here? You're helping me 'grasp things about my identity that had lain dormant'?

ANNE Perhaps as a by-product. More immediately, we're discussing my thesis.

PHILIP Oh yes, I forgot that's what we were doing . . . [*at this point, Philip accidentally topples over his as yet unfinished glass of wine on the camembert*] . . . Oh my God, I'm sorry—I didn't do that on purpose.

ANNE That's a more self-incriminating excuse than you realize. If conscious effort didn't bring about your misdeed, this renders more likely the possibility that clumsiness is constitutive of your way of being. Or maybe I'm just saying this because I'm familiar with your past, 'grace' not being the word that comes to mind when asked to describe your behaviour.

PHILIP [*ignoring Anne's speculations*] Oh no, the wine is dripping on my pants! If you'll excuse me for a moment, I have to clean this mess up [*Philip abandons his chair and proceeds to the 'toilettes' sign*].

ANNE Wait! . . . [*Philip, not yet having left the stage, stops and turns to Anne, surprised*] . . . You're coming back, aren't you?

PHILIP Yes, of course. Why?

ANNE I want you to stay—I'm not persuaded that you're persuaded by what I've been saying about my thesis.

PHILIP I'm not persuaded by what *I*'m saying, never mind what you're saying.

ANNE No, but I mean I wouldn't want you to think of our differences as being unbridgeable, which might cause you to want to leave.

PHILIP Don't worry [*winks at Anne*]—I'll come back.

[*Philip leaves the stage. Lights dim*]

Notes

1. De la Patrie is referring to Robert Bellah *et al.*, *Habits of the Heart* (Berkeley, Calif.: University of California Press, 1985).
2. Interestingly, the same accusation is made by Vincent Harding in a letter addressed to the authors of *Habits of the Heart*:

   You claimed to be researching and writing a book whose primary focus is cultural, whose fundamental questions have to do with what it means to be an American. Carrying out that task in the midst of one of the most fascinating and frustratingly multi-cultural and multiracial nations in the world, you are severely limited and confined by your chosen base of white middle-class Euro-Americans . . . We are not now and never have been a white middle-class nation. And in our perilous times it seems absolutely essential that all of us who write for the public about the definition of America must make it powerfully clear that our *only* humane future as a nation is located in a multicultural, multivocal, multiracial territory. Indeed, to ask in the 1980s what is an American, and even to begin to try to answer the question on exclusively white grounds is, in my view, both backward and dangerous. It is to deny a truly public philosophy. ('Towards a Darkly Radiant Vision of America's Truth: A Letter of Concern, An Invitation to Re-Creation', printed in Charles Reynolds and Ralph Norman, eds., *Community in America: The Challenge of* Habits of the Heart (Berkeley, Calif.: University of California Press, 1988), 68, 73; Harding's italics.)

3. This is similar to (part of) Robert Bellah's response to Harding's criticisms. See his 'The Idea of Practices in *Habits*: A Response', in Reynolds and Norman, eds., *Community in America*, 269–70.
4. In fact, as Bellah points out,

   A Japanese-American graduate student in my department is writing a dissertation on the Japanese-American community in San Francisco using *Habits* as a model. Another student, herself a Chicano, is investigating the Chicano middle-class. A group in Afro-American Studies at the University of Mississippi has asked me to bring the insights of *Habits* to their restudy of Allison Davis' classic work, *Deep South*.

   Bellah concludes his defence against Harding's accusations in the following way:

   In short, we did not intend *Habits* to leave anyone out, even though we focused mainly on one group, and we are extremely happy that the book is encouraging people of 'all colors and ambitions' to join in the discussion of the issues we have raised. (Ibid. 270.)

5. The editors of *Community in America* also make this point:

> *Habits of the Heart* is the kind of scholarship that periodically kindles broad public interest because it catches and focuses something out there ready to be kindled, a widely shared but not yet fully articulated sense that something urgent and important requires attention. *The Lonely Crowd, The Feminine Mystique, The Culture of Narcissism,* and *Roots* immediately come to mind as books that similarly have captured the public imagination. (p. 1)

Reynolds and Norman should have added that Allan Bloom's highly entertaining recent critique of American-style hedonism *The Closing of the American Mind* (New York: Simon and Schuster, 1987) even more spectacularly succeeded in capturing 'the public imagination'.

6. See Bellah *et al., Habits of the Heart,* 153, for a similar idea.

7. The reader dissatisfied with this vague and too inclusive definition of 'community of memory' may be appeased by a distinction De la Patrie makes between communities of memory and lifestyle enclaves in Act V.

8. This distinction is also made in Bellah *et al., Habits of the Heart,* 140.

9. Burke's phrase is also quoted in Alasdair MacIntyre, *Whose Justice? Which Rationality?* (London: Duckworth, 1988), 353.

10. See Reynolds and Norman, eds., *Community in America,* 290, and Bellah *et al., Habits of the Heart,* 27–8, 335–6, for similar ideas.

11. There may well be a natural tendency to interpret tradition in this manner, in the same way that we tend to interpret literary texts attempting to find motives, morals, and plots. It is to counteract this natural tendency, presumably, that Mark Twain, in the prefatory notice to *The Adventures of Huckleberry Finn,* felt compelled to warn in rather forceful terms against this mode of interpretation:

> Persons attempting to find a motive in this narrative will be prosecuted; persons attempting to find a moral in it will be banished; persons attempting to find a plot in it will be shot.

12. See Alasdair MacIntyre, *After Virtue,* 2nd edn. (Notre-Dame, Ind.: University of Notre-Dame Press, 1984), 34–6, 222, 254, and David Miller, *Market, State and Community: Theoretical Foundations of Market Socialism* (Oxford: Clarendon Press, 1989), 266–7, for similar proposals of public discourse within a shared tradition.

13. See Michael Walzer, *Interpretation and Social Criticism* (Cambridge, Mass.: Harvard University Press, 1987), 30, 88–90, for a similar idea.

14. There may be, of course, communities of memory which exclude a certain proportion of 'constituent members' from 'joining the argument about its tradition', an 'exclusionary principle' internalized by the 'excluded members'

themselves—that women are excluded from contributing to the understanding of certain religious practices within Islam would, on the face of it, seem to be one such case. Until one has actually talked to the 'excluded members' to find out if they agree with this 'exclusionary principle', however, one is entitled to remain sceptical of claims made in favour of their exclusion by 'non-excluded members'—Tabitha Troughton, who talked to Afghan women 'locked indoors' by fundamentalist leaders, found that 'all the women I talked to wanted their rights [to work, and practice their religion freely]', a demand grounded in the belief that 'the essence of Islam is egalitarianism.' Since 'the West [is] turning its back on the problem and their men [are] unable or unwilling to help,' 'Afghan women are realizing that they have to do it for themselves,' which involves 'Afghan women joining together to chant extracts from the Koran which praise women [and studying] Koranic law so that they can argue for their freedom' ('A Fundamental Fight for Women', *Guardian* (20 Sept. 1990), p. 38). For a book-length defence of the thesis that there are no true grounds in Islam for discrimination against women (such discrimination is rather the product of men who misunderstand their own religious heritage and do so for their own profit) by a feminist Muslim scholar, see Fatima Mernissi, *Women and Islam: An Historical and Theological Inquiry* (Oxford: Blackwell, 1991).

15. Evidence for Schwartzberg's assertion can be found in Anthony Smith, *The Ethnic Origins of Nations* (Oxford: Blackwell, 1986) and in Benedict Anderson, *Imagined Communities* (London: Verso, 1983).

16. Benedict Anderson also points to this example in *Imagined Communities*, 143. This is very much an exaggeration, however, as the Vietnamese sense of nationhood can be traced as least as far back as AD 938, when the Vietnamese revolted to win their independence from China. Neil Sheehan writes:

> During the next near millenium, from 938 until the arrival of the French in the 1850s, every new dynasty that came to power in China invaded Vietnam. The recurrent necessity to drive out big invaders from the north, and incessant warfare with less menacing neighbours in the course of their expansion southward down the Indochinese Peninsula, lent a martial cast to Vietnamese culture . . .
>
> The wars with the big power to the north also led the Vietnamese to elaborate a particular idea as the central concept of their military thought. The concept is that an ostensibly weaker force, properly handled, can defeat a stronger one . . . The martial prowess and tradition of resistance to outside aggression was institutionalized in precolonial Vietnam, ingrained in the folklore and mentality of the peasantry as much as it was in the heritage of the mandarin class. (*A Bright Shining Lie: John Paul Vann and America in Vietnam* (New York: Vintage Books, 1989), 159–61.)

Ho Chi Minh, a nationalist who as a young man in Paris joined the French Socialist Party 'because its more radical members were the only French political grouping that seriously advocated independence for the colonies' (ibid. 156), tapped this 'tradition of resistance to outside aggression', and became known as 'the father of modern Vietnam' (ibid. 168); many lives would have been spared had French and (then) American policy-makers understood and accepted this Vietnamese reality.

17. For an argument that, *contra* what Schwartzberg implies, it may still be rational to feel national loyalties even if those loyalties are backed up by false beliefs, see Miller, *Market, State and Community*, 242–3.

18. In actual fact, the nation commands an even more profound emotional legitimacy in parts of the non-Western world—China's sense of nationhood, for example, runs so deep that individual Chinese persons sometimes fail to make a linguistic distinction between their own lives and those of their ancestors, as when persons of Chinese descent living in Hong Kong, Malaysia, or Singapore say they plan on going back to (mainland) China even if *qua* individuals they have never set foot there.

19. The Canadian nation has recently done just that in the form of an official apology by the federal government and monetary compensation for the victims of this injustice.

20. For an argument that, *contra* De la Patrie, it is often, perhaps ordinarily, wrong to give priority to the claims of our compatriots in the present world system, see Robert Goodin's article, 'What is so Special about our Fellow Countrymen?', *Ethics* (July 1988), pp. 663–86.

21. See Charles Taylor, 'Cross-Purposes: The Liberal–Communitarian Debate' in Nancy Rosenblum, ed., *Liberalism and the Moral Life* (Cambridge, Mass.: Harvard University Press, 1989), 176, where a similar idea is expressed.

22. Schwartzberg would probably be surprised to find out that a similar point was made by the anti-liberal Alasdair MacIntyre in his Lindley Lecture entitled 'Is Patriotism a Virtue?', University of Kansas, 1984, pp. 16–17.

23. Solzhenitsyn has recently come out with a pamphlet entitled 'How we are to Rebuild Russia', which seeks to rebuild Russian national pride by drawing on pre-revolutionary models (he proposes to re-create the elected district councils of pre-revolutionary times and the Duma, the first Russian Parliament in 1905, and to revive the Orthodox Church), but without the anti-democratic and colonialist elements of Russian nationalism.

24. De la Patrie cannot deny, though, that the Statue of Liberty served as a source of inspiration for the students in Tiananmen Square. On the other hand, the communitarian might argue that it is generally more effective if critical tools are drawn from within one's way of life—in the Chinese example, the students did try to 'Sinologize' the Statue of Liberty by placing both hands on the torch (to illustrate the difficulty of achieving democracy in

China), but they could have done more, e.g. turned her facial features into Oriental ones.

25. Perhaps the Swiss may be generally unaware of the link between their everyday behaviour and the Swiss national commitment to cleanliness, but the same cannot be said of the alert seventeenth-century Dutch if Simon Schama's description of their mindset is not exaggerated:

> To be clean was to be patriotic, vigilant in the defence of one's homeland, hometown and home against invading polluters and polluted invaders. The Dutch could not help brandishing their brushes in the faces of grimier heathen folk. (*The Embarrassment of Riches: An Interpretation of Dutch Culture in the Golden Age* (New York: Knopf, 1987), 378.)

26. Switzerland's love of order can carry a high price for its non-conformist citizens: a Swiss tenant recently received an eviction order for not hanging the curtains straight in his Basle flat—see 'Curtains for Tenant', *Guardian* (24 Mar. 1990), 8.

27. If Alasdair MacIntyre's assertion that 'How much each of us cares for or is concerned about any person, group, institution, practice, or good is measured—cannot but be measured—by the degree to which we would be prepared to take risks and face harm and danger on their behalf' (*Whose Justice? Which Rationality?*, 40) is accurate, then concern for the nation runs very deep indeed.

28. Political autonomy, it should be noted, may not always be a feasible option for those nations which lack strong identification with the state (and who would ideally want their own national political institutions to serve as a mechanism for 'the argument about the good of the nation')—the Catholics of Northern Ireland, for example, may well have to settle for something like constitutionally enshrined minority rights.

29. Some examples include Christopher Lasch—'It [communitarianism] proposes a general strategy of devolution or decentralisation, designed to end the dominance of large organisations and to remodel our institutions on a human scale. It attacks bureaucracy and large-scale organisations, however, not in the name of individual freedom or the free market but in the name of continuity and tradition.' ('The Communitarian Critique of Liberalism', in Reynolds and Norman, *Community in America*, 174); Michael Taves—'It [communitarianism] involves an attempt to recapture political control in local communities' (Taves *et al.*, 'Roundtable on Communitarianism', *Telos* (Summer 1988), 2); and Charles Taylor—'If our aim is to combat, rather than adjust to, the trends to growth, concentration and mobility, and the attendant bureaucratic capacity and rigidity of representative democracy, then some measures of decentralisation are indispensable, with the consequent strengthening of more localised, smaller-scale units of self-rule' ('Alternative Futures', in

Legitimacy, Identity and Alienation in Late Twentieth Century Canada (Toronto: Knopff and Morton, 1986), 221–2.

More concretely, Michael Sandel favours the New England town-hall-type political structure, and Alasdair MacIntyre looks back nostalgically to the politics of the ancient Greek *polis*. And while Charles Taylor describes himself as being 'very sympathetic' to the idea of decentralizing to 'truly local communities' ('Alternative Futures', 229 n. 37), he argues in favour of decentralizing to provincial governments in Canada for the reason that Canadians lack strong identification with 'truly local communities'.

30. On a possible 'legitimation crisis' (with an emphasis on the USA), see Seymour Martin Lipset and William Schneider, *The Confidence Gap: Business, Labor and Government in the Public Mind* (New York: Free Press, 1983), ch. 12; and Daniel Yankelovich, 'A Crisis of Moral Legitimacy?', *Dissent*, 21 (Fall 1974), 526–33.

31. See John Dunn, *Interpreting Political Responsibility* (Oxford: Polity Press, 1990), 198, for a similar point. One worrisome aspect of the break-up of the Soviet Empire concerns precisely this 'democratization of responsibility for nuclear defence', and the possibility that violence could erupt between republics with the use of nuclear weapons. As US Secretary of State James Baker put it: 'We really do run the risk of seeing a situation created there not unlike what we've seen in Yugoslavia, with nukes—with nuclear weapons thrown in' (quoted in *The Straits Times* (10 Dec. 1991), 4).

32. See Michael Walzer, *Spheres of Justice* (Oxford: Basil Blackwell, 1983), esp. ch. 3 for a similar idea.

33. Richard Rorty makes the point that identification with 'fellow human beings' seldom provides the motivational force for generous actions:

> Consider . . . the attitude of contemporary American liberals to the unending hopelessness and misery of the lives of the young blacks in American cities. Do we say that these people must be helped because they are fellow human beings? We may, but it is much more persuasive, morally as well as politically, to describe them as fellow *Americans*—to insist that it is outrageous that an *American* should live without hope . . . [Our] sense of solidarity is strongest when those with whom solidarity is expressed are thought of as 'one of us', where 'us' means something smaller and more local than the human race. That is why 'because she is a human being' is a weak, unconvincing explanation of a generous action.
> (*Contingency, Irony and Solidarity* (Cambridge: Cambridge University Press, 1989), 191; Rorty's emphasis.)

That our sense of solidarity is strongest where 'us' means something smaller and more local than the human race provides a strong argument against the feasibility of a world-wide system of distributive justice (regulated by law), but of course it doesn't follow that the range of 'us' can't be extended in the direction of greater human solidarity for more narrow purposes, e.g. making people more sensitive to instances of cruelty in faraway lands (Rorty thinks that novels, with their detailed descriptions of particular varieties of pain and humiliation, are particularly suitable for this purpose).

34. David Miller makes a similar point in the context of his argument that the nation-state should be the site of distributive justice—see his 'The Ethical Significance of Nationality', *Ethics* (July 1988), 658–9. The city-state of Singapore, however, would seem to be an exception to this general rule.

35. See Bellah *et al.*, *Habits of the Heart*, 253–5, for a similar discussion of this idea.

36. Tax breaks delivered to the rich by the Reagan administration allowed them to reap most of the income gain in the 1980s, and the poor were especially hard hit by the failure of the minimum wage to rise from 1981 to 1989—families in the lower 40% of the income range saw their incomes actually drop (see the *New York Times* article 'Rich are Richer while Poor are Poorer in US, Report Confirms', repr. in *The Straits Times* (Singapore) (7 Mar. 1992), 6).

37. In the same vein, Will Kymlicka argues that it is best to live in a society which provides a wide range of options from which to choose a way of life, and that the state should ensure an adequate range of options:

> . . . everyone has an interest in having an adequate range of options when forming their aims and ambitions . . . there is no reason to suppose that governments couldn't develop a decision procedure for public support of the culture of freedom [i.e. a society which provides a rich array of possibilities] that respected the principle of neutral concern, that was endorsable as fair by everyone in society. (*Liberalism, Community and Culture*, 81.)

Not 'everyone' has an interest in living in a society which provides a rich array of possibilities as to modes of life, however, as there are many societies that fail to offer a 'wide range of projects and programs to which a life can be dedicated' and where the introduction of extra options as to modes of life is likely to lead to the destruction of the way of life of the 'narrow' culture— this is probably true of the Indian and Inuit societies that Kymlicka deals with in his book (few share his optimism that 'the Indian community has sufficient strength and integrity to survive the (desirable) transition to a situation where its members have all the resources of the modern world at their disposal' (p. 17), and most would agree that it would have been even more desirable from the point of view of 'the Indian community' had it never encountered 'the modern world'), and almost certainly true of the anti-technological 'Old Order Amish in America, [who] are morally committed to shielding their children from all knowledge that might lead them to doubt and all worldly influences that might weaken their religious beliefs' (Amy Gutmann, *Democratic Education* (Princeton, NJ: Princeton University Press, 1987), 29).

38. De la Patrie has captured Rawls's position (Rawls classifies liberty as a primary good, that is, one which any rational person will prefer more of to less, since individuals are not compelled to accept more if they do not want to nor does a person suffer from greater liberty, which is equivalent to asserting that a rational person always prefers to be offered a greater availability of choices), a position which is convincingly criticized by Gerald Dworkin in his article 'Is More Choice Better than Less?', in J. Howie, ed., *Ethical Principles for Social Policy* (Carbondale, Ill.: Southern Illinois University Press, 1983), 78–96.

39. Of course, the argument against a market for blood does not apply in countries such as China where few donate blood as an expression of social solidarity—in China, hospitals have to pay large amounts to buy blood from the general public (see David Bonavia, *The Chinese* (London: Penguin Books, 1989), 130) for the reason that Chinese people, imbued with the idea of traditional Chinese medicine that blood constitutes 'vital energy' of the body, can rarely be persuaded to donate blood by means of moral incentives. Although communist authorities have occasionally tried to move away from a system of straightforward cash payments for blood, they still have to rely on material incentives of some sort—at Beijing University, students are rewarded with free tickets for foods such as beef that are meant to 'replenish the blood supply'.

40. Singer's argument is also mentioned in Gerald Dworkin, 'Is More Choice Better than Less?', 87.

41. Ronald Dworkin would probably agree with Philip's viewpoint. Reviewing a book that traces the decline of egalitarian politics (which Dworkin endorses) in the United Kingdom, Dworkin writes:

> Americans dismayed by the failure of their own country to reduce inequality admired Britain's progress. They read the sociologist Richard Titmuss's exciting book, *The Gift Relationship*, which used the contrast between the British practice of donating blood for transfusions and the American practice of selling it as a metaphor for the difference between the two societies. (Review of Peter Jenkins's *Mrs. Thatcher's Revolution: The Ending of the Socialist Era*, *New York Review of Books* (27 Oct. 1988), 57.)

A communitarian would object to Dworkin's analysis on the following grounds—while this contrast may indeed illuminate an important difference between these two societies, the practice of donating blood reveals more about the strong spirit of social solidarity in pre-Thatcherite Britain than about the egalitarian politics of that society. In fact, were egalitarian politics applied more rigorously, this may well have had the unintended consequence of undermining the strong spirit of social solidarity characteristic of pre-Thatcherite Britain:

> Trying to define and enforce in detail some of our common feelings about equality may weaken the common sense of moral commitment and mutual solidarity from which these feelings grow. (Taylor, 'Cross-Purposes: The Liberal–Communitarian Debate', 162.)

More precisely, a government committed to equality above all else could not forbid the selling of blood on the market—a government that treats its citizens equally by not appealing to any particular conception of the good when it sets policy (a necessary component of equal treatment as interpreted by egalitarian-minded liberals of the Rawlsian mode—see Act II n. 4) could not forbid the selling of blood on the market, since one reason for doing so would be that a society with a strong, voluntaristic spirit of social solidarity is superior to a selfish society—which would serve to weaken the spirit of social solidarity for the Peter Singer reason that De la Patrie offers.

42. The American thinker Randolph Bourne proposed a similar scheme for the USA in 1916. He asks the question, 'How can we all together serve America by really enhancing her life?', and develops in response the idea of a domestic Peace Corps:

> I have a picture of a host of eager youth missionaries swarming over the land . . . [serving the country in such ways as] . . . 'food inspection, factory inspection, organised relief, the care of dependents, playground service, nursing in hospitals. (Quoted in Michael Walzer, *The Company of Critics* (New York: Basic Books, 1988), 48–9.)

43. The author Charles Moscos has recently surveyed the broad range of civic programmes in American history (see *A Call to Civic Service* (New York: Twentieth Century Fund/Free Press, 1988)), suggesting that these reflect a deep-seated American commitment to community service. Given the lack of institutional means (at the moment) that would enable Americans to realize that commitment, Moscos proposes introducing a universal, compulsory civilian service scheme in the USA.

44. Though De la Patrie's reasoning may on the face of it sound implausible, there are many cases where young people are made to do things whose worth they only come to appreciate later on in life—one often hears people say such things as 'I'm glad now that my mother forced me to take piano lessons, even though I hated it at the time', or 'I dreaded having to learn Latin in school, but it served me well and I'm sorry that my daughter is not made to do the same thing in her school', or 'though I would have preferred to have more choice of courses at university when I was there, I mourn the passing of the

core curriculum when I look at the culturally illiterate simpletons who now graduate from university', or even 'I wish I had been made to join a job training scheme when I dropped out of school instead of being handed out welfare cheques that I wasted on booze and poker games.'

45. If De la Patrie's suggestion that non-moral incentives such as subsidies for higher education may be necessary to attract citizens to community service work is accurate, this is an argument for making civic service compulsory (and therefore universal). Otherwise (i.e. if civic service is optional), the poor are likely to be disproportionately attracted to civic service, the drawing-card of this scheme being its material benefits (which well-off persons can do without)—it is for this reason that poor youth tend to be disproportionately represented in the American (non-conscription) military (see Benjamin Barber, *Strong Democracy: Participatory Politics for a New Age* (Berkeley, Calif.: University of California Press, 1984), 299).

46. Benjamin Barber advocates a compulsory service scheme for the USA that would include military service (thus eliminating the need for a volunteer army which makes military service a function of economic need) while reducing its importance *vis-à-vis* civil service (the armed forces would be only one of five branches of the compulsory service scheme which individuals could choose freely between except in times of congressionally declared wars)—see *Strong Democracy*, 298–303.

47. Randolph Bourne made a similar distinction in response to what he thought of as the state-inspired militaristic frenzy that led to World War I (see Walzer, *The Company of Critics*, 61–3).

48. It cannot be denied, however, that there are many who do not find the good in the public life of a citizen republic, or in any other form of politics, and to say that they have a dormant interest in 'acknowledging the nation's purposes as their own' would seem to stretch the bounds of plausibility. Dr Skreta is one extreme example: 'Politics [is] the least substantial and least valuable form of life. Politics is the dirty foam on the surface while real life takes place in the depths . . . When I put on my rubber glove and touch a woman's womb, I am much closer to the center of life than you, who have almost lost your own life in your concern for human happiness.' (pp. 81–2). Dr Skreta heads a fertility-restoring clinic for women in Milan Kundera's novel *The Farewell Party* (London: Penguin Books, 1984). Kundera, however, has recently been criticized for his apolitical stance from Paris while other prominent Czech intellectuals, most notably Vaclav Havel, stayed behind to engage in political activities for the good of their country, paying a severe personal cost.

49. See Michael Sandel, *Liberalism and the Limits of Justice* (Cambridge: Cambridge University Press, 1981), 179–83, for a similar point about the possibilities of friendship. Marilyn Friedman also invokes the concept of friend-

ship as a means of offering insights into the social nature of the self, but her analysis is marred by a mistaken account of friendship—she writes that 'Friends are supposed to be people whom one chooses on one's own to share activities and intimacies' ('Feminism and Modern Friendship: Dislocating the Community', *Ethics*, 99: 2 (1989), repr. in Shlomo Avineri and Avner de-Shalit, eds., *Communitarianism and Individualism* (Oxford: Oxford University Press, 1992), 113), but in most cases friends are not 'chosen' in the sense of making a conscious decision about something—rather, friendship is something that one 'slips into', more often than not as a result of chance meetings or shared experiences in childhood. One might reply that friendship is chosen in the sense that one can make a conscious decision to terminate a friendship, but there are occasions when it would be morally perverse (to choose) to abandon a friend (e.g. if a friend is in great need of help that one can provide), and besides friendships usually come to an end without anyone having made a conscious decision to end them—it can be assumed that De la Patrie and Schwartzberg's friendship would have withered away had they not run into each other by chance at *La Coupole*.

Act V: A Discussion about the Value of Language-Based Communities, the Gay Community, and the Family

SCENE: *the same.*

[*Philip enters the stage and reappropriates the seat he had vacated. His pants seem wet*]

PHILIP I apologize for my appearance. I used hot water and soap to wash out the wine stain, and I had no access to the hair-dryer that I would normally have employed to dry the clothes I spill things on.

ANNE Don't worry—I'm aware that contingent facts about your appearance, such as the clothes you're wearing, don't express constitutive features of your identity. At least I hope that's true for your sake, given the clashing outfit you've selected for today.

PHILIP Steeped as you are in the dominant 'shared meanings' of the day, you've no sense of avant-garde fashion . . . In any case, I'm still not at all clear as to how we're supposed to distinguish between constitutive features of our identity and contingent facts about our life.

ANNE I'd rather not get into this again. It will be sufficient to remind you that what we've been talking about thus far are essential components of the self, stripped of which we would no longer be the same person in the relevant sense. I've been referring to them variously as 'constitutive features of one's identity', 'constitutive attachments', and 'constitutive communities', but whatever label you use, these essential components—one's family, one's nation, one's religion, and so on—constitute what it is that's valuable in our lives.

PHILIP I'm not sure this is helpful, but the Spanish and Portuguese languages capture the distinction between constitutive attachments and contingent facts about oneself in a way that's not true of other Indo-European languages such as English, French, and German. In Spanish, for example, the verb 'ser' picks out constitutive attachments and the verb 'estar' picks out contingent facts about oneself, whereas both of the verbs are conflated into the verb 'to be' in English. Thus, the verb 'ser' would be used to translate 'I am a Canadian', which picks out a constitutive attachment, and the verb 'estar' would be used to translate 'I am in Max's store', which picks out a contingent fact about oneself . . . [*pause, as though Philip is thinking to himself*] . . . So you might want to say the following—the fact that we conflate the distinction in the English language may well explain why it is difficult for us to reflect upon our constitutive attachments, why our constitutive attachments matter less to us than to a Spaniard or a Brazilian for whom his family, nation, and religion matter a great deal, not just in the personal realm but also in the political life of those linguistic communities.

ANNE That's ridiculous! You can't seriously believe that the Spaniard is more in touch with her constitutive attachments because of some structural difference in our languages, or that Rawls, who overlooks the distinction between constitutive attachments and contingent facts about oneself when he divests persons of both of these in the original position, appeals more to English, French, and German speakers than to Spanish and Portuguese speakers for that same reason.

PHILIP I'm sorry—I was just trying to help.

ANNE Not to worry, as you're not the first to have engaged in such speculations. Some have suggested that Heideggerian thought, with its basic premiss that to think of 'being' one must 'live it', derives from a grammatical feature present in German but not in English—the German noun for 'being', 'Sein', is identical with the infinitive of the verb, in contrast with the static notion of 'being' in English, with the consequence that the dynamic process of 'being-there' is wholly operative only in German within the noun 'Sein'[1] . . . Having said that, this is a good occasion to get back to where we were before your last trip to the bathroom—I was about to go on to a more controversial example of a community of memory, namely, linguistic communities of memory.

PHILIP Fine, as long as you promise to stop talking about Heidegger . . . So tell me then, what's a linguistic community of memory?

ANNE Linguistic communities of memory, you won't be surprised to hear, are language-based communities of memory. Examples of what I have in mind include the German community of memory, the Basque community, and the Icelandic community.

PHILIP Before you proceed any further, let me bring up what I think is the failure of communitarians to take properly into consideration the Chomskian view on language and how it bears on politics, or rather, how it doesn't.[2] Chomsky, whose work still dominates the field of linguistics, posits a universal language 'mental organ',[3] which consists of abstract principles of a very general nature from which are generated particular languages that manifest themselves in a complex form at a critical age of about 2½ years old. That is, all humans share this language capacity, but which languages manifest themselves when and where depends on the particular language that's spoken in the environment the child happens to find himself in. The important point that communitarians should recognize is that particular languages should be treated as mere outputs of the universal language mental organ, ultimately reducible to that common element. Thus, if this view on language is correct, no great political importance, or any other kind of importance, should be attributed to particular languages, just as we attribute no special importance to eye colours or nose shapes. Having said this, do you still think that particular languages matter, that it makes sense to divide people into communities of memory according to the particular language that they happen to speak?

ANNE I told you that this issue would be controversial. However, I think that we can find common ground once we distinguish between two communitarian answers to your question. The first answer is that particular languages matter a great deal because of the truth of a very contestable philosophy of language that I'll present but not defend, the second is that one can remain agnostic with respect to competing philosophies of language while holding on to the view that languages matter, both subjectively and in the political realm. The contestable philosophy of language is the one you tried to foist upon me when you pointed out that difference between the Spanish and Portuguese languages and the other Indo-European languages you mentioned. This philosophy of language has been labelled the 'expressive theory of language' by Charles Taylor,[4] and its influential proponents in the past have included Herder and the later Wittgenstein.

PHILIP Please explain to me what you mean by the 'expressive theory of language', a theory that I've never heard of but which I was presumably aware of latently, since you say I foisted it upon you.

ANNE You'll recognize it when I articulate it. The expressive theory of language is that particular languages embody distinctive ways of experiencing the world, of defining what we are. That is, we not only speak in particular languages, but more fundamentally become the persons we become because of the particular language community in which we grew up—language, above all else, shapes our distinctive ways of being in the world. Language, then, is the carrier of a people's identity, the vehicle of a certain way of seeing things, experiencing and feeling, determinant of particular outlooks on life[5]. . .

PHILIP [*pause*] One implication of this view is that a change in one's language should result in a change of one's outlook on life. Didn't the post-revolutionary French hope to implement equality by means of forbidding use of the formal 'vous' in favour of the more egalitarian 'tu'?[6]

ANNE They failed, not surprisingly given the immensity of the task the revolutionaries took upon themselves—in France, even married couples address each other in the 'vous' form, and daring would be the child who would 'tutoy' her parent . . . In terms of implications, though, adherents of the expressive theory of language commonly adopt a policy of leaving individual words untranslated. The reasoning here would seem to be the following—since the languages of different people express very different visions of things, and individual words cannot be understood in isolation from the context in which they appear, even attempting to translate a word in abstraction from the role a certain word or words plays in the stream of thought or life of a people will cause more confusion than enlightenment.[7]

PHILIP Adherents of the 'expressive theory of language' seem to have found a place on the editorial board of the *New York Review of Books*,[8] which doesn't translate individual words, and sometimes even leaves whole sentences untranslated and unexplained. To be honest, I find this habit mighty irritating, for I frequently come across untranslated words in a language that I know, such as French, that can easily be rendered into English without significant loss of meaning.[9]

ANNE Of course, it's a separate question whether or not your knowledge of French is sufficient to allow you to make such an assertion.

PHILIP Four years in England haven't helped my French, as I've already said. In any case, my point is that whatever philosophy of language one happens to hold, it seems to me that the average reader will understand more if attempts are made at translation. And where problems occur, for instance, whether or not the idea of *Geist* in Hegel should be translated as 'mind' or 'spirit', an appropriate translation can be utilized after the ambiguities involved have been explained by the author.[10]

ANNE Perhaps, but it is sometimes better to keep terms in the original language if they are particularly difficult to translate. This is the case with Heidegger's idea of *Dasein*.[11]

PHILIP Your friend Heidegger is a special case. Unless you really believe that English and German express different and incompatible forms of life . . .

ANNE No, no, I never said that. Besides, English and German share common properties, both being languages of Indo-European extraction, which means that many words can be uncontroversially translated from one language into the other without significant loss of meaning. That's also why I still feel like the same person when I speak French and English—both of which I really do speak fluently as a result of my having decided to go to an English-language university.

PHILIP I'm not sure I understand . . .

ANNE I mean that English and French share the same base, so I don't feel like I'm tapping two different forms of life depending upon which language I speak.

PHILIP Ah, so you would endorse the expressive theory of language with respect to languages with different bases, for example, a language with an Indo-European base versus a language with a Chinese base.[12]

ANNE No—I said earlier that I would present that theory of language but not defend it.

PHILIP Look, you're not talking to your thesis examiner here. Tell me what you think—is it or is it not true that, say, a Chinese speaker will experience a different way of looking at things than we will simply as a consequence of the different languages spoken?

ANNE [*pause*] What I can say is the following—at least two commonly advanced claims by adherents of the expressive theory of language are importantly wrong, and a defensible reformulation of this theory, it seems to me, would have to do without these claims. The first claim is that language sets the limits to the world we can experience; it is not simply that language influences to a certain extent our conception of the world, but that language *alone* determines our particular way of seeing things, experiencing and feeling.[13] On the face of it, this would seem to be an absurd claim—can it be that your experience of the world stems solely from linguistic particularities of the English language? Yet many thinkers have taken this claim very seriously indeed, focusing on certain linguistic particularities, no matter what they are, and drawing conclusions about a speech community's conception of the world, on the assumption that nothing else besides language influences that speech community's experience of reality.

PHILIP Do you have any examples in mind?

ANNE Well, the anthropologist Benjamin Whorf drew from the fact that Hopi verbs have no tenses the implication that Hopi Indians have no conception of dimensional, linear time.[14]

PHILIP If Whorf is correct, I wouldn't want to set a dinner date with a Hopi Indian.

ANNE I doubt that Whorf is correct about the Hopi Indians, but in any case the assumption underlying his inference that Hopi Indians have no conception of dimensional, linear time can be criticized—there are many other languages whose verbs fail to distinguish between past, present, and future, and it certainly doesn't follow that speakers of those languages have no conception of dimensional, linear time. Think of Mandarin, the world's most widely spoken language—do Chinese speakers fail to distinguish between past, present, and future simply because Mandarin verbs have no tenses?

PHILIP So what are you saying then? That linguistic particularities do not bear in any way on one's experience of the world?

ANNE I wouldn't go that far. Linguistic particularities often do reflect a speech community's particular concerns—you've probably heard of the famous example that the Inuit have twenty-seven words to describe various types of snow,[15] but some grammatical features of language have nothing to do with our experience of the world. And granting that we may have a certain experience of reality not embodied in the particular language we happen to speak—Hopi Indians and Chinese speakers can experience linear time even if their verbs lack tenses—means having to drop the claim that language sets the limits to the world we can experience . . .

PHILIP So that's the first commonly advanced claim by adherents of the expressive theory of language that you disagree with. What's the second?

ANNE The second is this idea that it is language, above all else, which determines a people's distinctive cultural identity. If the way of being of a people is contained essentially in its language, and therefore one is introduced to a certain form of life by means of learning the language,[16] it should follow that pre-linguistic children do not yet partake of the form of life of the community in which they dwell. However, empirical research has revealed otherwise—3- to 4-month-old babies have already learned to be Japanese, American, or whatever the relevant community may be.

PHILIP I have to admit that I'm unfamiliar with the empirical research you're referring to. Most Japanese and American mothers, however, would probably be surprised to hear that their 3-month-old babies have already learned to think in Japanese and American ways, respectively.

ANNE It's a way of *acting* that's learned in the first instance, not a way of thinking, a belief system, a psychological disposition, or anything else that resides 'inside the head'; we can do without any mental content at this stage . . .

PHILIP [*interrupting*] I believe you were saying something about Japanese versus American babies.

ANNE Yes. My point is that contrasting child-rearing practices produce very different sorts of human beings, such that 3-month-old babies have already been socialized into a structure of shared social practices, a way of relating to others and the world that's permanently embedded . . . [*short pause*] . . . Comparing child-rearing practices in Japan and the United States, we find that the Japanese mother tries to soothe and quiet the child, almost as if she wants to turn out a passive, gentle, and contented human being[17] . . .

PHILIP [*interrupting*] What do you mean 'as if she wanted'? She doesn't want that?

ANNE I mean that all she's doing is acting as a mother should act, largely unreflectively, in a way specified by what she's learned from the world in which she dwells . . . The American mother is very different. She does more looking at and chatting to her baby, stimulating the baby to activity and vocal response, as if she wanted a loud, assertive, and relatively independent baby . . . [18]

PHILIP What if a Japanese mother stimulates her baby to activity and vocal response? Will she churn out a hamburger-eating, loud-mouthed American?

ANNE A Japanese mother wouldn't want to act like an American mother, and couldn't even if she tried; cultural traits, ways of acting that make sense to those sharing one's way of life, are picked up at a very early age, perhaps at 3 months of age, without ever the possibility of being understood and transferred as a whole from one person dwelling in a particular world to another dwelling in a different world. My description of the difference between Japanese and American mothers only scratches the surface.

PHILIP Don't you think that it's too deterministic to say that distinctive cultural traits have already been stamped in at 3 months of age?

ANNE Say what you may, the fact is that these early traits have far-

reaching implications, not the least of which is in the political realm—
the Japanese understanding of what it is to be human, as manifested in
the passive, contented, gentle, and socially mindful Japanese baby,
manifests itself in politics as a need for consensus; whereas the active,
independent, and aggressive me-first American baby will more often
than not end up thinking of politics as an arena for the negotiation of
individually held desires.[19]

PHILIP Personally, I think money and power matter more in politics than
child-rearing practices.

ANNE Whatever. I brought up the example of Japanese versus American
socialization to show that babies have learned to partake of the form of
life of the community in which they dwell before they've learned to
speak, which falsifies the idea that children are introduced to *a priori*
ways of seeing the world only when they learn the language of the community in which they're bred. Language, in short, can't be the primary
vehicle of culture, since babies learn their culture before they learn a
language.[20]

PHILIP I'm not too clear as to how you can reconcile this idea that language isn't the primary vehicle of culture with your earlier claim that at
least some linguistic particularities will reflect a community's concerns
. . .

ANNE Pay attention to the word 'reflect'. Rather than determining one's
experience of the world, language seems to play the role of reflecting—
and reinforcing—what's already there.[21] This isn't, please note, to deny
the importance of linguistic particularities—it can be a great source of
concern when language lags behind changes in the form of life of the
community. For example, while women seem to have largely won the
battle for equality, at least at the level of a shared meaning that is how
things ought to be, many of us are upset by persons such as yourself
who persist in failing to acknowledge the existence of women in your
use of personal pronouns . . .

PHILIP Not that again! I'll try to change, if only to reduce your blood-
pressure level.

ANNE I'll be on the watch for this . . . For the moment, however, let me
briefly remind you that I cast doubt on two claims commonly
advanced by adherents of the expressive theory of language, suggesting
that the idea that particular languages determine particular outlooks on
life would have to be weakened to the following form—some linguistic
particularities reflect and reinforce the concerns of a community, and

others do not . . . But in my thesis, I proposed a second communitarian answer to the question of whether or not particular languages matter, an answer which I endorse. On this view, I can remain agnostic with respect to the competing philosophies of language, while holding on to the idea that particular languages matter . . .

PHILIP [*interrupting*] Matter in what sense?

ANNE Matter in the sense that speakers of a particular language may well partake of a distinct community of memory. You'll recall that I defined a community of memory centrally by its feature of constituent members sharing a history that goes back several generations. And since it's an empirical fact that individuals who speak the same language can communicate meaningfully and therefore tend to learn and experience a similar history, it can be said that those speakers, sharing a common history that bears on how they interpret their lives, partake of what we can call a 'linguistic community of memory'. Think, for example, of French speakers in Quebec such as myself—we feel that we share a certain history that binds us together and sets us apart from the rest of Canada.

PHILIP Leaving aside the case of French Quebec for a while, there are occasions when a language is imposed from without on a group of people who do not share a history. How can it be said, for example, that when indigenous speakers of very different languages with a Mayan base are forced into so-called 'model villages' by the Guatemalan military, those indigenous people partake of the Spanish-speaking community of memory because their only common language is Spanish, the language of their oppressors?

ANNE It can't be said. What the Guatemalan military must be trying to do is to atomize and dissolve the various indigenous communities of memory, to purge them of their shared history, in order better to control them, or whatever. You can't force people to partake of a shared community of memory simply by making them speak the same language.[22]

PHILIP So then speaking the same language isn't a *sufficient* condition to partake of a community of memory. Just because we speak the same language it doesn't follow that we partake of the same community of memory. But is speaking the same language a *necessary* condition to partake of a community of memory?

ANNE No, no, of course not. I don't understand why you insist on fitting our topics under discussion into the straitjacket of necessary and sufficient conditions . . . It's not necessary to speak the same language in order to partake of a community of memory—think of the multilingual Swiss national community of memory,[23] or the Catholic religious community of memory whose constituent members need not and most often do not speak Latin.

PHILIP I'm confused. It's very hard to know when we're talking about a linguistic community of memory, not to mention the political implications that flow therefrom.

ANNE My dear Philip, I don't want to sound overly pedagogical, but I think I can get you to appreciate that it's really not that complex a question. We have a linguistic community of memory when speakers of a particular language think of themselves as sharing a distinct history that matters a lot to them. With respect to political implications, it follows at the very least that, since constitutive communities fill our lives with meaning, bearing crucially on our sense of psychological stability, linguistic communities of memory ought to be protected when they're threatened. The case of Iceland can serve to illustrate what I mean by this. Icelanders share a language and a literary tradition in that language, the Sagas, of which they're manifestly proud. However, they feel threatened by what is referred to as 'cultural imperialism', in the form of, for example, American and British television programmes. As a consequence, the government implemented measures of language preservation such as one requiring every television broadcast of foreign material to carry either Icelandic subtitles or an overlaid Icelandic commentary.[24]

PHILIP It's certainly original of you to bring up the case of Icelandic language rights at a time when most Francophones in Quebec would be concerned with the survival of the French language in Quebec.

ANNE Of course, I'm concerned with the survival of French in Quebec, but I thought we might get too sidetracked from my thesis if we were to handle this 'hot potato', as you Anglophones say. Besides, I have very little to say beyond voicing my support for governmental measures to protect the French language, whether this be making mandatory the use of French on public signs[25] or developing an immigration policy which favours French speakers.[26]

PHILIP The government can do what it wants, but the greatest threat to the survival of the French language in Quebec comes from the reluctance of the Québécois to have babies.[27] So if you're really concerned with the issue of the survival of French in Quebec, you should do your share. I'd like to help, but I'm not sure if an Anglophone Jew such as myself would be suitable for this purpose.

ANNE [*embarrassed*] Please, Philip, I'd rather our discussion be kept at a certain level of abstraction.

PHILIP As you choose, Anne . . . So let me ask you the following question—what if the need to protect a linguistic community extends to a call for political autonomy? Should French Quebecers, possessors of a shared language and history, separate from the rest of Canada?

ANNE Nothing in principle rules out political autonomy, but the Quebec case is a particularly hard one to settle. You'll recall the referendum for what the pro-independence Parti-Québécois government called 'sovereignty-association' in 1980. Individuals in Quebec had to answer what may have been an unanswerable question: given the fact that the Canadian national community of memory counts for less than the Quebec French-speaking community of memory in the minds of nearly all French Québécois, does the preservation of the Quebec French-speaking community of memory necessarily entail repudiating the Canadian nation, or can the two goods somehow be combined?[28] As you know, the Québécois as a whole voted 60 to 40 per cent in favour of the latter option.[29] They may have been wrong, however . . .

PHILIP I'll have you notice that you had a case here of conflicting goods, and that individuals had to choose between two incompatible options.

ANNE I never denied that higher goods could conflict, but I don't think that individuals choose between goods in the way you probably have in mind—responding to a cost–benefit calculus between various options. Most people operate according to what we can call an 'implicit hierarchy of goods',[30] which would take the following form in the case of the 1980 referendum: the greater the positive difference between the Quebec French-speaking community of memory and the Canadian national community of memory in one's hierarchy of constitutive higher goods, the more likely one voted in favour of sovereignty-association for Quebec.

PHILIP It sounds quite scientific. What was the cut-off point, to the nearest decimal point?

ANNE There's no need for sarcasm, Philip. I readily agree that this process cannot be a matter of scientific study, for the Heideggerian idea that action is first and foremost unreflected social practice rules out the possibility of a disengaged, fully explicit understanding of one's hierarchy of constitutive communities, not to mention understanding by others.

One's identity is much deeper and more many-sided than any possible articulation of it, as I've already said . . .

PHILIP Sometimes you take me too seriously. I try to make a joke, and you answer with Heidegger . . .

[*Waiter enters*]

WAITER [*to Philip and Anne*] Autre chose?

PHILIP I think we should have another bottle of wine.

ANNE I'm not sure if I have the time, as I have to get back to my family soon . . . [*adopting a patronizing tone*] . . . Are you sure you don't have a drinking problem? You had a reputation as being quite a drinker in your McGill days, and I wouldn't want to encourage that sort of behaviour.

PHILIP It's true that I drink a fair amount, but I don't think I'm a 'problem drinker' since problem drinkers tend to drink alone, which I don't do. I only drink in a social context, i.e. when I'm with other people . . . [*pause*] . . . Of course, that may help explain why I like being around other people.

WAITER [*impatiently*] Et alors?

PHILIP Well, Anne, should we get another bottle?

ANNE I'm still confused about your reasons for wanting to do so. I'm not sure if you seek more drink for the pleasurable anaesthesia that drink can bring, or whether you think more drink would fit into the context of social interaction in a Paris café.[31] I would only accept ordering another bottle if both of us regarded drinking as part of the practice of intellectual conversation, as one of its internal goods, *à la* Plato's Symposium.

PHILIP That's exactly what I had in mind. Shall it be white or red?

ANNE I suggest red, as we still have some camembert untainted with your spilt wine.

PHILIP Fine . . . [*to waiter*] . . . Un Beaujolais, s'il-vous-plaît . . . [*waiter leaves stage*] . . . [*pause*] . . . Reflecting upon what we've been discussing the last half-hour or so, my impression is that this notion of 'community of memory' is too diffuse and all-encompassing to be useful. As long as some people think of themselves as sharing a distinct history, they partake of a community of memory. That means racial communities, such as the black community, are communities of memory. What about the women's community? Is the gay community a community of memory? Where do we stop?

ANNE I didn't deal with those communities in my thesis. However, we have no special obligation to abide by the structure of my thesis indefinitely, so why don't I address your criticism by focusing on your example of the gay community. The answer to the question 'is the gay community a community of memory?' depends on one's views as to the nature of homosexuality. One school of thought denies that there are special sensibilities, insights, feelings, or experiences particular to gay people, and the other affirms the existence of a gay community with its own history and cultural heritage. According to the first school, usually called 'social constructionism',[32] there's no such thing as a person with an immutable trait of 'homosexuality'—the 'homosexual' is a socially constructed and historically contingent identity. In other words, homosexual acts are purely contingent characteristics of those who perform them, rather than being defining features of an ongoing community of people called homosexuals . . . On this view, then, a preference for homosexual, as opposed to heterosexual, acts is like a preference for a Beaujolais instead of a Bordeaux.

PHILIP That view sounds quite implausible, which I'm sure is what you wanted me to think. What's the second view?

ANNE The second view, held by an overwhelming majority of those who have performed homosexual acts throughout history, is that homosexuality is a necessary, constitutive element of those who prefer to perform homosexual acts.[33] Quite simply, most gays knew they were gay from as far back as they can remember,[34] an awareness that coloured their experiences of the world. Given this psychological fact, participants in the gay liberation movement thought that 'coming out of the closet' was crucial if gays were to shed self-hatred in favour of the self-respect that comes with public recognition of a community of memory.

PHILIP Now that you've articulated that view, it sounds even more implausible than the first one. Many people turn to homosexuality after having had bad experiences with opposite-sex partners.

ANNE Look, you'll just have to take my word for it—homosexuals do not choose to be gay any more than heterosexuals choose their preference for opposite-sex partners. It's not an intellectual decision, or something that one turns to after having tested other options. It's a constitutive feature of one's identity . . . [*pause*] . . . Heterosexuals should just accept that this is how most homosexuals think of themselves.

PHILIP I guess the fact that I doubted the constitutive conception of homosexuality proves that I'm not a true homosexual.

ANNE Yes, but I didn't need additional proof if the stories I heard about your days at McGill have any truth to them.

PHILIP [*blushes*] Don't believe everything you hear . . . [*pause*] . . . In a way though, it doesn't really matter what one's conception of homosexuality happens to be. For the liberal, at least, all that matters is that the state not intrude in the bedrooms of the nation if consenting adults engage in non-harmful activity.[35]

ANNE More than that matters for the communitarian. If it's true that homosexuals share a particular outlook on the world that has produced and is producing a distinct history, homosexuals should have access to structures that enable them to express their identity. And when a society fails to provide these structures, you'll most likely have a high proportion of frustrated and alienated homosexuals.

PHILIP Oh, oh. More of this 'damaged human personhood' stuff.

ANNE What's wrong with that? Don't you think it's better for homosexuals to have the opportunity to identify with and participate in the good of the homosexual community?

PHILIP It depends what you mean by that. If you mean that we should leave alone those who practice homosexuality in private, I see nothing wrong with that.

ANNE You don't understand yet. It's not just a question of tolerating homosexual acts, in the same way that a society might tolerate Nazi rallies or pornographic literature.[36] What I have in mind involves shaping a society that recognizes and respects its homosexual community, which might translate in practice into, for example, legislation that promotes schoolbooks which portray homosexuals in a positive light . . .[37]

[*Waiter enters the stage with a bottle of Beaujolais, which he serves to Anne and Philip*]

ANNE Merci.

[*Waiter smiles in response, then leaves the stage*]

PHILIP [*pause*] I still think that your 'community of memory' concept is too broad, too inclusive. Let's say that I play golf on Sundays, I talk mainly about golf to my friends, and I'm a member of a golfer's political action committee that pushes for subsidized golf clubs. Also, I've read golf encyclopedias to the point that I've memorized the history of golfing and I feel very much part of that history. Does that mean that

golfing is constitutive of my identity, that I partake of the golfer's community of memory?

ANNE Maybe, but I'd rather consider golfers as they are in the real world.
Golfers, bridge players, and the like belong to what the authors of
Habits of the Heart call 'lifestyle enclaves'.[38] Members of a lifestyle
enclave share some feature of what they think of as their private life, a
bond which is expressed through shared patterns of appearance, consumption, and leisure activities. Put colloquially, they meet to have
some fun, and that's that. Constituent members of a community of
memory, on the other hand, acknowledge a common past and certain
moral obligations that flow from belonging to those constitutive communities, obligations that are often carried beyond private life into
public endeavours. The Basque nationalist, the proud French speaker,
the committed Catholic, and the true homosexual, unlike the checkers
player or the member of the Led Zeppelin Fan Club, cannot conceive
of herself without those deep-down attachments . . . Before I give you a
chance to think of another objection to the community of memory
concept, however, I think it would be more fruitful, in view of our limited time, to go on to the third type of constitutive community, which
I've called 'psychological communities' in my thesis.

PHILIP [*pours himself more wine*] Fine. What's a psychological community?

[*Lights illuminate the De la Patrie table for the first time since the very
beginning of the play*]

ANNE By psychological community I mean a group of persons who participate in common activity and experience a psychological sense of
'togetherness' as shared ends are sought. Such communities, based on
face to face interaction, are governed by sentiments of trust, co-
operation, and altruism in the sense that constituent members have the
good of the community in mind and act on behalf of the community's
interest . . .

PHILIP [*interrupting*] . . . as opposed to the constituent members' selfish
interest?

ANNE I wouldn't want to make too much of the egoism versus altruism
distinction when it comes to constitutive communities. We identify so
strongly with constitutive communities that we deem the community's
purposes to be our own. I would not object that I was being used as a
means for another's ends if a disproportionate share of my family's

resources were being directed to caring for my sister if she, God forbid, were to suffer from a serious illness.

PHILIP What about if your sister gets served a larger portion of your favourite dish?

ANNE She'd probably give some to me, if only because she knows that I have a healthier appetite than she does.

PHILIP My point is that it's not all altruism even in the family context. If your sister was accepted by a college that had rejected you, you'd naturally feel a little jealous.

ANNE I do not think that one experiences what we think of as negative emotions such as jealousy, envy, spite, and anger when it comes to really important matters. Deep down, I'd still wish my sister success at college and feel bad for her if she failed or if she didn't get a job she was really counting on getting after college. And also, needless to say, I'd rescue my sister from a burning house before I'd rescue a stranger,[39] even if I'd just had a fight with her.

PHILIP So you deny that negative emotions such as the ones you mentioned can come to dominate families to such an extent that feelings of goodwill normally underlying family interaction will be dissolved?

ANNE No, of course not, but when you think about it the phenomenon you describe tends to occur when a constituent member appears to be benefiting undeservedly from an external circumstance. For example, an inheritance that's left in large part to one child normally causes the other children to feel jealous, sometimes resulting in serious, irreparable rifts between family members.[40] Along the same lines, development projects that target specific individuals instead of a local community as a whole, such as the Foster Child Aid Program, often do more harm than good, because other community members feel left out.

PHILIP [*looks over at the De la Patrie table*] Should we invite your sister over here? I wouldn't want to be held responsible for having undermined the moral cohesiveness of your family by having caused your sister to think that she hasn't benefited from your luck at having run into me.

ANNE Just as I wouldn't feel jealous if she ran into a friend of hers, it would make no sense if she were to feel jealous because I ran into you . . . But before we go any further, are you at least clear as to what I mean by 'psychological community'?

PHILIP I can't say I am.

ANNE I thought so. Let me tell you what psychological communities are not, and then provide some examples of what they are. They differ from communities of place by not being necessarily defined by locality and proximity—my sister might have moved to another country, but she still partakes of the De la Patrie psychological community. They differ from communities of memory by being based on face to face personal interaction at one point in time and consequently tend to be restricted in size to a few hundred people. Examples of such communities include the family, church groups, New England-type town halls,[41] long lasting civic associations, and work units.

PHILIP Work units?

ANNE Oh, sorry, that's a post-revolutionary Chinese practice that I shouldn't have brought up given the focus of my thesis. Briefly then, work units are the groups which provide workers in China with a sense of belonging and supply them with housing, health benefits, and so on. They are constitutive in the sense that they bear crucially on the identity of workers—without a work unit, a person's existence is barely recognized.[42]

PHILIP Perhaps belonging to an Oxford college is an example of a Western equivalent.

ANNE I wouldn't know. When I think of my psychological communities, I think of my family and my church group.

PHILIP One little point before we go any further—members of your church may well constitute a psychological community, but your church is also presumably the site where you seek the good of your religious community of memory. We seem to have some overlap between types of constitutive communities here.

ANNE I never claimed that there couldn't be an overlap of that sort, but one can always distinguish between partaking of a religious community of memory, which includes strangers, and seeking the good of the local institutional branch of that religion, which can be called a psychological community if the ties between its constituent members are long-existent, based on face to face interaction, and governed by sentiments of fellow-feeling as shared ends are sought.

PHILIP OK. So psychological communities are small-scale groups that members feel very attached to, different from communities of memory. But are you not overlooking another important distinction, namely, that between groups one is born into such as the family and those that one joins by choice such as a church group or a local Rotary club?

ANNE I wouldn't want to emphasize that distinction. A community is constitutive to the extent that one experiences one's own nature as bound up with its good, and the reasons we initially joined a community that comes to be constitutive are largely irrelevant because they do not necessarily bear on or explain the current constitutive state of the community. For example, someone like yourself may choose to join a certain synagogue as a result of being attracted to a female member of that congregation, but once you find out that she's married and unavailable you may decide to remain part of that synagogue anyway, and after some years of having participated in seeking the good of that group and helping to realize its purposes, you may come to feel that the synagogue is so central to your identity that you couldn't conceive of yourself without it.[43]

PHILIP I think that's stretching the bounds of plausibility a little, although you're correct in assuming that belief in God would not be a motivation of mine were I to join a synagogue. In any case, your example made me realize that I seem to have less 'constitutive psychological communities' than you do. In fact, one can go further than that to point out that some of us have none, such as the guy who was shunted from foster-home to foster-home as a child and has spent his adult life sipping booze under a bridge, firmly resisting encroachments on his private sphere of being. Now, my question is the following—do you have any arguments in favour of the proposition that one should have constitutive psychological communities, as opposed to having none?

ANNE My empirical response to your example is that even such people as you describe tend to want to belong to what we might call a 'psychological community of bums'.[44]

PHILIP Let's assume that this bum is all alone, that he doesn't talk to anyone, and that he's happy that way.

ANNE You won't like this, but we'd most likely have a case of a 'damaged human personhood'.

PHILIP [*sighs*] I should have guessed.

ANNE Well, this might seem like a facile response, but few would dispute the idea that solitary bums—and, more generally, those who are totally self-absorbed and incapable of developing meaningful attachments to others—are damaged in some very deep way.[45]

PHILIP [*raises voice*] And those people should be shipped to mental hospitals where your guardians of virtue would heal them, notwithstanding their own desires.

ANNE Please, Philip, there's no need to get alarmed. People can change for the better without being institutionalized in mental hospitals—for one thing, I've already alluded to the importance of deliberation among friends about moral commitments, with one friend helping the other grasp something about her identity that had lain dormant. And besides, some people are too far gone to change.

PHILIP [*pause*] Essentially, then, your argument in favour of the proposition that people ought to join psychological communities is that doing so is a condition of psychological health. If you don't join, you're mentally ill.

ANNE I wouldn't put it so crudely, but it's true that I'd be puzzled if you were to deny that a fully developed human being in Western societies participates in the life and purposes of psychological communities . . . But there's another argument to be made in favour of psychological communities, this time at the macro-level. Such communities, or what Tocquevillians would call intermediate structures, serve to pressure, check, and restrain the tendencies of the centralized state and other large-scale agencies to assume more and more power over our lives.[46] By instilling a concern for goods beyond narrowly conceived self-interest, psychological communities provide the best bulwark against the Hobbesian condition that communitarians fear most—the atomized, mass society of mutually antagonistic individuals, easy prey to despotism and the all-embracing uniformity of *Gemeinschaft*-type communities as a perverse expression of the need for community.

PHILIP If you put it that way, it's hard to disagree.

ANNE Well, you don't have to disagree with everything I say.

PHILIP [*pause*] OK. Let's assume that your arguments in favour of psychological communities are correct. One would expect individuals to realize that their real interest lies in nurturing the psychological communities to which they currently belong and seek to join new ones if they feel a void in their lives. What happens, however, if this doesn't happen? We can't force people to participate in psychological communities, so what political implications flow from your pro-psychological-community arguments?

ANNE Well, for one thing, political legislation can help to restructure education in such a way that people's deepest needs of membership and participation in psychological communities are tapped at a young age. For instance, classrooms can be organized so that students co-operate on assignments, with exam results counting for the classroom as a whole instead of the current system of awarding grades to individual students. Motivation to seek the good of the classroom as a whole can be generated by implementing a reward scheme for the best classrooms of a school in academic and sporting activities, and meting out collective forms of punishment to the members of classrooms that perform less well.

PHILIP So an element of competition comes into the picture . . .

ANNE Yes, well, for the purposes of instilling a spirit of concern for intersubjective goods, all that matters is that psychological communities be internally governed by co-operative and altruistic behaviour. Besides, it's hoped that by adulthood seeking the good of psychological communities will have become an end in itself for properly trained members, such that competition between psychological communities will prove to be unnecessary at this stage.

PHILIP Don't you think that's a little utopian? I've yet to hear a good response to the élitist critique of mass participation in political life and within social institutions and groups generally. Specifically, we can extend Robert Michels's 'iron law of oligarchy',[47] that all lasting social and political organizations develop oligarchic tendencies due to the organizational requirements of efficiency and the apathy of the masses, to include the small face to face groups you call psychological communities. Thus, hierarchies must come to reign in psychological communities if they're to last, with the leaders formulating their own set of interests that may oppose those of the majority of constituent members of psychological communities. It follows that the communitarian ideal of a society composed of psychological communities that serve as forums for widespread, civic-minded participation will never get off the ground . . .

ANNE I can't logically refute that argument, but I'd like to point out that even if Michels, who ended his days as a cheerleader for Mussolini,[48] is right, it doesn't follow that maximal participation ought not to be striven for any more than the conclusion that no one ought to strive for sainthood follows from the premiss that no one can be a saint. Put positively, even if our deepest aspirations are unrealizable in their fully developed form, we should still strive to realize those aspirations.

PHILIP In short, it's better to be a hypocritical communitarian than an honest élitist.

ANNE That's true, but I'd want to claim more than that—I think that a communitarian society of participatory psychological communities is realizable in more or less developed form, depending on whether or not the structures are such that individuals have the opportunity to express their communitarian impulses. To illustrate the importance of structures, let's get back to education, comparing two departments at a university we're both familiar with, McGill. The psychology department, housed in the functional but characterless Stewart Biology Building, has some 900 students, few of whom get to know each other. Consequently, psychology students act as atomized individuals in mass society. A cloud of competition hangs over psychology classes, some of which have over 300 students. The psychology library is a veritable Orwellian den, with electronic 'beepers' strategically positioned to prevent people from stealing books . . .

PHILIP [*interrupting*] One of my girlfriends at McGill was a psychology student. Actually, she was a bit too cheerful for my taste. But now I wonder—how could she be having such a good time in that sinister place?

ANNE Please bear with me. The psychology library imposes a stiff 25 cents a day fine for late books, and in fact the student will not be issued grades for her transcript unless all her books are returned. Despite these preventive measures, however, many books go missing, some of which are stolen or never returned, others are purposefully misplaced so that competing students will have difficulty finding them . . . [*short pause*] . . . The religious studies department, on the other hand, is a well-established, comfortably small department, housed in the beautiful neo-Gothic Birks Building, a building which shows the influence of William Morris's anti-modernist arts and crafts movement.[49] New students get to know each other after a few weeks, many of them work on co-operative projects or develop their ideas in the hospitable atmosphere of the religious studies discussion room . . .

PHILIP [*interrupting*] Yes, I've been there myself. The coffee's not very good, mind you . . .

ANNE And the religious studies library, in contrast to the psychology library, relies upon the student's goodwill to ensure that books are returned on time. A return date is stamped on the book, but the student is not fined if the book is returned late. Not only is there no 'beeper' to prevent the student from stealing any books, but the older and more valuable books are stored in the basement two floors down, and the student is offered a key if she desires to use this section of the library. The library relies upon the student to find her books, lock the basement section of the library, and walk past the exit of the Birks

Building and two floors back up to the library to sign out the books and return the basement key! This system of voluntary adherence to the rules of the library has lasted for well over half a century, by the way.

PHILIP I don't like to play the role of demystifier, if that's a word,[50] but don't you think that the religious studies library can work in this way because there's less demand for books, as compared to the psychology library?

ANNE No, as both libraries have roughly the same proportion of books and articles per student.

PHILIP What's your source for this information?

ANNE If you want to know, I wrote a paper about this, which included a comparison and attempted explanation of the theft rates at both libraries. There are interesting side details, such as the fact that more books about Judaism go missing from the Religious Studies Library than books about Christianity, but . . .

PHILIP [*interrupting, raises voice*] That's because hostile Christians are confiscating books about Jews!

ANNE It could be. Getting back to what I was saying, the most salient fact I found in my paper was the following—despite the psychology library's very tight security, this library has a significantly higher theft rate than the religious studies library. So what we have to explain is why the religious studies students act in a non-self-interested fashion— clearly it would be in the self-interest of each student to 'free-ride' by either stealing the books from the library, which is nearly risk-free, or by returning the books when one has finished using them irrespective of whether or not the due date has expired. The reason for this socially mindful behaviour, I believe, is that religious studies students feel part of a psychological community, a feeling which depends on the small-scale educational structure within which they find themselves.[51] If put in a large-scale anonymous educational context such as the psychology department, their behaviour would degenerate into that of competitive, mutually antagonistic individuals, with only certain legal regulations containing a 'war of all against all' that would otherwise break out.

PHILIP Mmmh, interesting speculations—one might reach similar conclusions if one compared Oxford's Bodleian Library with college libraries. In any case, let me ask you something: if structures determine behaviour, or what you've called 'ways of being', then why do you focus primarily on the latter in your thesis?

ANNE I never said that structures 'determine' behaviour, only that certain structures better enable the realization of deep needs than others. If you imprison a normal person, this will likely induce anti-social behaviour not expressive of that person's true nature—simply extend this uncontroversial point to structures such as large-scale university departments that oppress their subjects in more insidious ways . . .

[*At this point, Marie, Anne's twin sister, walks over to Anne and Philip's table*]

MARIE Anne, n'oublie pas . . .

ANNE [*interrupting*] Marie, this is Philip, my anglophone friend from Montreal . . .

MARIE Pleased to meet you . . . [*Philip smiles at Marie, who unsuccessfully strains to conceal her suspicion*] . . . Anne, we left you some mussels, and if you want them, you'd better come now as we're leaving soon.

ANNE Thank you. I'll be back in a few minutes. Philip and I have nearly finished our talk . . . What kind of mussels, by the way?

MARIE Mussels with a Spanish-style vinaigrette.

ANNE Great! I'll be with you in a moment.

MARIE OK, but please hurry. *On s'inquiète un peu.*

[*Marie returns to her parents' table*]

PHILIP Your sister seems to think that a craving for mussels would be more likely to cause you to go back to your family's table than would a felt obligation to be with your family at mealtime.

ANNE Neither is true. I'd want to go back because I love Marie, Maman, and Papa, not because of some edible reinforcement or a sense of obligation to be with my family at mealtime, if by that we mean that I'd be forcing myself to do something I don't really want to do. In fact, I can't think of anything I'd rather do than nurture and cultivate my family ties.

PHILIP But you must admit that selfish motivations, such as a craving for mussels, can coexist with more noble sentiments such as love of family.

ANNE Selfish motivations would be subordinate to the noble sentiments in the context of a healthy, working psychological community, and do not normally apply, let me repeat, when it comes to important matters of life and death. This is particularly true for that model psychological community known as the family.

PHILIP [*pause*] I feel like I'm making the same point as before, but there are two senses, it should be said, of what is meant by 'the family'. There's the family one is born into and brought up in, and there's the family we voluntarily create by choosing a marriage partner and having children.

ANNE And I feel like I'm answering in the same way to your attempted chosen community versus unchosen community distinction. First of all, the second type of family you describe is not as 'chosen' as one might think. Typical reasons for marrying someone include 'it was love at first sight', 'he reminds me of my father', 'she was the girl next door' . . .

PHILIP [*interrupting*] Don't forget 'I knocked her up.'

ANNE Yes, that too. The point is that choice, meaning something like cost–benefit decision making, does not come to bear when those reasons apply. Even if, in response to the question 'why did I marry *X*?', I can articulate reasons about the person *per se*, such as '*X* is intelligent', '*X* is attractive', '*X* has a good sense of humour', '*X* is a good cook', or whatever, I still feel deep down that the reasons do not do justice to my partner's many-sided, concrete individuality. Moreover, it goes without saying that the children we have together are not chosen in the genetic lottery, nor do I think many of us would like to live in a society whose technology allowed us to choose our children according to certain criteria . . .

PHILIP If choice is so irrelevant with respect to marriage, why not bring back the practice of arranged marriages? You'd have the support of my mother, for one, who'd like nothing better than to marry me off to a nice Jewish girl of her choice.

ANNE Actually, it's a shame that the liberal emphasis on the autonomous, choosing self has rendered obsolete the practice of arranged marriages. There's nothing intrinsically illegitimate about parents helping their children find suitable marriage mates, yet somehow this practice has come to be seen as infringing upon the rights of the individual.

PHILIP [*raises voice*] You wouldn't mind being forced to marry someone whom your parents think you should marry!

ANNE [*patiently*] It doesn't have to be forced—the individuals involved can retain their veto power over who it is they are to marry. My point is that we've lost a valuable mechanism for helping people find marriage partners, leaving discothèques and the like as structures where freely choosing individuals are to find suitable people with whom to spend the rest of their days.

PHILIP Most people don't go to discothèques to find marriage partners.

ANNE Whatever . . . Getting back to your point about there being an important difference between the family one is born into and the one that's been contracted into as an adult, the most pertinent response would be that the same sorts of moral ties and psychological sense of 'togetherness', the same spontaneous affection and spirit of generosity, in short, the same experience of self-sacrificing love, come to character- ize relations between both types of families, irrespective of differences of origin.

PHILIP I think you're idealizing family relations . . . My mother claims she's motivated by self-sacrificing love, but you can be sure that by let- ting me know how much she does for me she expects something in return. And no matter how much I do, I always seem to end up feeling guilty for not having done enough.

ANNE So what do you want instead? That family members respond to each other on the basis of abstract principles of justice, of rightful obligations and claims rather than on the basis of love?[52]

PHILIP That would be good. Next time I visit my mother and she wakes me up at some unreasonable hour like 10 a.m. for some vacuuming because she wants a clean house, I'll reach into my back pocket, pull out my rights trump card, and veto her request on the grounds that she's treating me as a means to her ends, rather than as an end in myself, deserving of equal respect. Of course, she'll threaten to with- draw the matzo ball soup that she'd promised to make for supper . . . Maybe you're right after all, we ought to respond to each other on the basis of love rather than on the basis of abstract principles of justice.

ANNE Thank you. I'm glad we agree on what ought to be the ideal family situation.

PHILIP More seriously though, I'm not sure that we agree. By glorifying the family, communitarians overlook feminist criticism that points to the family as the seat of much exploitation and alienation.[53]

ANNE [*raises voice*] You don't have to tell me about feminism!

PHILIP Sorry. Just trying to help.

ANNE Well, let's take up your point, abstracting from the fact that it's you who made it. My response would take the following form: the ideal family situation, according to our shared understanding of what family relations ought to look like, consists of family members responding to each other on the basis of freely expressed love. Where that's not true, e.g. in the patriarchal family context where the male coerces, either insidiously or explicitly, the female into submission, deviations from the ideal ought to be criticized . . . Communitarians, in short, welcome feminist criticism of the family.[54]

PHILIP Maybe. How, then, can you reconcile the 'ideal family situation' with the 'constitutive conception of homosexuality'?

ANNE What do you mean?

PHILIP Well, if the family is a key component of the good life, you must want to criticize 'true homosexuals' unable to partake of that institution for leading bad lives.

ANNE Not at all. There's no reason, in principle, why the family ought to be composed only of heterosexuals. In fact, among homosexuals the trend seems to be towards coupling into family-type cells characterized by intimacy, affection, unconditional acceptance, and loyalty.[55] And this is being recognized in law in some places, including the supposedly conservative America of the 1980s.[56]

PHILIP [*pause*] Look, I wouldn't want to attack the ideal family situation as you describe it, but you should at least recognize that many people have had, to put it crudely, a bad upbringing, and the best thing for them to do if they're to lead decent lives is to escape the grip of their family.

ANNE The attempt to 'escape the grip of one's family' or to 'overcome its influence' is generally fruitless and self-destructive. Let's take the case of Ernest Hemingway. The adult Hemingway dramatically flouted the standards of his puritanical and punitive father and of his ambitious, domineering mother, yet, in doing so, he remained caught in their grip. In particular, the values he professed such as hedonistic thrill-seeking, hypermasculine bravado, and misogyny functioned, according to an excellent new biographical study of Hemingway by Kenneth Lynn,[57] as preventives against self-insight into his androgynous core.

PHILIP His androgynous core?

ANNE Yes. He was always confused about matters of sexual identity as a result of his upbringing, notwithstanding his melodramatically male façade. In any case, my point is that Hemingway would most probably have led a happier, more authentic life expressive of his deepest commitments had he acknowledged the influence of his family and sought to make the best of it, instead of endlessly striving to escape from the grip of his family, which led to frequent bouts of impotence and ultimately suicide.[58]

PHILIP It's too bad Hemingway never ran into Dr Freud before he decided to kill himself.

ANNE You're not convinced . . . So let me ask you—do you think it's outrageous to propose that one can avoid a lot of torments by being true to one's identity? Think of James Joyce, who confronted his transsexual fantasies with humane humour as well as passion,[59] or of Rilke, who wholly embraced his feminine side both in his life and work.[60] Surely they led healthier lives than the macho Hemingway . . .

PHILIP Let's try to be clear here. I'm not against being true to one's identity if it means, say, dealing in a rational way with the fact that one has had an emasculating mother. But what if a child has had a particularly unlucky upbringing, such as having suffered frequent beatings from a parent, being locked up for months at a time in a dark closet, or whatever. Should that person acknowledge and embrace what he's learned from his parents?

ANNE I don't mean to sound callous, but some people are, to borrow a line from Hemingway himself, 'bitched from the start', such that there can be no positive outcome no matter what's done later on.[61] That's one reason you need prisons and mental hospitals. Luckily, though, most people seem to have had a fairly decent upbringing, and legislators should do their best to promote the institution of the family so as to increase this number.

PHILIP [*pause*] I'm wondering whether your placing so much emphasis on 'the family' as the model psychological community undermines the rest of your communitarian project. That is, I'm quite sure that you wouldn't want to say that the family is a sufficient attachment to have, yet there's a trade-off between attachment to one's family and attachments to other of these so-called constitutive communities. Put differently, withdrawal into what's known as the private sphere of the family means less dedication to the public sphere.

ANNE Well, I share Tocqueville's point of view that . . .

PHILIP [*interrupting*] Never mind Tocqueville! I'm getting tired of your recourse to authorities of various sorts.

ANNE I have to leave very soon, so let's not get too impatient. I'll leave out Tocqueville's name if you wish. My response, then, would be to urge you to look at the world as it is—when the family structure decays, as in American ghettoes, atomism and nihilism eat into the fabric of society. Far from there being a conflict between love of one's family and other commitments, in the real world a secure family environment seems to be the springboard for communitarian attachments.[62]

PHILIP I don't know which 'real world' you're referring to. I know that in my case being devoted to my family, and my mother in particular, would leave very little time for politics and other pursuits. But let's go down to the smallest family unit, that of two newly-weds deeply in love. Surely there's a trade-off between romantic love and other attachments—being in love diminishes attachments to others, sometimes overwhelming all facets of one's life.

ANNE [*confident tone*] Retreat into dualistic intersubjectivity can't last forever—it either progresses to include other attachments or it collapses under its own weight.

PHILIP Did you and Jean-Guy break up, if you don't mind me asking?

ANNE [*sadly*] Yes, I'm afraid.

PHILIP [*insincerely*] Oh, I'm sorry.

ANNE It happened when he left for Toronto.

PHILIP Well, at least you're free now.

ANNE If this is freedom, I'm not sure I like freedom.

PHILIP [*pours more wine into Anne's glass*] OK, how about one last question with reference to the family: how does the communitarian conception of the family as a model psychological community bear on politics?

ANNE If the agreed-upon end is a society of secure, strongly constitutive families, political measures should be implemented that help realize that end.[63] This brings us once again to the issue of limiting choice. It's not implausible to suggest that the easy availability of legal marriage dissolution reduces the probability of a successful long-term marriage, for such availability is likely to affect the expectations brought to the marriage, the inclination to tolerate imperfections of the marriage partner, and the sense of commitment to the marriage.[64] If the state sanctions my walking out of a marriage after a little spat with my mate, I'm more likely to do so . . .

PHILIP [*interrupting, raises voice*] Are you suggesting that divorce be made illegal?![65]

ANNE Laws don't have to be so crude to serve their purpose. But divorce can be made a more time-consuming procedure, thus allowing for a certain period of reflection before the knot is permanently untied . . .[66]

[*Waiter arrives on stage to clear away the dishes from the De la Patrie table. Anne's parents seem to be engaged in a heated argument about something or other*]

PHILIP [*glancing at the De la Patrie table*] It seems like your family is getting ready to leave.

ANNE Yes, I guess I'll have to go too. We won't have time to run through other examples of constitutive psychological communities that I dealt with in my thesis. I hope, though, that you will have taken something valuable from this discussion of ours. I wouldn't want to think I've been wasting my time telling you about my thesis . . .

PHILIP Well, I have to admit that I'm not clear as to how the bits of your thesis fit together. I don't have a sense of the 'big picture', so to speak.

ANNE [*pause*] OK. Let me do the best I can. We have very little time left, so please don't interrupt me . . . [*hurriedly*] . . . We began with the 'ontological debate' between those of you who would give primacy to the choosing agent, and 'communitarians', who point to the social embedding of selves. But I emphasized that 'ontology' could do nothing more than clear the ground to lay bare the options which it is meaningful to support by advocacy, and I demonstrated how this could be done by invoking two 'ontological' claims to remove from contention certain interpretations of liberalism founded on a highly individualistic view of the person—firstly, that we more often than not act in a way specified by social practices, which shows the impossibility of leading a life largely on the basis of individual decisions about what to do, and secondly, that one's social world provides some sort of orientation in moral space, which shows that the ideal of a self who would freely invent her own moral outlook or conception of the good cannot do justice to our actual moral experience . . . Next, we turned to a methodological issue, how best to carry out political reasoning. I favoured the approach which involves the interpretation of shared meanings bearing on the political life of one's community, as opposed to those who would derive a political order on the basis of the assumption that particular individuals enter into society armed with pre-existing needs, wants, and desires; that we're first and foremost social beings, bound up in the particular world in which we find ourselves, would seem to rule out this latter possibility . . . [*gasping for breath*] . . . And after that—following your second escape to the bathroom, I believe—we moved on to 'communitarian advocacy', or the moral stand in favour of communal life. I advanced the claim that we need to experience our lives as bound up with the good of the communities out of which our identity has been constituted—a claim justified by its consistence with 'communitarian ontology' and its congruence with a deeper understanding of what really matters to those of us living in the modern world—and I distinguished between three kinds of 'constitutive communities': communities of place, or communities based on geographical location; communities of memory, or groups of strangers who share a morally significant history; and psychological communities, or communities of face to face personal interaction governed by sentiments of trust, co-operation, and altruism. Along the way, I pointed to various examples of political practices which favour those structures that allow people to live their lives in conformity with their deeply felt attachment to constitutive communities . . .

[*Anne's family get up to put on their jackets*]

PHILIP [*short pause*] So that's your thesis?

ANNE Roughly speaking, yes.

PHILIP You know, Anne, before you go, I ought to express one final reservation about your thesis. I'm afraid that this objection will go to the very heart of the communitarian enterprise.

ANNE Oh, oh. Go ahead, but make it quick.

PHILIP OK. This idea that government officials ought to enact laws which allow people to actualize their supposed commitment to 'constitutive communities' rests, of course, on the assumption that we do in fact experience our lives as bound up with the good of the various constitutive communities you mentioned. But surely there are some of whom this is not true—what can you say to someone who truly believes that his family or nation means very little to him? The response that we should seek the good of constitutive communities because our deepest aspirations lie in doing so simply won't do the trick, I'm afraid.

ANNE That's not really a new point you're making . . . [*pause*] . . . OK, I didn't think I'd have to do this, but your recurrent objection forces me to invoke the appendix to my thesis.

PHILIP An appendix?

ANNE Yes. You recall the communitarian critique of the original position, the position behind a veil of ignorance within which a rational, self-interested individual not fundamentally committed to particular persons or communities or conceptions of the good would assent to principles of justice?

PHILIP I think so. Essentially, it's that this procedure requires abstracting from one's deepest intuitions about one's identity and conception of the good life, with the consequence that actual individuals could not be persuaded to live by the principles of justice that result therefrom.

ANNE Good memory. Another way of stating the communitarian critique of the original position is the following: since we never find ourselves in this position in real life, moral reasoning in the original position fails to satisfy the communitarian requirement that a theory must be expressed in a form comprehensible to the agents addressed, and which allows them to recognize it as a description of their own situation and use it as a guide for action[67] . . . However, I'd like you to notice that I haven't objected to universal moral reasoning *per se*. It's conceivable, after all, that there is a universal position of a different sort, one in which we are all likely to find ourselves at some point in life.

PHILIP [*interrupting*] But . . .

ANNE No buts. I think (*a*) that there is such a position and (*b*) that this position satisfies the communitarian requirement by being compelling to real-life, concrete individuals . . .

[*Marie walks over to Philip and Anne's table*]

MARIE [*to Anne*] We're going now. We ate your share of the mussels. Are you joining us?

PHILIP [*to Anne*] No, you can't go now! This sounds like the most interesting part of your thesis.

MARIE Anne, it's really getting late, and don't forget that we have to attend Grandmaman's funeral tomorrow morning . . .

ANNE [*pause*] How about if I meet you later at the hotel? I won't be long.

MARIE Are you sure you know what you're doing? Because we've been noticing that you're drinking more than usual, and . . .

ANNE [*interrupting*] Don't worry, Marie. It's just that I have to satisfy Philip's curiosity before I go.

MARIE [*upset*] Look, you do what you want. But we hope to see you soon . . .

ANNE Au revoir . . .

[*Marie leaves the stage, along with Anne and Marie's parents who wave to Anne as they depart*]

PHILIP Thank you for staying on. If we run on too late, you can always stay at my place.

ANNE [*too defensively*] No, absolutely not! I must go back to my family tonight.

PHILIP Well, you can decide later . . . [*pours more wine into their glasses*]
. . . So tell me—what's the universal position that, as you put it, real-
life, concrete individuals would find appealing?

ANNE It's called the final position, or what most people know as 'the
deathbed'. Many of us actually do find ourselves in the final position,
reflecting upon our past life and what has really mattered to us . . .

PHILIP [*interrupting*] Many? Are there some who escape death?

ANNE No, not death, but not everyone finds themselves in a position
where they're on the verge of death with the capacity to reflect upon
their past life—some die instant deaths in unlucky circumstances, others go senile. It's the possibility of finding oneself in the final position,
a possibility that everyone shares, which makes the final position very
real to everyone. And that's its advantage over the original position—
whereas the latter appeals mainly to political philosophers with a taste
for mental gymnastics, it requires no special difficulties to imagine ourselves in the final position.

PHILIP Mmmmh . . .

ANNE Why don't we try to imagine ourselves in the final position, and
see what conclusions we can generate. When we reflect upon our past
life from that position, ponder what has mattered to us, and what we
would have done differently,[68] it seems to me that we wouldn't say to
ourselves 'I wish I had had a Porsche instead of a Volkswagen' or 'if
only I'd been promoted to assistant manager'[69]—such matters would
seem irrelevant to us . . .

PHILIP I guess I agree with that.

ANNE Yes. The reason for that, I believe, is that death points to the
need for significance in life.[70] Having said that, let me ask you
the following question: 'what would matter to you in the final position?'

PHILIP Nothing would matter. I'd probably be thinking 'I don't want to
die. I'm afraid of death.'

ANNE You wouldn't be thinking that if you'd led a good life. A person
with a good conscience usually overcomes the 'fear of death' phase,[71]
ultimately accepting the inevitability of death with a balanced peace of
mind.[72]

PHILIP As I don't want you to think I'm leading a bad life, I won't dispute your assertion.

ANNE Come on Philip, this is serious—it's not just a question of what I
want you to think.

PHILIP I'm sorry, I don't normally think about death, my outlook on life being sufficiently bleak as it is.

ANNE You don't normally think about death because death tends to be covered up in Western societies, which leads to all sorts of distorted interpretations of what matters in life. It would be instructive to compare the way we deal with death in Western societies with the public presentness of death in such societies as India, where dead bodies are routinely paraded down main streets.[73] You can be sure that you couldn't muster up the same enthusiasm to purchase the latest video recorder had you been woken up on a certain day by a noisy death ritual on the front lawn of your Westmount[74] home.

PHILIP I do not, let me set the record straight, get enthusiastic about purchasing video recorders.

ANNE Fine. Now tell me what sorts of things you'd be committed to on your deathbed.

PHILIP [*pause*] Well, if I was a Christian like you, and I'd led a good life, I might be thinking, 'after all these years of self-sacrifice, I'm really looking forward to having some fun in heaven'.

ANNE But you're not Christian, and . . .

PHILIP [*interrupting*] If I was Hindu,[75] I'd be curious about my next incarnation—will I come back as a tree, a frog, or a Brahmin?

ANNE [*losing patience*] Just assume reincarnation theory is false . . . Please, Philip, you said yourself you're not religious, and it's not likely that you're going to discover a sudden commitment to religion on your deathbed.[76] So tell me what would really matter to you in the final position, without offering a religious answer you don't believe yourself. Take your time if you have to . . .

PHILIP [*pause*] My family would matter. I might be thinking 'I regret not having spent more time with my mother.'

ANNE [*excitedly*] Yes, yes, your family would matter! You see, it's constitutive communities that would matter to us in the final position! What would concern us are such matters as 'I hope I've done enough for my children', 'I'm proud to have been a Swede' . . .

PHILIP [*interrupting, incredulous tone*] I'm proud to have been a Swede?!

ANNE Yes, it sounds funny to us, but that's how Swedes really think. Substitute 'Canadian' if you prefer.

PHILIP Even that's pushing it a little. I can accept that, perhaps, a Canadian who fought against Nazis in World War II might be thinking 'I'm proud to have fought with the Canadian army against the

Nazis', but I can't believe that an ordinary Canadian citizen would be thinking 'I'm proud to have been Canadian' on his deathbed.

ANNE Maybe you're right, particularly if that person's a francophone from Quebec.

PHILIP My point is that most people would take more pride in their personal achievements on their deathbed. For example, I'd care more about being remembered for the various political philosophy books I plan to write than about having been a 'good Canadian citizen'.

ANNE You'd take pride in your political philosophy books because of what they would have done to make the world you knew a better place, not in your political philosophy books *per se*. In other words, writing political philosophy books is the principal way in which you were being a 'good Canadian citizen'.

PHILIP [*pause*] Basically, then, you're suggesting that we should ask ourselves in real life 'what would matter to me in the final position?' And if what we're currently doing would seem irrelevant from that standpoint, we should restructure our goals in accordance with what would matter in the final position.

ANNE Exactly, exactly. The final position is a device to help us determine what we ought to want in real life—seeking the good of constitutive communities—which should take priority over what we actually want if these conflict. In practice, this might just mean your going to the park with your family instead of the gambling-house with your friends.[77]

PHILIP [*lengthy pause, as though he's immersed in deep thought. Laughs to himself. Short pause*] And now, Anne, let me tell you about my thesis . . .

[*Lights dim*]

THE END

Notes

1. George Steiner, for one, suggests this is in his book *Heidegger* (London: Fontana, 1978), 48–9. This grammatical feature of the German language may help explain why Heidegger said that when the French, who share with the English a static notion of 'être', began to think, they spoke in German (see 'Heidegger and Nazism: The Dark Side of Being', *International Herald*

Tribune (11 Dec. 1987), 9), although Heidegger's opinion about the French may perhaps better be explained by the following Franz Kafka quip: 'If the French were German in their essence, then how the Germans would admire them' (*The Diaries of Franz Kafka: 1910–23*, ed. Max Brod (London: Penguin Books, 1972), 30).

2. Chomsky himself says that there is only a 'tenuous connection' between his work on language structures and his political writings. See his *Language and Responsibility* (New York: Pantheon, 1977), 3–8.

3. For a (Wittgensteinian) critique of Chomsky's view that the language faculty is an (internal) organ like the heart on the grounds that this view rests on an ultimately incoherent distinction between knowledge of a language and the ability to use it, see Anthony Kenny, *The Legacy of Wittgenstein* (Oxford: Basil Blackwell, 1987), 137–47.

4. See Charles Taylor, *Human Agency and Language: Philosophical Papers, 1* (Cambridge: Cambridge University Press, 1985), 9–10, 71, and 234, and his *Hegel and Modern Society* (Cambridge: Cambridge University Press, 1979), 17–18, 162–3, where this philosophy of language is presented and defended.

5. Hans-Georg Gadamer succinctly summarizes this philosophy of language:

> . . . I have tried to present in *Truth and Method*, through the aspect of lin-
> guisticality that operates in all understanding, an unambiguous demon-
> stration of the continual process of mediation by which that which is
> societally transmitted (the tradition) lives on. For language is not only an
> object in our hands, it is the reservoir of tradition and the medium in and
> through which we exist and perceive our world. ('On the Scope and
> Function of Hermeneutical Reflection' (1967), in *Philosophical
> Hermeneutics*, trans. and ed. David E. Linge (Berkeley, Calif.: University
> of California Press, 1976), 29.)

6. Schwartzberg may have read Robert Darnton's article 'What was Revolutionary about the French Revolution?':

> The French Revolution wanted to make everybody 'tu'. Here is a resolu-
> tion passed on 24 Brumaire, Year II (November 14, 1793), by the depart-
> ment of Tain, a poor, mountainous area in Southern France:

>> Considering that the external principles of equality forbid that a citi-
>> zen say 'vous' to another citizen, who replies by calling him 'toi' . . .
>> decrees that the word 'vous', when it is a question of the singular
>> [rather than the plural which takes vous], is from this moment ban-
>> ished from the language of the free French and will on all occasions be
>> replaced by the word 'tu' or 'toi'.

> A delegation of sans-culottes petitioned the National Convention in 1794
> to abolish the '*vous*', '. . . as a result of which there will be less pride, less

discrimination, less social reserve, more open familiarity, a stronger lean-
ing toward fraternity, and therefore more equality'. (*New York Review of
Books* (19 Jan. 1989), 4.)

While legal attempts to abolish use of the formal '*vous*' in post-revolutionary
France have proved to be laughable failures, it does not follow that successful
implementation of a more egalitarian society will not change that society's
language in a less hierarchical direction—for example, use of the formal
'*usted*' is gradually disappearing in post-revolutionary Cuba (see Martha
Gellhorn, 'Cuba Revisited', *Granta*, 20 (Winter 1986), 109).

7. Wittgenstein himself sets the task for the translator:

> whether a word of the language of our tribe is rightly translated into a
> word of the English language depends upon the role this word plays in
> the whole life of the tribe; the occasions on which it is used, the expres-
> sion of emotion by which it is generally accompanied, the ideas which it
> generally awakens or which prompt its saying, etc., etc. As an exercise ask
> yourself: in which cases would you say that a certain word uttered by the
> people of the tribe was a greeting. (From the *Blue and Brown Books*;
> quoted in Hanna Pitkin, *Wittgenstein and Justice* (Berkeley, Calif.:
> University of California Press, 1972), 176.)

If a (correct) translation of a word from another language must take into
account 'the role this word plays in the whole life' of a people, it is little wonder that adherents of the expressive theory of language have avoided the task
of finding equivalent words in their own language.

8. See Gore Vidal's review of 'Selections from the First Two Issues of the *New
York Review of Books*', in *New York Review of Books* (27 Oct. 1988), 82–3, for a
humorous parody of this *New York Review of Books* practice.

9. Alasdair MacIntyre could answer Schwartzberg's point in the following way:
while English, French, and other late twentieth-century international languages such as Spanish, German, Chinese, and Japanese have been developed
in such a way as to allow translatability from one into another without significant loss of meaning, this is not true of local, dialecticized 'languages-in-use'
which express and presuppose by their vocabulary and linguistic uses a particular system of well-defined beliefs that could not be rendered into another
language without problematic (contestable) interpretative glosses and expla-
nations. (For MacIntyre's distinction between the tradition-less 'internationalized languages of modernity' and tradition-constituted 'languages-in-use',
see *Which Justice? Whose Rationality?* (London: Duckworth, 1988), 327–8,
373–4, 379, 388, and 395–6. It should be noted, however, that MacIntyre does
not name French as one of the 'internationalized languages of modernity',
which hints at the arbitrariness of a distinction few contemporary linguists
would accept.)

10. That is what Peter Singer does in his book *Hegel* (Oxford: Oxford University Press, 1983). Singer settles on the word 'mind' after having explained the ambiguities involved in translating Hegel's idea of *Geist* (pp. 45–7).

11. For an argument that it is 'utterly implausible' to translate many of Heidegger's key notions and formulations, see George Steiner, *Heidegger* (London: Fontana, 1978), 17–19.

12. It is interesting to note that Heidegger, who explicitly endorses the expressive theory of language with respect to languages with different bases ('Some time ago I called language, clumsily enough, the house of Being. If man by virtue of his language dwells within the claim and call of Being, then we Europeans presumably dwell in an entirely different house than Eastasian man', 'A Dialogue on Language', in *On the Way to Language* (New York: Harper and Row, 1982), 5), none the less allows for the possibility of a 'dialogue from house to house' (ibid. 5).

13. This claim is made by e.g. Peter Winch and Stephen Mulhall:

> . . . in discussing language philosophically we are in fact discussing *what counts as belonging to the world*. Our idea of what belongs to the realm of reality is given for us in the language that we use. The concepts we have settle for us the form of the experience we have of the world . . . there is no way of getting outside the concepts in terms of which we think of the world . . . the world *is* for us what is presented through those concepts. (Peter Winch, *The Idea of a Social Science and its Relation to Philosophy* (London: Routledge, 1958), 15; his emphasis.)

> Wittgenstein's remark that essence is expressed by grammar (*Philosophical Investigations*, 371) . . . entails a view of language as the bearer of conceptual structures which *alone* determine the bounds of sense in experience, which provide the *only* content that can be given to the idea of the *essence* of entities and processes. (Stephen Mulhall, *On Being in the World: Wittgenstein and Heidegger on Seeing Aspects* (London: Routledge, 1990), 127; my emphasis, except for that on 'essence'.)

While proponents of the idea that language sets the limits to the world we can experience principally draw their inspiration from Wittgenstein, it should be noted that Wittgenstein himself never advanced this claim, nor did he (explicitly) present any other doctrine about the relationship between language and the world (see Pitkin, *Wittgenstein and Justice*, 4, for a similar point).

14. Whorf's point about the influence of the Hopi language on the Hopi conception of time is described (and endorsed) in Pitkin, *Wittgenstein and Justice*:

> [Whorf] argues persuasively that Hopi is a 'timeless language'. We have already noted that Hopi verbs lack tense, failing to distinguish among

past, present, and future. The Hopi language 'recognizes psychological time, which is much like Bergson's "duration", but this "time" is quite unlike the mathematical time, *T*, used by our physicists. Among the peculiar properties of Hopi time are that it varies with each observer, does not permit of simultaneity, and has zero dimensions; i.e. it cannot be given a number greater than one' . . . Hopi grammar makes it easy to distinguish among momentary, continued, and repeated events, and to indicate the actual sequences of reported events, so that 'the universe can be described without recourse to a concept of dimensional time.' (105–6, quoting Whorf.)

15. Famous, but a distortion of the facts according to Geoffrey Pullman in his book *The Great Eskimo Vocabulary Hoax: And Other Irreverent Essays on the Study of Language* (Chicago: Chicago University Press, 1991). Pullman argues that people have overestimated the number of Inuit words for snow, and that anglophones have just as many words for snow as the Inuit.

16. Hans Georg-Gadamer, Hanna Pitkin, and Alasdair MacIntyre assume that language is the principal vehicle of a people's cultural identity, and therefore that one is introduced to a certain form of life by means of learning a language, as the following passages demonstrate:

> We grow up, and we become acquainted with men and in the last analysis with ourselves when we learn to speak. Learning to speak does not mean learning to use a pre-existent tool for designating a world somehow already familiar to us; it means acquiring a familiarity and acquaintance with the world itself and how it confronts us. (Gadamer, 'Man and Language', in *Philosophical Hermeneutics*, 62–3.)

> What we can say and think is very largely determined by the language we have available. If we are American we can think in terms of 'fairness', as a German cannot, but we cannot think in terms of '*Gemütlichkeit*'. We become the particular persons we become as we grow up because of the language community in which we grow up . . . The culture, like the language that carries it, is first imposed on (or at least offered to) the individual from the outside, but eventually it becomes a part of his very self. (Pitkin, *Wittgenstein and Justice*, 194–5.)

> Learning its language and being initiated into their community's tradition or traditions is one and the same initiation. (MacIntyre, *Whose Justice? Which Rationality?*, 382.)

(It is interesting to note that even Ronald Dworkin, normally associated with the 'liberal' side of the 'communitarian–liberal debate', approvingly articulates a claim equivalent to the idea that language is the principal vehicle of a people's cultural identity: 'the center of a community's cultural structure is its shared language' (*A Matter of Principle* (Cambridge, Mass.: Harvard University Press, 1985), 230).

17. The same seems to be true of Chinese babies:

> ... Chinese babies are on the whole ... remarkably docile: they are acting the role which parents and society prescribe—for them to be obedient and cute—and are trained from infancy to restrain from tantrums or let them be subdued in the pillow of all-encompassing maternal care. (David Bonavia, *The Chinese* (London: Penguin Books, 1989), 59.)

18. De la Patrie is almost certainly thinking of the W. Caudill and H. Weinstein article, 'Maternal Care and Infant Behavior in Japan and in America':

> [A] Japanese baby seems passive ... He lies quietly ... while his mother, in her care, does [a great deal] of lulling, carrying and rocking of her baby. She seems to try to soothe and quiet the child, and to communicate with him physically rather than verbally. On the other hand, the American infant is more active ... and exploring of his environment, and his mother, in her care, does more looking at and chatting to her baby. She seems to stimulate the baby to activity and vocal response. It is as if the American mother wanted to have a vocal, active baby, and the Japanese mother wanted to have a quiet contented baby. In terms or styles of care-taking of the mothers in the two cultures, they get what they apparently want ... a great deal of cultural learning has taken place by three to four months of age ... babies have learned by this time to be Japanese and American babies. (Repr. in C. S. Lavatelli and F. Stendler, eds., *Readings in Child Behavior and Development* (New York: Harcourt and Brace, 1972), 78; this passage is also quoted in Hubert Dreyfus's *Being-in-the-World*, 17, but not for the De la Patrie reason to argue against the expressive theory of language.)

One interesting implication can be derived from Caudill and Weinstein's research—if it is true that babies (only) begin to exist (in the Heideggerian sense of partaking of a particular way of being) soon after birth when they get socialized into a specific cultural understanding as embedded in a structure of shared social practices, this may help underlie the widely shared intuition that it's much worse to kill a live baby than a foetus; in other words, an argument against those who oppose abortion on the grounds that there is a deep continuity between the life of a foetus and the life of a live baby is that a human only becomes a particular being when she is 'in the world' (out of the womb), and it's not nearly so bad to kill a foetus (which is only human in the abstract) as it is to kill a baby which exhibits a particular way of being.

19. A similar point is made in Dreyfus, *Being-in-the-World*, 18. Incidentally, it is difficult to reconcile De la Patrie's explanation of 'individualistic' politics in

the USA with her scenario in Act IV that American citizens be engaged in politics as members of a nation committed to advancing its common good (the former would in all likelihood rule out the possibility of the latter).

20. De la Patrie does not mention another reason to make us doubt the proposition that language is the primary vehicle of culture—if culture is somehow 'contained' within language, it should follow that, as Pitkin puts it, 'In mastering a language, we take on a culture' (*Wittgenstein and Justice*, 3). But this inference does not seem to be true—one can be a fluent German speaker with only a very limited understanding of German culture. (Do people with a special talent for learning languages also (necessarily) have a special talent for learning about other cultures?) Wittgenstein, it is interesting to note, grants the possibility that one can master a language without understanding the way of being (the culture, the traditions) of a people: '. . . one human being can be a complete enigma to another. We learn this when we come into a strange country with entirely strange traditions, and what is more, *even given a mastery of the country's language*. We do not *understand* the people. (And not because of not knowing what they are saying to themselves.) We cannot find our feet with them' (*Philosophical Investigations* (Oxford: Blackwell, 1958), ii. 223; my emphasis, except for that on 'understand').

21. The Heidegger of *Being and Time, contra* the later Heidegger who conceived of language as the vehicle for the way of being of a culture, thought of language in De la Patrie terms as more of a reflection and reinforcement of already imprinted social practices, with words merely pointing out what *Dasein* has already 'understood':

> But in significance itself, with which Dasein is always familiar, there lurks the ontological condition which makes it possible for Dasein, as something which understands and interprets, to disclose such things as 'significations'; upon these, in turn, is founded the Being of words and of language. (*Being and Time*, 121.)

That there was a turn in Heidegger's thought in this respect recognized by Heidegger himself is confirmed by a comment that the later Heidegger wrote in the margin of the passage quoted above in his own copy of *Being and Time*: 'Not true. Language is not tiered. Rather it is the primordial essence of the truth as the there' (quoted in Dreyfus, *Being-in-the-World*, 354 n. 1).

It should be noted that while a more intense love of the German language (see Act V n. 1) may have been one consequence of the later Heidegger's view that particular languages determine a people's way of being (including its 'thinking about being', or lack thereof), the later Heidegger reserves his highest praise for ancient Greek, the erosion of which, he believed, had seriously altered and damaged subsequent Western European history (see Steiner, *Heidegger*, 15, 27–9, 32, 36–7, 53–4, 69). The later Heidegger thought that modern man's survival depended upon the rediscovery of the original meaning of ancient Greek words, going so far as to claim that Western history may turn on the proper translation of the verb 'to be' in a pre-Socratic fragment (ibid. 43)! For an argument that Heidegger's 'privileging' of Greek and German on the grounds of their special relation to 'Being' was arbitrary, see Jacques Derrida, *De l'esprit* (Paris: Gallile, 1987), 110–16.

22. However, the Guatemalan military justifies its attempted destruction of indigenous communities on the grounds that this is necessary in order to create a national Guatemalan community (see Ken Anderson *et al.*, 'Roundtable on Communitarianism', *Telos* (Summer 1988), 6). And while De la Patrie may be right that individuals cannot be made to partake of a community of memory simply by forcing them to speak a non-native common language, it does not follow that the Guatemalan military will not succeed in forging a national community several generations down the line.

23. For a discussion of the origins and the evolution of the multilingual Swiss nation, see Benedict Anderson's *Imagined Communities* (London: Verso, 1983), 123–6. It is interesting to note that before 1848, Switzerland was not even segmented into linguistic zones ('Language was a matter of personal choice and convenience', p. 125), as ancient religious cleavages were much more politically salient than linguistic ones.

24. The case of language-protection laws in Iceland is also discussed in Brad Leithauser, 'Iceland: A Nonesuch People', *Atlantic Monthly* (Sept. 1987), 32–41.

25. It should be noticed that De la Patrie does not defend the more difficult to justify ban on English as a second language on public signs.

26. In actual fact, Quebec immigration officials award three points for good English, fifteen for French, plus five more if the applicant's husband or wife can also speak French.

27. This helps to explain why the Quebec government offers cash incentives for parents to have larger families, with payments for parents who have three or more children ranging from $3,000 to $4,500 per baby (see 'Cash Incentives for Large Families', *Canada News* (Aug. 1989), 32).

28. On the task of having to combine in our lives moral outlooks that seem to demand incompatible things of us, see Charles Taylor's article 'The Diversity of Goods', in *Philosophy and the Human Sciences: Philosophical Papers, 2* (Cambridge: Cambridge University Press, 1985), esp. 234–6. On the particular issue that De la Patrie lays out, Taylor has campaigned vigorously for the latter option—more precisely, a Quebec with greater autonomy *within* Canada—with the 'no' side during the Quebec referendum for a mandate to negotiate for 'sovereignty-association' in 1980, and more recently in favour of the (failed) Meech Lake constitutional accord which would have granted Quebec the status of a 'distinct society' (within Canada).

29. In actual fact, many Québécois voted against 'sovereignty-association' for economic reasons, convinced that a 'yes' vote would severely damage the Quebec economy and their own personal financial situation in particular; most notorious at the time was the federal government's scare campaign designed to persuade the elderly in Quebec that a 'yes' vote would result in a loss of their pensions. In other words, the vote might have been closer if more Québécois had thought of the issue of political autonomy for Quebec as essentially a matter of identity, as De la Patrie would have it.

30. For an argument that values can (in principle) be ranked on a single scale, see James Griffin, *Well-Being* (Oxford: Clarendon Press, 1986), ch. 5.

31. For a similar distinction, see Robert Bellah, 'The Idea of Practices', in Charles Reynolds and Ralph Norman, eds., *Community in America: The Challenge of Habits of the Heart* (Berkeley, Calif.: University of California Press, 1988), 286–7.

32. For the most elaborate defence to date of the constructionist position, see David F. Greenberg's *The Construction of Homosexuality* (Chicago: University of Chicago Press, 1988), and for a critical review of this book see John Boswell (himself a writer on homosexual history), 'Gay History', *Atlantic Monthly* (Feb. 1989), 74–8:

> . . . constructionism deprives gay people of history and heritage . . . if there are special sensibilities, insights, feelings, or experiences particular to gay people—as there might be to women, blacks or Jews, for example—and if the essentialists [i.e. those who assume that homosexuality is an ongoing 'essence' of some number of individuals throughout history] are right, then the many gay people who have been prominent and influential in Western culture, from Socrates to Keynes, have introduced something of what is special about their outside status into the mainstream of culture, as 'inside' contributors to the cultural heritage of their society. (pp. 74–5)

33. This is also suggested in Francis Fitzgerald's book, *Cities on a Hill* (London: Picador, 1987), 29, 42, 47, 57.

34. Many homosexuals have interpreted this psychological experience to mean that they were born with their sexual orientation, an interpretation for which there is growing scientific evidence—one recent study has reported a difference between homosexual and heterosexual men in the hypothalamus, a part of the brain that develops at a young age, and another study has found greater rates of homosexuality in identical twin brothers of homosexual men than in non-identical twin brothers and adoptive, genetically unrelated brothers of homosexual men. In short, say the authors of the latter study, 'science is rapidly converging on the conclusion that sexual orientation is innate', a fact which has social and legal implications:

Homophobes sometimes justify their prejudice against homosexuals by alleging that homosexuality is contagious—that young homosexuals become that way because of older homosexuals, and that homosexuality is a social corruption. Such beliefs form the core of the organized anti-homosexual movement. If homosexuality is largely innate, this would prove that these claims are groundless. (Michael Bailey and Richard Pillard, 'Homosexuality Seems to be Innate', *International Herald Tribune* (19 Dec. 1991), 6.)

35. Actually the liberal position on homosexuality entails more than Schwartzberg's claim. Since the state ought not to appeal to particular con-ceptions of the good as justification of its policies, liberals would oppose anti-homosexual policies even with implications outside the bedroom, such as when Ronald Dworkin (see his review of Peter Jenkin's book, *Mrs. Thatcher's Revolution: The Ending of the Socialist Era, New York Review of Books* (27 Oct. 1988) excoriates the Thatcher government for having passed Clause 28 of the Local Government Act, a clause which forbids local councils to 'promote' homosexual relationships through distributing literature suggesting that such relationships can form an acceptable basis for family life (presumably on the grounds that homosexual relationships cannot form an acceptable basis for family life; it must also be assumed that local councils do not violate liberal neutrality by justifying their 'pro-homosexual' policies on the grounds that homosexual relationships can form an acceptable basis for family life but instead that homosexuals are merely receiving their fair share of resources to lead the lives they prefer).

36. Michael Sandel criticizes liberals who argue for the toleration of homosexual acts in private merely on the grounds that each should have the freedom to live the life he chooses as long as he does not harm others, arguing that the liberal case for toleration is unlikely to win for homosexuals more than thin and fragile toleration. He points to a New York case which vindicated privacy rights for homosexuals by drawing an analogy with a case which upheld the right to possess obscene material in the privacy of one's home, thus demean-ing homosexual intimacy by placing it on a par with a right to (obscene) sex-ual gratification in private and allowing the US Supreme Court to strike down the New York State ruling by ridiculing its (perceived) assumption of there being 'a fundamental right to engage in homosexual sodomy'. Instead, Sandel argues that a fuller respect for homosexuals' relationships would require at least some appreciation of the life homosexuals live, which involves articulating the human goods that homosexual intimacy may share with het-erosexual unions (see his 'Moral Argument and Liberal Toleration: Abortion and Homosexuality', *California Law Review*, 77 (1989), esp. 533–8). Having said all this, David F. Greenberg has found (in his *The Construction of Homosexuality*) that economic climate matters more than anything (including

legislation and court judgements) in terms of whether or not homosexuality will be tolerated. More precisely, it is generally the case that in times of economic deprivation a stricter moral climate, with associated sanctions against homosexuality, takes hold.

37. The 'social constructionist' school of thought might go along with this and other 'pro-homosexual community' proposals, but the two schools would approach the issue differently—e.g. the 'immutable trait' school might draw on earlier examples of homosexuals (Socrates *et al.*) so as to 'portray homosexuals in a positive light', but the 'social constructionists' could not do so, for they deny that homosexuality is an ongoing 'essence' of some number of individuals throughout history.

38. See Bellah *et al., Habits of the Heart,* 72–4, 83, 104, 154, 179, 238–9, 291–2, 335.

39. William Godwin would have denied the justice of this act if the stranger involved was more valuable to society than De la Patrie's sister. Godwin believed that only social utility could be (justly) employed to adjudicate between the competing claims of different individuals, and he supported this point by providing the (now famous) example of someone being morally compelled to save a bishop from a burning palace instead of his valet (a being of less social worth than a bishop), even supposing that the valet had been the rescuer's brother or father (see William Godwin, *Enquiry Concerning Political Justice* (Oxford: Clarendon Press, 1971), 70–1).

40. While it may be that relations among family members tend to be governed, at the deepest level, by feelings of goodwill (something that family members engaged in seemingly important squabbles should keep in mind!), and that the displacement of feelings of goodwill can often be attributed to preventable external circumstances, it cannot be denied that there sometimes exist (deep) springs of sibling rivalry. Those 'springs' seem to have 'sprouted' in the mind of the young Charles Dickens as he watched his 14-year-old sister Fanny receive a silver medal for good conduct and a second for piano performance at the Royal Academy of Music. Dickens's biographer writes of his impressions:

> He may not have wished that his sister was in the blacking factory [at the time, the 12-year-old Charles was doing dirty and demeaning work in a shoe-polish factory], but he certainly wished that he was on that stage receiving prizes. He could not think of himself 'beyond the reach of all such honourable emulation and success . . . I felt as if my heart were rent. I prayed, when I went to bed that night, to be lifted out of the humiliation and neglect in which I was. I never had suffered so much before.' (Fred Kaplan, *Dickens: A Biography* (London: Hodder and Stoughton, 1988), 42–3; my brackets.)

41. For a discussion of New England town halls and other small-scale political councils modelled upon the participatory political structures of the Greek

polis, see the excerpt from Hannah Arendt's 'On Revolution' reprinted in Michael Sandel, ed., *Liberalism and its Critics* (Oxford: Basil Blackwell, 1984), 239–63.

More recently, Benjamin Barber writes: 'the first and most important reform in a strong democratic platform must be the introduction of a national system of *neighbourhood assemblies* in every rural, suburban and urban district of America. Political consciousness begins in the neighbourhood' (*Strong Democracy: Participatory Politics for a New Age* (Berkeley, Calif.: University of California Press, 1984), 269, Barber's emphasis). However, Barber goes on to develop an intimidatingly high-tech proposal of 'electronic town meetings' which make use of 'Warner Amex's "QUBE" system [which] provides subscribers with an input module that permits multi-choice voting, computer information retrieval, and a variety of home shopping and security services' (ibid. 275).

42. See Bonavia, *The Chinese*, 60.

43. A phenomenon of this sort was well demonstrated in the otherwise abominable film *Oxford Blues*. A crass American, played by heart-throb Rob Lowe, goes to Oxford in search of his 'dream girl', a member of English Royalty with the title of Lady Victoria. By the end of the film, Lowe's dream girl has dropped out of his life-plans, and Lowe seems to have adapted to his college milieu. Activities that were once subordinated to the purpose of pursuing his dream girl, such as rowing, have unintentionally become ends in themselves for a Lowe now fully accepted by his college community as one of theirs.

44. While it is unfortunate that De la Patrie's 'empirical response' contains no evidence to support her claim, William Kennedy's compelling portrayal of bums' lives in his Pulitzer-Prize-winning novel *Ironweed* (Middlesex, England: Penguin Books, 1986) does lend some credibility to her speculations—Francis Phelan, Kennedy's life-like protagonist, ends up returning to the home and family he had fled twenty years previously after having failed to find solace in an illusory 'brotherhood of the desolate' (p. 23).

45. While Thoreau of Walden Pond may come to mind as a counter-example to De la Patrie's assertion (i.e. he looks like an 'undamaged human personhood' who 'firmly resists encroachments on his private sphere of being'), Nancy Rosenblum explains that

> The author of *Walden* introduces himself as a quietest withdrawn from social affairs, immersed in nature or in inspired acts of literary creation, but it soon becomes clear that Thoreau's hut at Walden Pond and *Walden* itself are designed to be provocative. His privatization is exhibitionist, a public act calculated to engage others . . . Thoreau's experiment in neighbourliness at Walden Pond was a public, even exhibitionist, act that exemplifies a 'life of exposure'. It has something of 'épater la bourgeoisie' in Thoreau's conspicuous idleness, the constant affront of his hut situated

close to the town road, and his jeremiads. Thoreau's main business in the woods, composing *Walden*, was ultimately directed toward his Concord neighbors. He did not want to be left alone entirely and he certainly did not want to leave others be. He was a militant, not quietist. (*Another Liberalism: Romanticism and the Reconstruction of Liberal Thought* (Cambridge, Mass.: Harvard University Press, 1987), 104, 112.)

46. See Bellah *et al.*, *Habits of the Heart*, 38, for a similar point.

47. The 'iron law of oligarchy' is developed in Michels' book *Political Parties* (New York: Free Press, 1962), 342–56.

48. See ibid. 32–3, 38.

49. More precisely, the Birks Building was designed by Montreal architect Harold Lee Fetherstonhaugh, who had studied with Perry Erskine Nobbs, one of William Morris's disciples. Features of the building which show the influence of the arts and crafts movement include the decorative detail of wood and stone carving, wrought iron, oak panelling, plaster moulding, and leaded clear and stained-glass windows. (See the pamphlet, 'The William and Henry Birks Building', prepared by McGill's Faculty of Religious Studies.)

50. It is not, according to the latest edition of the *Concise Oxford Dictionary*.

51. It can also be argued that lack of theft in the religious studies library stems from a more self-interested reason: many religious studies students calculate that it is in their long-term interest not to steal books, as they think one theft would lead to another, and so on, with the whole happy structure crumbling in the end. This explanation of lack of theft, however, would seem to rest on the not altogether plausible assumptions that (1) a religious studies student thinks that if she steals books, others will (*a*) notice and (*b*) do the same (the religious studies student fears (*b*) presumably because of the potential inconvenience of missing books, or perhaps she wants to avoid the probable response of the library authorities, namely the installation of strategically positioned 'beepers', and therefore the loss of the possibility of stealing books in a risk-free environment), and (2) the number of religious studies students who refrain from stealing books because they think that the theft of a few books will cause others to (*a*) notice and (*b*) do the same is great enough to enable us to say that it is many students thinking (*a*) and (*b*) which explains the relative lack of theft in the religious studies library (as compared to the psychology library).

52. See Michael Sandel, *Liberalism and the Limits of Justice* (Cambridge: Cambridge University Press, 1981), 33–4, 69, for a negative answer to this question. Will Kymlicka (*Liberalism, Community and Culture* (Oxford: Clarendon Press, 1989), 113–14) seems to take Sandel's passage on the family to be a defence of the idea that relations in 'the community' should be modelled on the ideal family situation, when Sandel simply means, it seems to me, to show, by invoking the counterfactual example of family relations

governed by principles of justice instead of love, that an increase in justice does not necessarily imply an unqualified moral improvement, and may in fact be a vice.

53. For example, Barbara Ehrenreich criticizes those: 'who romanticise the traditional family as a haven for non-market values [for consistently overlooking] the economics of the situation. The wife's dependence on her husband—whatever feelings may or may not be involved—is also a financial dependence. The husband, in turn, is dependent on his employer so that the family as a whole might as well be married to capital.' ('On Feminism, Family and Community', *Dissent*, 30 (1983), 104–5).

54. For a similar response, see M. Elizabeth Albert, 'In the Interest of the Public Good', 88–9, and Robert Bellah, 'The Idea of Practices', 283–4, both of which can be found in *Community in America*.

55. Though this trend is partly due to the AIDS scare (see Fitzgerald, *Cities on a Hill*), it is not implausible to speculate that most gays prefer coupling in family-type cells once this is tried out to a life of random release of libido impulses in bathhouses.

56. e.g. the US Court of Appeals extended privacy rights to homosexuals by arguing that qualities prized in conventional marriages, such as 'the unsurpassed opportunity for mutual support and self-expression that [the marital relationship] provides', can sometimes be present in homosexual unions as well: 'For some, the sexual activity in question here serves the same purpose as the intimacy of marriage' (from *Hardwick* v. *Bowers*, 706F. 2d 1202 (1985); Michael Sandel also quotes from this case in his paper 'Moral Argument and Liberal Toleration: Abortion and Homosexuality', 535). And in 1989 the New York State Court of Appeals ruled that non-legalized homosexual partners who live as a man and wife should be treated on the same terms as those who have gone through a marriage ceremony for purposes of a family member inheriting a deceased person's rent-controlled apartment. This decision was justified as follows: a family 'should not be rigidly restricted to those people who have formalised their relationship . . . by marriage', since one now defines family life in terms of the 'exclusivity and longevity of a relationship', on the 'level of emotional and financial commitment', on 'how a couple has conducted their everyday lives and held themselves out to society', and the 'reliance placed upon one another for daily family services.' (The passages from the case are also quoted in Keith Botsford's article 'Gays Go to Court to Seek Salvation', *Independent* (22 July 1989), 19.)

57. De la Patrie is thinking of Kenneth Lynn, *Hemingway* (New York: Simon and Schuster, 1987). See Frederick Crewes, 'Pressure under Grace', *New York Review of Books* (13 Aug. 1987), 30–7, for a very positive review of Lynn's biography.

58. Lord Baden-Powell, the founder of the Boy Scouts, is another 'repressed

homosexual who sublimated his desires on a grand scale' (from Ian Buruma's review of Tim Jeal's book *The Boy-Man: The Life of Lord Baden-Powell*, in *New York Review of Books* (15 Mar. 1990), 18). Baden-Powell's sublimation took the form of a neurotic homophobia and a longing for a pre-modern (male-dominated) order of purity, self-reliance, comradeship, and discipline that, Buruma notes, 'might well have ended up in the same moral world as the Hitler Youth or the Red Pioneers' (p. 19) had it developed under different conditions.

59. Benjamin De Mott also brings up the case of James Joyce as contrasted with that of Hemingway in his review of Lynn's biography of Hemingway in *Atlantic Monthly* (July 1987), 91–2.

60. Rilke's biographer notes that Rilke's mother expressed disappointment over his not being a girl (see Wolfgang Leppmann, *Rilke: A Life*, trans. Russell M. Stockman (Cambridge: Lutterworth Press, 1984), 81), and that she paid so little attention to him that he felt she had only loved him 'when there was a chance to present me in a new little dress to a few admiring friends' (ibid. 7). While Rilke's distorted relationship with his mother may have prevented him from loving women to the point of abandon (see ibid. 42–3), he never completely turned on women *à la* Hemingway (Hemingway's mother had also dressed him up as a girl). Rilke married, advocated 'the ideal of husband and wife as colleagues and of their parallel rather than joint development, in which there would be room for growth as well as for the preservation of the partner's own individuality' (ibid. 39; see also 146–7), he wrote plays dealing with women's self-awareness and self-realization in various forms (ibid. 87), and he even wrote poems in which he sought to transplant himself into the innermost being of young girls on the threshold of awakened sensuality (ibid. 86).

61. Robert Alton Harris is one uncontroversial example: his parents frequently beat him about the head, leading to brain damage that altered his personality. As a 37-year-old, Harris killed two 16-year-old boys, then laughed as he finished off the hamburgers they had been eating (see Christopher Reed's article 'Murderer to Die in "Liberal" State', *Guardian* (20 Mar. 1990)). Harris was eventually executed (to great controversy) by the state of California in April 1992.

62. While De la Patrie probably means to contrast children raised in 'broken families' with those raised in 'secure family environments' in terms of the effect on subsequent communitarian attachments, another contrast can be made—that between children raised in 'secure family environments' and those raised in communal child-rearing structures such as the 'children's houses' of Israeli kibbutzim. Bruno Bettelheim's research as described in his book *The Children of the Dream* (London: Thames and Hudson, 1969) suggests that the latter do at least as well as the former in terms of devotion to

their communities (of place) and their nation, and he speculates that the educational methods of kibbutzim can be applied to 'slum children of America' in order to breed future citizens (see pp. 1, 4).

63. Liberals, it should be noted, would be forced to oppose this communitarian move into politics: any legislation whose justification rests at least in part on the grounds that family-type relationships are being promoted violates the liberal dictum that a government should not appeal to any particular conception of the good when it sets policy.

64. The easy availability of legal marriage dissolution is an example of a cost that Gerald Dworkin calls 'increased choices that diminish welfare' in his article 'Is More Choice Better than Less?', in J. Howie, ed., *Ethical Principles for Social Policy* (Carbondale, Ill.: Southern Illinois University Press, 1983), 89.

65. In a polemical critique of 'anti-liberal' communitarians, Stephen Holmes asks a similar question: 'Does moral revulsion at "radical separation" among citizens require making divorce . . . illegal?' ('The Community Trap', *New Republic* (28 Nov. 1988), 25).

66. It should be noted that De la Patrie assumes that variations in the strictness of divorce laws influence the degree of marital breakdown in any given society, an assumption for which there is very little historical evidence according to Roderick Phillips (see his book *Putting Asunder: A History of Divorce in Western Society* (Cambridge: Cambridge University Press, 1988)). Notwithstanding this historical generality, Gwynn Davis criticizes current divorce laws in England for encouraging marital breakups that need not have occurred. Specifically, petitioning for divorce on grounds of adultery or 'unreasonable' behaviour allows for a quick divorce, with the consequence 'that the need to take rapid decisions in the course of the legal process of divorce leaves some people with a sense that they acted precipitately . . . Indeed it is so quick that if a person who initiates the divorce is ambivalent about the marriage (as many are) and consults a solicitor in order to seek advice, she may find herself with a divorce which she never really wanted' ('Season of Discord', *Guardian* (15 Dec. 1989), 36; and see Gwynn Davis and Merwyn Murch, *Grounds for Divorce* (Oxford: Oxford University Press, 1988)). Instead, Davis favours a proposal drawn up by the Law Commission in 1988 that would allow more time for reflection without requiring the spouses to undergo an unpleasant public airing of their differences. The Law Commission's recommendations on reforming divorce law were published in full on 1 November 1990, and its proposals seem 'almost certain to be accepted by the Government' ('Quickie Divorces Face Axe', *Guardian* (2 Nov. 1990), 2).

67. Raymond Geuss calls this requirement the 'hermeneutic requirement' in *The Idea of a Critical Theory* (Cambridge: Cambridge University Press, 1981), 85. Against the view that the original position lacks relevance for actual people

thinking about justice, since it requires us to ignore our particular context, Susan Moller Okin argues that the original position in fact requires us to think about justice 'through empathy with persons of all kinds in all the different positions in society . . ., to think from the point of view of everybody, of every "concrete other whom one might turn out to be" ' ('Reason and Feeling in Thinking about Justice', *Ethics* (Jan. 1989), 248). This interpretation of the original position still does not mean that the original position can readily be used as a guide for action, however—in practice, an American thinking about justice, say, would have to consider the identities, aims, and attachments of approximately a quarter of a billion people!

68. It can be argued that the final position cannot replace the original position since they are serving entirely different purposes—whereas the FP is intended to help us discover what it is that really matters to us, what sort of life we think is most worth living, the OP is intended to help us answer what is just, what is our fair share of rights and resources. In response, De la Patrie might reply that the FP can also help us think about matters of justice—individuals who have restructured their goals in accordance with what would matter in the FP (see the last two pages of Act V) will (as a by-product) also lose inappropriate interest in the things (e.g. money and power) that cause people to want more than their fair share. (Also assuming that good persons will lack most discernible reasons that lead people to be ordinarily unjust, Plato (in book 4 of *The Republic*) poses and answers the basic questions about justice in terms of the good agent, focusing on the character, education, and moral psychology of the good person instead of beginning with the question 'what is the right thing to do?' and answering in terms of duties and obligations owed to others—see the discussion in Julia Annas, *An Introduction to Plato's Republic* (Oxford: Clarendon Press, 1981), ch. 6.)

69. De la Patrie's claim is consistent with Pascal's observation that the same person who spends so many days and nights in fury and despair at the prospect of losing some petty office hardly ever bothers to think about the prospect of his eventual extinction (see Michael Ignatieff's *The Needs of Strangers* (Middlesex, England: Penguin Books, 1984), 75)—were that person to think of his eventual extinction, he would be aware of the 'pettiness' of the particular office that he happens to be holding, and only worry about losing that office if losing it affected those things that would matter in the final position (e.g. the family—see the last few pages of Act V; if losing a 'petty office' would result in the inability to feed one's family, then losing that office would indeed be a source of worry for someone who thinks about the prospect of her/his eventual extinction).

70. A very Heideggerian idea, De la Patrie should have mentioned: Heidegger devotes chs. 1 and 2 in division II of *Being and Time* to a discussion of the idea that Dasein must face up to the anxiety that accompanies the realization

of its own extinction, with the positive consequence that this anxiety 'liberates him *from* possibilities which "count for nothing", and lets him become free *for* those which are authentic' (p. 395, Heidegger's italics).

It should be noted, however, that Heidegger and De la Patrie have different ideas with respect to the content of 'authentic possibilities'—Heidegger insisted that the existence an individual should perpetuate in the face of the ever-present possibility of one's own death requires that one recognize one's essential, unavoidable involvement in the destiny of one's language-based community (see Catherine H. Zuckert, 'Martin Heidegger: His Philosophy and his Politics', *Political Theory* (Feb. 1990), 57 and above, Act I n. 43), whereas De la Patrie, it will be recalled, argues that the good life involves seeking the good of *many* constitutive communities.

71. Evidence in favour of De la Patrie's claim comes from Dr Elizabeth Kübler-Ross's experience with dying patients in the USA. She found that dying patients, if given some help in working through the stages of denial, anger, bargaining, and depression reach a stage where they have found some peace and acceptance (see Elizabeth Kübler-Ross, *On Death and Dying* (London: Tavistock Publications, 1970), esp. ch. 7).

72. David Hume's peace of mind at the time of his death, as described in Ignatieff, *The Needs of Strangers*, 83–8, illustrates De la Patrie's idea.

73. An example of what De la Patrie describes comes from the recent film *Salaam Bombay*. This funeral rite was also practised in China until recently.

74. Westmont is a wealthy, largely anglophone neighbourhood within the greater metropolitan area of Montreal.

75. If Philip was Hindu, it can be argued that he would not find the deathbed such a compelling position from which to 'reflect upon his past life and ponder what has mattered to him', as the idea of the deathbed would seem to rest on a (Western) conception of death as the end point of life—the Hindu who conceives of death as a mere staging-post on the way to the next incarnation would in all likelihood attribute no great importance to the deathbed.

76. *Contra* De la Patrie, some may say that even those hostile to religion discover religion from the position of their deathbed. However, the case of Benjamin Tucker, an exponent of individualist anarchism in his lifetime, falsifies this objection—Tucker went out of his way on his deathbed to proudly reaffirm his anti-religious stance, calling for his housekeeper to witness that he had not recanted: 'I do not believe in God,' he told her (from James Joll's review of Paul Avrich's book *Anarchist Portraits*, *New York Times Book Review* (27 Nov. 1988), p. 24).

77. A more important example might be someone who spends so much time at work that he fails to sufficiently nurture his family ties, realizes from the death-focused perspective that in the end family matters more than work, and decides to cut down on work hours in order to spend more time with his

family. This seems to have happened to a Belgian businessman who decided after being taken hostage (and seeing his partner killed) to cut down his work-week from 70 to 35 hours so as to spend more time with his wife and children (his wife said that they would have been divorced if he had not been kidnapped; 'The Hostages Speak', BBC2, 20 Aug. 1990, 8.10 p.m.). The case of the Belgian businessman, however, suggests that simply 'imagining' what would matter to us in the final position might not be sufficient to cause us to restructure our priorities in accordance with 'what really matters'—it may be that one has actually to be in a position where death is felt to be a highly likely, short-term probability.

Appendix 1: Some Questions about Justice and Community

Will Kymlicka

August 1990: A café in Montreal. Anne De la Patrie, having recently defended her Ph.D. thesis at McGill, is sitting with Louise, an old friend of the family, who is a social worker, and part-owner of a women's bookstore in Montreal. Anne had given Louise a copy of the thesis in May, since she knows that Louise has a passing interest in political philosophy, and they have met for lunch to discuss it. They have already eaten, and Louise pulls out her copy of the thesis, which is full of 'post-it notes' attached to various pages.

ANNE [*slightly apprehensive*] You seem to have lots of comments, particularly on Act II.

LOUISE Actually, my first question concerns the focus of the thesis. You call this 'Communitarianism and its Critic',* but you seem to focus almost entirely on *liberal* critics. You don't discuss any feminist critics of communitarianism. Indeed, I was disappointed to see that well over 90 per cent of your bibliography is composed of works by men, and that almost no mention was made of the differences in the way men and women are 'socially embedded'.

ANNE Unfortunately, political philosophy remains a male-dominated profession, and the communitarianism debate has, so far, been dominated by (male) liberals and communitarians, with little input from feminists.

LOUISE I'm sure we've had a few books into our store lately that criticize communitarianism from a feminist perspective. Books by Iris Marion Young and Susan Moller Okin come to mind.[1] But in any event, surely the older feminist literature on the way men and women are socialized is very relevant.

ANNE Well I did try to incorporate some feminist perspectives—for example, the use of non-sexist language.

LOUISE But you don't consider one of the reasons why non-sexist language is important. Sexist language obscures the fact that women's experience is often different from men's, and that these gender differences generally work to women's disadvantage. Attending to these differences is part of the definition of

---

* The title of my D.Phil. thesis. Due to the appearance of 'Louise', I have entitled the book 'Communitarianism and its Critics' (Daniel Bell).

a feminist outlook, and it is quite absent from your thesis. The history of the feminist movement, by the way, seems to contradict the basic 'ontological' claim in Act I of your thesis.

ANNE In what way?

LOUISE You argue that we don't choose how we walk or dress, and that we only question these practices when they 'break down' (pp. 33–4). But consider the way I became a feminist. George and I had just married, and I was working as a social worker to help put him through graduate school, although it was expected that I would give up the job once he had completed his work, and that I would stay home and raise children. As you know, this was quite normal in the 1950s and early 1960s. A good friend of mine suggested that I read Betty Friedan's *The Feminine Mystique*, which I did out of curiosity. While initially sceptical, once I started reading her account of the ways women's development is stunted by our 'feminine' socialization, I was immediately convinced of its essential truth. It made so much sense of my experiences, from childhood forward. So I began to question my various 'feminine' traits, including the way I dressed, walked, talked, made eye contact with people, etc. I felt I had to change all these traits, since they were submissive traits—traits which allowed and encouraged men to ignore or interrupt my conversation, or which made me more vulnerable to physical attack, etc. I know from my conversations with other women, and from books in our store, that many women responded in this way to Friedan's book, or to other popular feminist books (*Sexual Politics, The Women's Room*, etc.). We picked up a book out of curiosity, and ended up questioning our entire repertoire of learned behaviours, not because these behaviours had 'broken down', but because we were persuaded that they were damaging us.

ANNE But surely, if Friedan was right, then your learned behaviours *had* broken down. Your modes of talking or dressing were not helping you cope with the world, but rather were making it impossible for you to achieve your aims in life.

LOUISE That's true in a sense, but not in the sense you suggest in the thesis. I was certainly frustrated at the time, although, like most women, I had repressed the depth of the frustration. I was frustrated at the way male professors had ignored me or belittled my contributions to class, and at the way George's colleagues treated me as if I were invisible. But the fact is that I had always felt that frustration, way back to childhood, when my brother received more encouragement for his academic and athletic accomplishments than I. But like most girls and women, I had assumed that this was a problem with *me*—that I wasn't deserving of the same respect as my brother, or male colleagues. I began to think that I was somehow deficient. I never thought that the problem lay with the social construction of femininity. This, of course, is why Friedan's book was so powerful for many women. We had low self-respect, and assumed that our difficulties from childhood forward were due to personal failings. But she

showed that our difficulties were due to our socialization as women, and that
we had to fight to recognize and reform the many ways in which we were
socialized to be submissive or passive, etc. Now according to your thesis, any
attempt to 'escape the grip' of our constitutive identities results in becoming a
'disturbed' or 'damaged' person (p. 100) . . .

ANNE [*interrupting*] Well, I didn't mean . . .

LOUISE Actually, Anne, you are quite right. We in the feminist movement quickly
found out that it is disturbing and painful, and indeed impossible, entirely to
escape the grip of our socialization. Femininity had become constitutive of our
identity, and it is profoundly damaging to have to fight against it. The description you give of the 'acute form of disorientation' (p. 100) which results from
trying to escape from our socialization is mirrored in many feminist writings.[2]
But your discussion is one-sided. You focus on the damage created by trying to
escape our socialization, but ignore the damage caused by *not* escaping it. Once
I'd recognized how domination and subordination were built into the social
construction of masculinity and femininity, I could not go back. When George
tried to discourage me from keeping my job after his graduation, I knew that
our marriage could not be one of equals, and that he wanted a feminine wife.
So, as you know, we got divorced. (He recently married one of his graduate
students.) I, and others in the women's movement, had to try to find new ways
of dressing and talking, new forums for interacting, drawing support from each
other. As you know, our bookstore was part of this creation of a women's community in Montreal. We were 'damaged' and 'disturbed' by trying to escape
patriarchy, but we were even more damaged and disturbed within patriarchy.
You never once in the thesis consider how people can be damaged by their constitutive attachments, how these attachments can systematically undermine
people's sense of self-respect, and make them subordinate to others. Feminists
will insist that we be free to question our constitutive attachments, not just
when they break down, but even when they are working as expected, for the
subordination of women is built into our everyday expectations about men's
and women's behaviour.

ANNE Does that mean that you endorse the liberal conception of the person as
someone who freely chooses all aspects of her life?

LOUISE Of course not. If liberals deny that vast areas of our life are governed by
learned dispositions that have not been consciously chosen, then clearly they
are wrong.[3] What we need is a conception of the self that recognizes that we
have constitutive attachments, and that they are damaging to give up, but that
these attachments can themselves be damaging, and hence that we must be free
to question and possibly reject them even when they don't 'break down'.

ANNE Perhaps I overstated the ontological point. But I think we agree about practical politics. For example, my notion of constitutive 'psychological communities' allows for the possibility that people can *construct* a constitutive
community, such as the lesbian feminist community in Montreal, and that over

time this community would deserve support. Also, I defend the legal recognition of lesbian families. Moreover, I agree that the patriarchal family should be reformed, since the coercive power of men over women violates our 'deepest self-understanding' of the family as based on freely given love (p. 180).

LOUISE But this last point relies on the very dichotomy you elsewhere criticize liberals for relying on—that is, between free choice and coercion (p. 40). George was not coercing me to subsidize his education, or type his term papers. This sometimes happens, but feminists believe that subordination occurs even where there is no external coercion. Subordination, feminists believe, is built into the very construction of femininity and masculinity (and hence 'husband' and 'wife'), and many women accept their subordinate role in the family as natural or appropriate. It is true that most women want their husbands to do more domestic work, and to give them more emotional support, etc. But it doesn't follow that the status quo is based entirely on coercion.

ANNE Are you denying that the patriarchal family, or the homophobic denial of family status to lesbians, violates our deepest shared understandings?

LOUISE Well this raises the whole question of political justification, discussed in Act II of your thesis. You argue that political justification must appeal to the deepest shared understandings within each community. I must say I find the notion of 'deepest' shared understandings very obscure. I'm not clear on what distinguishes 'deep' from 'shallow' understandings. There are a variety of ways one might measure 'depth', but I'm not sure that any will suit your purposes.

ANNE As you know, I take the idea of 'deep' understandings from Walzer, but I must admit I myself am a little unclear about his metaphor of depth.

LOUISE It might mean historical depth: that is, the longer a social practice (or interpretation thereof) goes back in time, then the deeper it is in our society. But this of course won't provide grounds for criticizing patriarchy—patriarchy goes back far longer than our commitment to equal opportunity for women, and homophobia goes back far longer than any commitment to gay rights. A cursory summary of family law would reveal that changes in the direction of sexual equality or gay rights are just piecemeal reform on the surface of an institution that has been patriarchal to the core for centuries.

ANNE That clearly can't be what Walzer means. I think he means deeper in the sense of more important to us, what we are most strongly committed to, even if this conflicts with historical practices and institutions.

LOUISE Actually I read an article arguing that Walzer is ambiguous on just this question of whether shared understandings are embedded in historical institutions or whether they are found within the beliefs of members of the community.[4] But in any event, what does it mean to be more strongly committed to something? The average male claims to be committed to sexual equality, but the evidence is that they *in fact* want and expect a wife who is submissive, that they find sexual stimulation in the harming of women, and that they pay less attention to women's conversation and writings, etc. Moreover, they are threatened by women who insist on being treated as equals, and seek to find and defend spheres where they can avoid such women. It seems to me, therefore, that most men's strongest commitment is to patriarchy, not sexual equality.

ANNE Are you saying that men do not believe in sexual equality, and that they only claim to do so? I'm sure that most men sincerely believe in sexual equality.

LOUISE But this is my whole point—people have different kinds of understandings at different levels. At one level, men believe in sexual equality—they do not consciously accept any of the traditional justifications for women's inferiority. But at another level, they do not believe in sexual equality. They put less credence, for example, in what women say; they assume that women want to be controlled in various ways; they assign lower marks to school papers with women's names on them, even when the papers are identical to those written by men. So men both do and don't believe in sexual equality. Now the question is, which of these beliefs is 'deeper'? If by deeper we mean that which most determines their conduct, that which most informs and structures their everyday interpretation of events, then it seems clear that it is patriarchal beliefs which lie deepest in many men. The belief in sexual equality, while sincere, is relatively superficial.

ANNE Clearly Walzer can't mean 'deepest' in terms of what lies deepest in one's personality, or in terms of what lies deepest in society's institutional history. Perhaps one's deepest understandings are those that one can most fully and consciously endorse, that one thinks are most rationally defensible. If so, then it is important that men no longer publicly affirm patriarchal beliefs. Even if they act in patriarchal ways, they do not, and cannot, think of themselves as patriarchal. This would conflict with their deepest understandings in the sense of what they can consciously and rationally endorse. Deepest understandings, then, would be those beliefs that we can consciously articulate and rationally endorse as our guiding principles.

LOUISE Yes, it is true that most men do not consciously subscribe to patriarchal ideologies. Patriarchy maintains itself through its historical embeddedness in social institutions and its psychological embeddedness in individual personalities, neither of which requires patriarchy to be consciously endorsed as a belief system, and indeed that belief system is often consciously disavowed. But this raises a deep conflict in your argument. In your 'ontological' argument, you argue that people cannot articulate the 'essence' of their constitutive attachments (p. 98), and indeed you emphasize the 'relative unimportance of beliefs' (p. 97) in determining one's identity, and hence in determining the obligations that go with that identity. This is crucial to your argument against the liberal conception of self-determination: you say we cannot stand back from our constitutive attachments and evaluate and reject them because we cannot even articulate them (p. 97). But now it seems that our 'deepest' understandings have to be those that *are* articulated and consciously endorsed. It is only at the level of conscious affirmation, rather than unconscious behaviour, that our society is egalitarian. If our essential identities and understandings are those that resist articulation but none the less structure our everyday lives, then our society is essentially patriarchal, which of course is just what feminists believe. You yourself note this contradiction later on. You note that Walzer's theory presupposes that we can articulate our deepest understandings, and respond that while our identities resist a 'full and definitive statement', we can none the less articulate the 'relevant parts' of the shared tradition (p. 127). This is a remarkably cursory treatment of a deep problem. How is it that we can't articulate the 'essence' of our identity, but we can articulate its 'relevant parts'? What is the difference between the essence of an identity and its relevant parts? And if we can articulate the relevant parts of our identity, then why aren't liberals correct in saying that we can stand back and evaluate it?

ANNE So you're saying that I'm caught between a rock and a hard place. If I emphasize the ontological claim that our deepest identity and goals are those that structure our being in the world but which resist articulation, then I have no basis for saying that our shared understandings support reforming the patriarchal family in the name of sexual equality. If on the other hand I emphasize the Walzerian claim that our deepest understandings are those we articulate and consciously affirm, then I no longer have an argument against the liberal view that we can evaluate and possibly reject our deepest attachments. Is that it?

LOUISE Exactly. As I argued earlier, I think any feminist would take the second route, and insist that we can evaluate our constitutive attachments, since this is just what the feminist movement seeks to do. I should add that the problem is even greater for your recommendation to legalize gay marriages. There is little support for that proposal amongst the general population at the level of either historical practice, personal psychology, or conscious belief. I have no idea how you would try to defend that recommendation in terms of shared understandings.

ANNE I argue that the goods realized in homosexual relationships are the same as those realized in heterosexual marriages, and so consistency requires people to accord homosexual relationships the same privileges as heterosexual relationships.

LOUISE Oh yes, I remember. There are two problems with that argument: firstly, it is often not true that gays see themselves as pursuing the same goods as heterosexuals (as you note on p. 181); and secondly, it is not true that heterosexuals view the family as simply a sphere of love and care between people committed to each other. If that was the everyday conception of the good of marriage, then it would be arbitrary to deny it to homosexuals (or to polygamous relationships). The fact is that heterosexuals believe that the heterosexual family is distinctly valuable because it unifies sexuality and reproduction, because children have a genetic as well as social bond with their care-givers, because it is endorsed by the Bible, and for a million other reasons that do not apply to gay couples. You pick out one aspect of the heterosexual commitment to the family, and argue that since that aspect can also apply to homosexuals, therefore heterosexuals should accept gay rights. But you don't provide any evidence that the particular aspect you pick out is the one which is 'deepest' in society. And it seems clear to me that it is not deepest, on any of the three measures of depth we've discussed (history, psychology, conscious belief). This is like Walzer's dubious argument that Americans' 'shared understandings' include a commitment to economic democracy.[5] He takes one aspect of one argument for political democracy, and argues that since it can also be applied to the workplace, we should all support economic democracy. But he gives no evidence for the claim that the argument he has identified is 'deepest' in terms of explaining our commitment to political democracy.

ANNE Well I agree with you on economic democracy (Act II n. 21). In fact, I admit in the thesis that sometimes the reformer is 'taking sides, as opposed to claiming that her interpretation captures the "deepest", "most authentic" morality of her people' (Act II n. 41). If our deepest understandings are homophobic, the gay rights reformer may appeal to an understanding of sexuality and family life which has relatively little popularity in society, and seek to make it more popular, with the eventual goal of making it the 'deepest' understanding in society. So I agree that the ultimate standard for political argument is not always the 'deepest' standard.

LOUISE Yes, I remember that claim in your thesis, even though you hid it away in an endnote. In fact, I was quite startled when I read it, since it seems to give the entire game away. In the main text, you claim that reformers must appeal to what is 'most congruent' with the community's 'deepest aspirations' (p. 65). On this view, the deepest understandings of the community define what is right for it, and so arguments of justice must (by definition) be couched in terms of congruence with those deepest understandings. There is no way to identify what is right except by reference to deepest understandings. This is the view that Ronald Dworkin criticized in his famous *New York Review of Books* exchange with Walzer.[6] According to Dworkin, no matter how deep a certain practice or belief is, we can still question its justice. Depth does not make something right. It is possible that something relatively shallow in our culture is more just, and should replace the deeper practice or belief. As Dworkin put it, Walzer talks about our deepest understanding of justice, but ignores one of our most deeply held beliefs about justice—namely, that congruence with our community's deepest self-image is no guarantee of justice.[7] In conceding this in your note, you seem to be siding with Dworkin against Walzer.

ANNE But, as I state in that note, the reformer is still appealing to some aspect of her culture's morality. She is appealing to one cultural standard to criticize another standard. She is not entirely stepping outside her culture.

LOUISE Well it's of course true that people can only criticize social practices by drawing on the ideas about justice they have learned in their community.

Walzer sometimes makes it sound as if that is a controversial claim, but I can't believe anyone denies it.[8] The question is not where our ideas come from, but how we evaluate them. What Dworkin claims is that justice cannot be equated with, or defined in terms of, 'congruence' with a community's deepest understandings or deepest self-image. Since acts which are congruent with a community's deepest self-image can none the less be unjust, we must test our deepest self-image against other possible standards of justice (e.g. our shallower self-image). The fact that something is congruent with a community's deepest self-image does not foreclose the argument about its justice. That is all that Dworkin was claiming, and your note seems to concede his claim.

ANNE But if the reformer's proposals are not in line with society's self-image, they aren't likely to be effective (pp. 65–6).

LOUISE That just shows that some requirements of justice may go unfulfilled for a long time. The efficacy of a justice claim and its legitimacy are two separate questions. Again, a glance at the history of the feminist movement would attest to the importance of this distinction. I think a similar problem affects your discussion of national projects (p. 132), where you say . . .

ANNE [*interrupting*] Yes, yes, I see the analogy. But I don't see how any of these criticisms actually bear on the specific policy recommendations I make in the third part (Acts III–V) of my thesis.

LOUISE I agree. I think that your recommendations stand or fall independently of Walzer's theory of shared understandings. Indeed, I think your recommendations are much stronger if they are detached from Walzer's theory. You've argued that people's good is tied to their participation in constitutive communities (Acts I and III), and that the state should take various measures to protect those communities (Acts III–V). I think that this is a good argument (subject to the qualifications I made earlier), whether or not our community's shared understandings recognize the good of constitutive communities (Act II). In the case of homosexual psychological communities, for example, it seems obvious to me that the community does not recognize their value. But that is a flaw in the community's understandings, not in your argument for gay rights. The fact is that we live in a very individualist culture (i.e. mainstream white North American culture), and our deepest understandings do not give due weight to community. We have trouble understanding arguments about the value of community—it is not part of our political repertoire. Tying your argument to Walzer is unnecessary, and indeed counter-productive.

ANNE Do you accept my policy recommendations then?

LOUISE In part. But I must say that I found your recommendations rather tame, in light of your earlier arguments.

ANNE What do you mean?

LOUISE Most of the recommendations (e.g. mandatory national service; cooperation-promoting education) are designed to give young people opportunities to discover the value of participating in constitutive communities. Once they have experienced this, you hope they will choose to maintain their ties to their communities. But one could imagine more radical proposals. If, as you think, it is pointless and damaging to try to escape the grip of one's constitutive communities, then why not prevent people from leaving their community, except under very strict conditions? If the only good reason to leave one's physical community is economic livelihood or political persecution (p. 108), then why not restrict mobility rights except under those conditions? And if people cannot escape their religious community (p. 95), then why not legally prohibit both proselytization (i.e. attempting to induce people to leave their religious community) and apostasy (i.e. abandoning one's faith and leaving one's religious community)?

ANNE But as I tried to explain in the thesis, the state can act in less coercive ways.

LOUISE I agree it *can* act in less coercive ways, but why *should* it avoid coercion? If you think that people are damaged by leaving their communities without adequate reason, why not protect them from damaging themselves? Why rely on the notoriously unreliable mechanism of the individual's own assessment of her best interests? We know that some people will be tempted into harming themselves if they are exposed to proselytizers, so why not prohibit proselytization and apostasy?

ANNE Freedom of religion is one of our deepest shared understandings.

LOUISE That is true, but your thesis doesn't explain *why* it is one of our deepest values. Your thesis explains why the members of religious communities should be free to practice their shared beliefs. But you don't explain why proselytizers should be free to induce people to leave their religious community, or why apostates should be free to go. Allowing apostasy and proselytization corrodes people's ties to their religious community. Liberals argue that freedom to challenge religious orthodoxy is important because some people worship false gods out of ignorance and superstition, and hence are harmed by their current attachment to a particular religious community. Freedom to question the community's beliefs, and to hear the proponents of other religions, helps dispel religious corruption, and spreads enlightenment. You obviously reject that argument for proselytization and apostasy. So why not prohibit them?[9]

ANNE As Walzer argues, freedom of mobility, including religious mobility, is one of our deepest values, and it is simply unfeasible to try to compel people to stay in their communities.

LOUISE But there are lots of things we could do to ensure that people stay in their communities that are feasible. For example, why not allow parents to control the content of their children's education so as to ensure that they are not tempted to leave their home or religion? We could allow parents to withdraw their children from school as soon as they have learned whatever skills are needed at home, even if this leaves children completely unequipped to deal with the larger world. Would you support that?

ANNE Well I do support it in the case of the Amish (Act IV n. 37). I'm not sure whether I'd support it for every other group.

LOUISE The point is that your practical recommendations are misleadingly tame. If you reject the liberal conception of the person as self-determining, and think that people who seek to escape the grip of their constitutive communities are damaged in the process, then you should follow the logic of that argument to its conclusion.

ANNE But people belong to different constitutive communities, including communities that they have joined later in life (p. 173), and in different locations (p. 111). People may have valid reasons for leaving their home, religion, family, even though this will be painful. I never meant to imply that people's lives always got worse when they leave their communities. I wouldn't deny that some local communities are so narrow in their way of life that the occasional resident will rationally want to move permanently to the big city, or that some families are so abusive that the occasional child or wife will rationally want to cut all ties. So there is no need to confine people to their original communities, so long as we support the establishment and maintenance of new communities, like the feminist community in Montreal.

LOUISE I certainly agree with that. But now we're in danger of losing your argument for even non-coercive measures to keep people in their communities. If the damage done by leaving a constitutive community can be outweighed by the damage done by staying inside it, and if the benefit of staying inside a particular community can be outweighed by the benefit of joining another community which is more nourishing of one's particular talents or aspirations, then why not ensure that everyone has the opportunity to learn about other ways of life, and the capacity to stand back from and evaluate the benefits of staying in their original community? And surely this is what liberals aspire to?

ANNE Let me summarize what you've said so far: (1) you think that my ontological claim about our social embeddedness is overstated, since people can seek to articulate and question their learned behaviours even when they have not broken down, and moreover that some people have good reason to engage in this questioning, since their learned behaviours can be damaging to their sense of well-being; (2) you think my Walzerian theory of shared meanings is obscure, since I give no criteria for distinguishing which meanings are deeper than others. Moreover, you think that this theory conflicts with my ontological claim, since the former appeals to articulated and consciously endorsed beliefs, whereas the latter denies that our fundamental identity and values can be articulated; (3) you think my practical recommendations are plausible, but that my ontological claim justifies far greater restrictions on personal liberty, and I have given no reason why we should respect certain commonly accepted civil liberties. On the other hand, you think my recommendations are too strong in terms of my Walzerian theory of shared understandings, since there is no evidence that our shared understandings support gay rights or feminist reforms of the family. Is there anything else?

LOUISE Well, I wasn't sure whether to mention this, since I'm not sure what role it plays in your thesis. You have another argument against liberalism in the first section. You argue that many people in our culture do not value self-determination—the two examples you give are your grandmother and Mother Teresa. However, neither example is really developed, and I'm not sure what conclusions you want to draw from them.

ANNE I was trying to show that many people in our society reject the liberal conception of the person.

LOUISE Well that depends on what the liberal conception of the person is. If you mean the view that choice is an intrinsic value to be exercised for its own sake, then the two people you mention certainly reject that view. But so do many liberals, including Rawls. If you mean the view that people have an interest in being able to question and revise their ends, then it's not clear that either example works. In the case of Mother Teresa, her decision to move to Calcutta is just the kind of change of life-plan that liberals insist people must be free to make. Presumably she had constitutive attachments to her original life and work, but liberals insist that this should not foreclose her freedom to radically revise her plans.

ANNE But she says it was God's choice, not hers.

LOUISE This is just semantics. The fact is that she chose to move, although of course God's calling was her reason for choosing. She may not view it as a free choice, in Sartre's sense of that word, but rather as a commandment or calling. But, as Rawls discusses, the kind of choice liberals want individuals to have is the freedom to pursue their calling, not choice for the sake of choice.[10]

ANNE What about my grandmother?

LOUISE Well, I didn't know your grandmother, so I can't really comment. I think we often exaggerate the extent to which our grandparents were unreflectively committed to their way of life, and the extent to which they were free from doubts about its value. We get a lot of diaries these days in our store, and it is remarkable how often seemingly traditional women questioned (in the privacy of their diary) the legitimacy of various cultural rules or church policy. Of course, this may be a biased sample. And it is certainly true that some people lead their lives unreflectively. Indeed, this is the liberal nightmare, as in *Brave New World* or *1984*, where people are discouraged from questioning authority. This sort of blind obedience is what liberals were fighting against during the Enlightenment when they attacked the superstitions used by the Church to keep their flock in tow. Liberals believe that recognition of the importance of reflection is an historical accomplishment, and fear that various forces in society are endangering that historical accomplishment. So it will not surprise liberals to hear that some people unreflectively do what they are told, and it will not lead them to give up their belief in the value of reflective choice. The liberal believes that people (including your grandmother) can find themselves in social relationships that are harmful or manipulated, and hence they can have reasons for wanting to be able to question the value of those relationships. What you want to argue, I assume, is not just that there are people who lead their lives unreflectively, but that this was the best life for them. You clearly believe that people like your grandmother would have been harmed rather than benefited by having the capacity and opportunity to stand back and evaluate their way of life. But you don't defend that claim, or even clearly state it. I think these examples need to be fleshed out if they are to succeed in dislodging the liberal commitment to reflective choice.

In any event, I don't understand what this has to do with Christian benevolence (p. 43). Some people reflectively choose to lead a life of Christian benevolence. Some people unreflectively lead a life of unChristian selfishness. I don't see what the connection is between these two issues.

ANNE Well, I don't agree with everything you've just said, but I can see that perhaps I need to add a few more sentences to explain my position fully.

LOUISE I wish you the best of luck with the revisions. Thanks for giving me a copy of the manuscript—I enjoyed reading it, and I'm sure it will be an excellent book when it is published. If you promise to add a discussion of the feminist critics of communitarianism, I promise to order lots of copies for our bookstore.

ANNE I promise.

[*Lights dim*]

Notes

The dialogue in this appendix was originally written as a reader's report on Bell's manuscript for Oxford University Press. As a result, it was written primarily to stimulate discussion, rather than to state carefully my own views on the subject. One of my initial responses when reading the manuscript was that it was misleading for Bell to present his communitarian views in the voice of a woman, particularly since I felt he failed adequately to consider the interests and experiences of women, and ignored recent feminist critiques of communitarianism. It occurred to me that a vivid way of expressing that concern was to write my report in the form of a dialogue between Anne and a feminist activist named 'Louise'. As a reader's report, this strategy may have been an effective way of raising certain questions. I am less comfortable, however, with the idea of publishing the report, since it contains the very danger I was trying to point out in Bell's manuscript. The views I attribute to Louise are partly inspired by recent feminist critiques of communitarianism, but these critiques have been adapted for my own purposes. Hence the views I attribute to Louise should not be taken as representative of feminist views of communitarianism. For excellent discussions of communitarianism from a feminist perspective, see the works cited in note 1 below.

1. Iris Marion Young, *Justice and the Politics of Difference* (Princeton: Princeton University Press, 1990), esp. ch. 8; Susan Moller Okin, *Justice, Gender and the Family* (New York: Basic Books, 1989), ch. 3. See also Marilyn Friedman, 'Feminism and Modern Friendship: Dislocating the Community', *Ethics*, 99: 2 (1989), 275–90; Donna Greschner, 'Feminist Concerns with the New Communitarians', in A. Hutchinson and L. Green, eds., *Law and the Community* (Toronto: Carswell, 1989).

2. See Marilyn Frye, *The Politics of Reality: Essays in Feminist Theory* (Trumansburg: Crossing Press, 1983).

3. Do liberals deny this? Liberals believe that people can and should consciously adopt a 'conception of the good life'—i.e. a conception of what sort of life is worth leading. This is quite consistent, it seems to me, with recognizing that many areas of a good life are governed by unchosen habits and routines. Bell doesn't give any references to liberals who believe that meaningful autonomy requires that every aspect of one's life must be consciously chosen.

4. As Joshua Cohen notes, Walzer tends 'to identify the values embodied in institutions and practices with the values of members'. Joshua Cohen, 'Review of *Spheres of Justice*', *Journal of Philosophy*, 83 (1986), 457–68, repr. in Will Kymlicka, ed., *Justice in Political Philosophy*, ii (Aldershot: Edward Elgar Ltd., 1992), 323–4.

5. M. Walzer, *Spheres of Justice* (Oxford: Basil Blackwell, 1983), 295–303. For a comprehensive critique of Walzer's argument for workers' control, see Richard Arneson, 'Is There a Right to Workers' Control?', *Economics and Philosophy*, forthcoming. As Arneson notes, the particular argument Walzer identifies to defend industrial democracy would also defend legislation requiring churches to be internally democratic.

6. Ronald Dworkin, 'What Justice Isn't', reprinted in Ronald Dworkin, *A Matter of Principle* (Cambridge, Mass.: Harvard University Press, 1985), ch. 10.

7. According to Dworkin, Walzer's theory is 'incoherent', for it 'ignores the "social meaning" of a tradition much more fundamental than the discrete traditions it asks us to respect. For it is part of our common political life, if anything is, that justice is our critic, not our mirror, that any decision about the distribution of any good—wealth, welfare, honors, education, recognition, office—may be reopened, no matter how firm the traditions that are then challenged, that we may always ask of some settled institutional scheme whether it is fair' (ibid. 219).

8. Bell claims that various liberals deny it, but he provides no references for that claim. It seems to me that most people recognize that political argument must appeal to ideas about justice that can be found within the community.

As Joshua Cohen notes, 'There are certainly serious disagreements about the enterprise of political philosophy. But it is wrong to say that they are importantly about where "to *begin* the philosophical enterprise" ' ('Review of *Spheres of Justice*, 467, quoting Walzer). Even dedicated universalists like Plato and Kant accept that moral argument must begin with 'local and particular ethical opinions'. They simply believe that moral reasoning may lead us to reject those original starting-points, no matter how deep they are in our culture.

9. This is a serious question, not only for communitarians, but also for those liberals who seek to defend liberalism on purely 'political' grounds. For example, Rawls, in his most recent work, argues that the only way to ensure social stability in a religiously diverse society is to protect freedom of conscience. He thinks that this political argument is the best argument for religious toleration, and that liberals need not, and should not, make the separate argument that religious liberty is needed to enable individuals to revise their religious commitments. He wants to avoid this second argument, because he accepts the possibility that people are unable to stand back and rationally revise their basic commitments. In other words, he thinks that liberals should defend religious liberty on the ground that it enables diverse religious communities to practise their shared creed, not on the ground that it enables individuals to freely affirm or revise their religious beliefs. The problem, however, is that Rawls's political argument cannot in fact defend freedom of conscience. It can defend the right of religious communities to practise their religion, but it cannot defend proselytization and apostasy. If we wish to defend these practices, we must defend the claim that people have the capacity to question and revise their basic commitments, and often have good reasons to exercise that capacity. Or so I argue in 'Two Models of Pluralism and Tolerance', *Analyze & Kritik*, 14: 1 (1992), 33–56.

10. I discuss liberal views of the value of freedom of choice in *Liberalism, Community, and Culture* (Oxford University Press, 1989), 48–50.

Appendix 2: A Reply

Daniel Bell

February 1992: The renowned Punggol Point seafood restaurant in Singapore. Louise, travelling with her fiancée Thérèse, has just arrived in Singapore. Her bookstore hard-hit by Canada's seemingly interminable recession, Louise has come to Singapore to consider the possibility of moving shop. She had heard of Singapore's booming economy from her friend Anne De la Patrie, currently in Singapore writing a book on communitarian politics in Asia.

LOUISE [*having just spotted her friend*] Anne! . . . [*they embrace*] . . . What a long trip! I thought we'd never make it here.

ANNE I'm so glad you came. But where's Thérèse?

LOUISE She's sleeping over at the hotel. The trip here knocked her out.

ANNE Oh? She didn't mind your joining me for a meal? I guess you haven't told her about us two . . . or perhaps she's not the jealous type.

LOUISE Actually, she does get jealous, but in this case exhaustion trumped jealousy. Besides, the past is the past, and she feels more secure now that we've got engaged. As soon as Quebec legalizes lesbian marriages, we're tying the knot.

ANNE Strange. Last time we met, you criticized my recommendation to legalize gay marriages on the grounds that gays do not see themselves as pursuing the same goods as heterosexuals. But now you seem to think of marriage as an expression of commitment and loyalty, which is precisely how heterosexuals look at marriage.

LOUISE First of all, I said that it is *often* not true that gays see themselves as pursuing the same goods as heterosexuals. This leaves open the possibility that sometimes gays do see themselves as pursuing the same goods as heterosexuals. In my case, I view the family as a sphere of love and care between people committed to each other, but other gays do not see themselves as pursuing the goods of intimacy and loyalty. Secondly, I noted that heterosexuals are committed to the family for a whole host of reasons, so you can't just pick out one aspect of the heterosexual commitment to the family, and argue that since that aspect can also apply to homosexuals, therefore heterosexuals should endorse gay marriages.

ANNE With respect to your first point, the fact remains, as I noted in my thesis (p. 181), that an increasing number of gays do seem to be coupling into family-type cells characterized by intimacy, affection, unconditional acceptance, and loyalty, which helps to explain why many gays are campaigning for the legalization of gay marriages. Gays want the self-respect that comes with public recognition of their attempts at establishing families, but of course this issue need not concern the minority, heterosexual or homosexual, who do not see themselves as pursuing the goods of intimacy and loyalty . . . [*short pause*] . . . Nor am I convinced by your second argument. You claim that heterosexuals value the family not just because the family is viewed as a sphere of love and care between people committed to each other, but none of the alternative reasons you mentioned seem nearly as central as that one. How many people value the family because it unifies sexuality and reproduction? This sort of reasoning might appeal to government planners and anthropologists, but no one would think of the worth of their own marriage in such terms. Do heterosexuals really believe that the family is especially valuable because children have a genetic as well as a social bond with their care-givers? Few would deny that families with adopted kids can be just as 'valuable' as families with biological ties to their children, certainly not to the point of withholding legal recognition of such families. You also suggested that heterosexuals value the heterosexual family because it is endorsed by the Bible. As you well know, very few of us think like that anymore, and besides even Christian theologians don't endorse the marriage alliance for that reason[1] . . . So while I have no evidence off-hand to back up my claim, it does seem to me that heterosexuals value the family first and foremost because it's viewed as a sphere of love and care between people committed to each other, and that if people really thought about it, they would realize that it's arbitrary to deny it to gay couples.[2]

LOUISE I'm not too sure what you mean by 'first and foremost', as opposed to a secondary reason. This goes back to my earlier point about your confusing use of the term 'deepest shared understandings'. You provided no criteria for distinguishing between 'deep' and 'shallow' understandings.

ANNE [*pause*] I didn't think we'd immediately launch into the subject of my thesis again, but since we've started, let me tell you what's been on my mind for some time now. I appreciated the detailed criticisms you made of my thesis, but I realize now that I may have been suffering from what scientists have called a 'post-lunch dip', a physiological response whereby one's critical faculties are somewhat dulled after a big meal. I accepted without reply many of your criticisms, but I subsequently realized that I should have . . .

LOUISE [*interrupting*] Fine, fine. Do you mind addressing the substance of my argument? I was saying that you didn't provide criteria for distinguishing 'deep' from 'shallow' understandings.

ANNE Well, we talked about three criteria last time, and only the last one makes sense to me. You began with the idea that 'deep' understandings might mean historical depth, discounting that criterion because it won't provide grounds for criticizing patriarchy. I agree with your point, and I'd like to support it further by referring you back to my discussion of health care in the USA, where I emphasized, following Walzer, that it's the present-day appreciation of the importance of medical care in the USA which would justify the creation of a national health service (p. 58). It wouldn't have been appropriate to enforce the idea of a medical profession that's to treat patients in proportion to their physical illness in times when the chance for a long and healthy life wasn't a socially recognized need (Act II n. 28), so what matters is the contemporary interpretation of a social practice. Incidentally, I predicted that one can expect change on this front (p. 61), a prediction which seems to be coming true. Even George Bush felt the need to propose a health-care plan for the middle class and the poor.[3]

LOUISE Actually, it's hard to know whether it's moral outrage at the fact that close to 40 million Americans can't afford decent health care which has made health care a pressing political issue,[4] or if it's simply because the American health-care system has become an unbearable burden on the American economy.[5]

ANNE Perhaps, but efforts to reduce costs without addressing the issue of the uninsured won't be tolerated, whereas efforts to provide minimally decent care for all that do not decrease costs might well be, which suggests that it's the moral issue which matters most in the final analysis . . . [*short pause*] . . . Going back to this issue of distinguishing between 'deep' and 'shallow' understandings, you also mentioned the idea that 'deep' understandings are those that lie deepest in one's personality. But I said in my thesis that we shouldn't take seriously the slaveholder's grandson who admits to his wife that he 'wishes for the old days' (p. 63), so we should remove that criterion from contention. We're left, then, with the third suggested criterion: deepest understandings are those beliefs that we can consciously articulate and rationally endorse as our guiding principles, a criterion which I endorse. I pointed out last time that 'it is important that men no longer publicly affirm patriarchal beliefs', and you'll recall that I also provided several examples to show that 'shallow' understandings are those that can't be said in the open—in Congress, Parliament, or the letter pages of a newspaper (p. 64).

LOUISE I'm glad to hear that, but as I said earlier, this raises a deep conflict in your argument. You can't both say that our deepest understandings are those that we articulate and consciously affirm *and* say that our deepest identity and goals are those which structure our being in the world but which resist articulation.

ANNE That sounded convincing when I first heard it, but I'm not so sure anymore. It's true, I did say that constitutive communities provide a largely background way of being in the world, with the implication that it's not possible to stand apart from those communities so as to subject them to evaluation and possible rejection (p. 95). And yes, I also pointed to the relative unimportance of beliefs in determining crucial features of our identity, meaning that we are who we are largely because of unselfconsciously followed behaviours stamped in at a very early age, like the 3-month-old distinctively Japanese baby (pp. 161–3). With respect to the 'female community', if you will, this would mean that I can't really be clear about 'what it means to be a woman' and subject this feature of my identity to willed rejection. But why should that conflict with the point that we've come to reject the various reasons why women should assume inferior roles in society to men? Can I not both feel that femininity is something deep inside me, not open to willed rejection, *and* reject the idea that women are somehow biologically endowed to do dishes and change diapers? I do experience my life as bound up with the good of the female community for now and the foreseeable future, but why should that prevent me from joining the 'fight to recognize and reform the many ways in which we were socialized to be submissive or passive'?

LOUISE [*losing patience*] You missed my point. If we fight to recognize and reform the many ways in which we were socialized to be submissive or passive, this involves 'questioning our entire repertoire of learned behaviours', so that there'd be nothing left of 'femininity' after the job is done. This is what we have to do to attack patriarchy. Either we can articulate most, if not all, of 'what it means to be a woman', so as to achieve sexual equality, or else we resign ourselves to accepting that most of what it means to be a woman lies at the level of unconscious behaviour, and we forsake the goal of sexual equality. We can't have it both ways.

ANNE This is where we part company. While I can't provide any general criteria for distinguishing between the 'essence' of a constitutive community and relevant parts which need to be articulated at a certain point in time to achieve concrete political objectives, I do think that there's much more to being a woman than acting and thinking in a submissive way, just as there's more to being a black than taking orders from a white master.

LOUISE I can neither prove nor disprove what you're implying about a latent feminine 'essence', but it doesn't really matter. Your 'communitarian feminism' would make no difference at the political level, so you might as well join the liberal feminist camp.

ANNE Actually, there is a difference. Whereas communitarians would side with feminists who consider the problem to be the devaluation of women's qualities and activities by a male-dominated culture, liberal feminists see the gender system itself as the problem, aiming for nothing less than an androgynous society where sex differences no longer exist,[6] a society where one's sex would have no more relevance than one's eye colour or the length of one's toes.[7] The liberal goal, in my opinion, is neither feasible nor desirable.[8] It's not feasible because, let me repeat, being a woman provides a largely background way of being in the world. I can try to reject those values and social practices which 'keep us down', but I couldn't entirely escape the grip of my femininity. At the end of the day, I'll still experience my life as bound up with the good of the female community, I'll identify with Mary Wollstonecraft and Harriet Taylor in a way that, say, John Rawls wouldn't, my best friends will likely be women, and so on. Even in a society completely free from sexual discrimination, I wouldn't

expect an equal distribution of men and women at Formula One car-racing
extravaganzas, or even in your own field of social work, for that matter.[9]

LOUISE So what you're saying is that we should try to escape patriarchy on the
grounds that we've come to reject patriarchal beliefs justifying the subordination of women, but that there's more to being a woman than the subordination
built into the social construction of femininity, much of which lies at the level
of unconscious behaviour, and so it would be foolish even to imagine the possibility of ridding ourselves of the entire repertoire of learned feminine values
and behaviours.

ANNE Well spoken, but I haven't said anything about the desirability issue . . .

LOUISE [*interrupting*] You need not. Last time we spoke, I acknowledged that it is
profoundly damaging to have to fight against our femininity.

ANNE But the damage is far worse than what you suggested. Quite simply, it
means losing touch with the deepest sources of one's being, the very core of
one's self. I'll refer you to the example of Simone de Beauvoir. Thinking that
the oppression of women could be overcome only by shunning everything associated with femininity, de Beauvoir deliberately avoided the 'burdens' of marriage and motherhood. She spent most of her time in the company of men,
and looked forward to a future society without feminine values and social practices, women having been completely assimilated into the world of men. Yet de
Beauvoir's own intellectual interests—women and the elderly—and the com-
passionate way she dealt with those subjects, suggest that she was drawing on
caring social values deep inside her, the same social values largely sustained by
women in human history but which she so forcefully renounced at the conscious level.[10]

LOUISE Overlooking that armchair psychoanalysis of yours, I'd like to point out
that contemporary feminists of a liberal persuasion aim for a society where
one's sex plays no role in determining which values and life-projects one
adopts, and not for a future that completely rejects hitherto 'feminine' social
values. More importantly, the damage that learned behaviours can cause to
women's sense of well-being, even when those learned behaviours haven't broken down, is far greater than the damage caused by a de Beauvoir-type attempt
at escape from 'feminine' socialization. I made this point last time we spoke,
but you didn't provide a satisfactory answer.

ANNE Well, I've had some time to mull over this issue, and I think that my
answer will turn on how it is that we interpret this idea of learned behaviours
not having broken down. If we interpret it to mean that both men and women
really accept a patriarchal social system, I'm not too sure how we can say that
women are somehow 'damaged' by the system . . .

LOUISE [*raises voice*] Are you saying that if women don't protest, we can assume
that they partake of patriarchal 'shared understandings', so patriarchy can be a
just social system? But even if patriarchal understandings appear to be shared,
in the sense that there seems to be public agreement that principles about

rights and equality shouldn't be extended to women, those understandings are often the outcome of the domination of men over women, the latter being silenced or rendered 'incoherent' by the former. Those to whom gender structures deny education are far less likely to acquire the tools needed to express themselves in ways that would be publicly recognized.[11]

ANNE I agree with that, and we should be very wary of assuming that people are satisfied if no audible sounds of protest are heard.[12] In fact, it's probably safer assuming the opposite until we have evidence to the contrary. Even in what appear to be the most patriarchal of societies, there have been stirrings of protest. You may have read recently that researchers have uncovered hundreds of poems, stories, and letters written over the past thousand years in a unique script used by Chinese women to record their emotions and share them with female friends. One theme shines through many of the writings—unhappiness with their lot in China's male-controlled society.[13] This stunning discovery shows two things: (1) we shouldn't assume that people denied access to formal structures of education are necessarily inarticulate, and (2) my point that women aren't damaged by a system where both men and women really accept patriarchy, though theoretically valid, is probably meaningless in practice, because it's questionable whether there ever has been such a society.

LOUISE It's nice to see you making such an effort to stay within the progressive camp, but the price you pay is inconsistency. Earlier you said that shared understandings are those that we can articulate and consciously affirm, which means that we should look at what's being said in public, but now you're suggesting that we should turn to what people do in secret to find out how they really think.

ANNE In liberal democracies, people generally support the 'system of public discourse', if you will—what's being said in newspapers, universities, houses of government, and so on, does seem to reflect to an important extent what people really think, so it's important to look at what's being publicly affirmed or criticized. In ancient China, by contrast, women were obviously dissatisfied with the 'system of public discourse', inventing their own secret script as a means to express themselves. Once Chinese women gained the opportunity to study in schools where standard writing was taught, the use of the script declined,[14] presumably because they felt relatively satisfied with 'mainstream' channels of discourse.

LOUISE [*pause*] Forgetting about China for a while, I'm not so sure that in our own culture there are feminist 'shared understandings', even at the level of public discourse. In fact, there are fundamental disagreements not only between men and women on the subject of gender in our society, but even within the ranks of the oppressed. Anti-feminist women, far from rejecting as unjust traditional views on the subordinate role of women, regard the economic dependence of women and the dominance of the world outside the home by men as natural and inevitable. Given such opposite poles of opinion about the very nature of sexual difference and the appropriate social repercussions, how would you adjudicate between such widely disparate viewpoints?[15] This goes back to what I was saying last time about your having given the entire game away by conceding that the reformer is taking sides, as opposed to claiming that her interpretation captures the 'deepest', 'most authentic' morality of her people. That is precisely what the liberal claims—political argument involves appealing to ideas about justice that can be found within the community, but justice cannot be defined in terms of 'congruence' with a community's deepest understandings or deepest self-image, as it's possible that something relatively shallow in our society is more just, and should replace the deeper practice or belief.

ANNE Actually, liberals normally claim much more than that, when they apply their ideas about human rights to certain countries regardless of the traditions in those countries, for example. Moreover, why should liberals accept the point 'that people can only criticize social practices by drawing on the ideas about justice they have learned in their community', for that would imply that someone can't go abroad, pick up some new ideas about justice, and criticize social practices by drawing on those new ideas. Perhaps liberals and communitarians will dispute the circumstances in which this ought to be done, the liberal critic not ruling out principled commitment to 'foreign' ideas totally antithetical to the habits and traditions found within her community, but both sides will surely want to grant the possibility of drawing on ideas about justice that can be found outside the community . . . [*short pause*] . . . But to address your point about how to adjudicate between conflicting understandings, I did suggest one way in my thesis that I should have brought up last time we spoke. In fact, this alternative holds a lot of promise, I believe—we can move beyond the now stale Walzer/Dworkin dispute about justice . . .

LOUISE Please refresh my memory.

ANNE I'm referring to 'transition arguments', ones that compare systems of thought and/or morality with each other (see the end of Act II). A morality can be superior to another on this view if one can demonstrate progress from position X to position Y but not the other way around. So one can show how women gain by moving from a patriarchal system to one that provides women with equal power—they can develop their talents in the spheres of work and government, they wouldn't be so vulnerable to domestic violence and sexual assault, and so on—whereas one would be hard pressed to construct a plausible narrative of progress the other way around.[16]

LOUISE I'm not too sure that such 'narratives' would ever convince anti-feminists . . . [*feeling tired*] . . . Perhaps we can continue this conversation another time. It's been a long trip, and . . .

ANNE [*interrupting*] We're nearly finished. Let me respond to what you said about my policy recommendations, which you criticized for being either too tame or too strong, depending on which 'communitarian' justification is invoked. I've already dealt with your point that my recommendations are too strong in terms of my Walzerian theory of shared meanings because there is supposedly no evidence that our shared understandings support gay rights or feminist reforms of the family. With respect to the legalization of gay marriages, I argued that most of us value the family because we see it first and foremost as a sphere of love and care between people committed to each other, with the implication that it would be unjust to deny it to homosexuals. You mentioned some other reasons to value the family that do not apply to gay couples, but those reasons sounded either too cold, counter-intuitive, or outdated . . . For feminist reforms of the family, I pointed to a public anti-patriarchal consensus in liberal democracies as significant evidence. As you persisted in claiming that there's fundamental disagreement on this point, I suggested transition arguments showing that feminism represents a gain in understanding as a way out . . . [*Louise yawns*] . . . Now let me deal with your argument that my recommendations are rather tame in light of my ontological claim that it is pointless and damaging to try to escape the grip of one's constitutive communities. You're entirely right that one could imagine more radical proposals compatible with my ontological argument, but I'm not too sure what you mean when you say that I 'should follow the logic of that argument to its conclusion'. I repeatedly noted in my thesis that ontological issues and advocacy issues are distinct in the sense that taking a position on one does not force your hand on the other, that ontology can do no more than structure the field of moral and political possibilities in a more perspicuous way (see e.g. Act I n. 14), so you can't criticize me for not having endorsed a certain political implication compatible with the stand I took at the ontological level. Moreover, why should I endorse the most radical imaginable proposals involving the greatest amount of state coercion if less radical proposals will do?

LOUISE My point was that you've given no reason why the state *should* avoid the greatest amount of coercion.

ANNE Of course there are reasons, such as the fact that overwhelming state coercion would in all likelihood not serve the communitarian aim of fostering deeper communal attachments, but I didn't feel there was a need to dwell on this issue because basic civil and political liberties are taken as self-evident truths in liberal democracies, not in need of any justification.[17] Perhaps if I thought that few have developed 'the capacity to stand back from and evaluate the benefits of staying in their original community', and that this was a serious problem, I would have tried to give reasons why the state shouldn't prevent people from leaving their community. But more serious in my opinion is that few have the opportunity to nurture and sustain the deeply felt bonds to the various communities that constitute their identity, and it is to respond to the loss of community and the consequent broadly felt sense of social malaise in the West[18] that I proposed several policies which might foster a greater sense of community. I didn't even consider excessively coercive measures that would have had no chance of being taken seriously, but can I really be blamed for that? . . . [*short pause*] . . . By the way, you said that you find my recommendations 'plausible', but there's no way you could endorse, say, mandatory national service 'designed to give young people opportunities to discover the value of participating in constitutive communities' on liberal grounds. Liberal neutrality, as you know, rules out the justification of policies by an appeal to the supposed superiority of a certain way of life. The state should not favour, say, Mother Teresa over 'someone whose only pleasure is to count blades of grass in various geometrically shaped areas such as park squares and well-trimmed lawns',[19] nor should it subsidize theatre instead of professional wrestling on the grounds that theatre is a more valuable activity.[20] Given that I explicitly justified the policy of mandatory national service by appealing to the value of participating in constitutive communities, how can you endorse that policy without abandoning the idea of liberal neutrality?

LOUISE Well, there might be more neutral ways of justifying that policy such as . . .

ANNE [*interrupting*] But my point is that liberal neutrality will rule out many proposals meant to respond to this loss of community, and if it's not this one, it'll be others. You're going to have to accept that it's necessary to cheat a little on state neutrality—which need not entail trampling upon basic civil liberties—if you want to join the conversation about practical ways of implementing communitarian aims. And if social malaise won't force you to consider 'non-neutral' measures, economic considerations will. One hears a lot these days about the West's competitive deterioration in the world economy compared to the more group-oriented societies of East Asia,[21] and the East's competitive superiority is leading many in the West to question the absolute primacy of individual rights over the common purposes furnished by an active, planning state. Already we're learning from the East about the need for a national industrial strategy laid down in collaboration with business and labour, for business alliances which provide the security and stability necessary for risk-taking and long-term investment, and for more teamwork and loyalty within companies,[22] just to name a few of the measures aimed at improving economic productivity.

LOUISE Liberal neutrality does not preclude any of the measures which you've just mentioned.

ANNE Perhaps. But the governments of Japan, Singapore, Taiwan, and South Korea have stressed group identity and certain communal values thought to underlie economic success, implementing paternalistic measures which would have been ruled out of court by true blue liberals. Just to take some Singapore examples: the government gives housing benefits to those who care for their elderly parents, a policy justified by an appeal to the traditional Asian family-support system; worried about the large number of unmarried female graduates, the government's 'Social Development Unit' arranges for single university graduates to meet on subsidized 'romantic cruises'; the government gives priority for public housing to those who want to remain in the neighbourhood in which they already live so as to foster the sense of belonging to a community. Now I say that we should look at such policies and perhaps learn from them, rather than rejecting them a priori because they're justified by an appeal to a certain conception of the good.

LOUISE You said that we can 'cheat a little on state neutrality' without trampling upon basic liberties. When I went through Singapore customs this morning, a customs officer confiscated my copy of *Cosmopolitan* on the grounds that I was bringing the 'wrong values' into Singapore. I was outraged, and . . .

ANNE [*interrupting, as though surprised*] You read *Cosmopolitan*, that heterosexist magazine that is basically about how women should stay sexually attractive for their man! I wouldn't have thought that was your sort of reading material . . .

LOUISE [*blushes*] Well, I wouldn't normally, but I was interested by an article about women and business . . . In any case, my point was that banning *Cosmopolitan* is not exactly what you'd expect of a government committed to protecting basic liberties.

ANNE I said *need* not trample upon basic liberties. Allowing *Cosmopolitan* to circulate freely will not deal a fatal blow to Singapore's 'traditional family values', in my opinion.

LOUISE [*recovering her courage*] You're right—it may in fact reinforce them, if one such value is the view that women exist to serve men's needs. None the less, one can infer certain things about a state which bans *Cosmopolitan* on the (mistaken) assumption that it threatens 'traditional family values'. I doubt that the government offers subsidized 'romantic cruises' to lesbian couples, for example. And I don't even want to think about what this means for my plans of opening up a women's bookstore in Singapore . . .

ANNE We'll talk about that later. For the moment, I'm arguing that it might be worth looking at certain policies which you might not otherwise have considered had you dogmatically insisted on liberal neutrality.

LOUISE [*pause*] In any event, I still haven't heard anything which would make me reject the liberal view that people have an interest in being able to question and revise their plan of life. As I said last time, you would have to show that people have been harmed, rather than benefited, by having the opportunity to stand back and evaluate their way of life.

ANNE Some people have in fact been harmed by having the opportunity to learn about other ways of life, a pre-condition for evaluating one's own. The aboriginal people of the Americas, for example, were probably harmed by their encounter with the choices of the modern world (Act IV n. 37).

LOUISE Well, you can't undo history. Certainly for the large majority of people today, they've benefited by having the opportunity to stand back and evaluate their way of life.

ANNE Don't be so sure. You see, there's a crucial difference between us. Whereas you want to found our social and political system on the principle that we should have the opportunity to stand back and evaluate our way of life, and you would strike down any practices or policies which conflict with what flows from that principle, I say that we have other interests, such as the need to nurture our communal attachments, which matter just as much, if not more, than your favoured principle. And there's no special reason to give ultimate priority to what flows from your principle in cases of conflict, particularly when basic liberties are not involved. If your principle means that we can't compel an 18-year-old 'grass counter' to do community work for a year, you'll have a hard time persuading the communitarian to join your side.

LOUISE Which principle you would give priority to, I guess, would depend on what you'd consider to be the most serious problem facing our times. Liberals believe that recognition of the importance of reflection is a great historical accomplishment, and we fear that various forces in society are endangering that historical accomplishment. Measures which deal with this problem ought to have priority.[23]

ANNE That's a pretty eccentric opinion, I have to say, nearly as eccentric as J. S. Mill's belief that the dearth of eccentrics was the chief danger of his time.[24] Many of us think that the 'chief danger' of our time is the social malaise, and possibly the economic decline, traceable ultimately to the loss of community, and consequently that's what the government ought first and foremost to be dealing with, rather than worrying about the right of the 'grass counter' or the professional wrestling fan to make use of her leisure time as she sees fit . . . Louise? Louise?

[Louise has fallen asleep, finally having succumbed to the effects of jetlag. *Lights dim*]

Notes

1. St Augustine, for example, writes that the marriage alliance should be 'contracted for the purpose of having children' (*Confessions*, trans. R. S. Pine-Coffin (London: Penguin Books, 1961), 72).

2. Louise notes parenthetically that if heterosexuals view the family as a sphere of love and care between people committed to each other, it would also be arbitrary to deny it to polygamous relationships. But the everyday conception of the good of marriage involves loyalty and commitment as well as love, and such notions lose a lot of their meaning when they are applied in the context of polygamous relationships. We tend to praise and admire couples engaged in lasting relationships, but would we attend the golden anniversary of a man with three wives (or a woman with three husbands)?

3. See Robert Pear, 'Why Bush Joined the Health-Care Debate, and Why He had to Fudge the Details', *International Herald Tribune* (8–9 Feb. 1992), 5. Pear comments that Bush joined the debate because it has become politically necessary for candidates to discuss health care in general, but that he had to

fudge the details because 'it is virtually impossible for them to make specific proposals without offending somebody'. None the less, the fact that Bush finally joined the national debate on overhauling the health-care system 'increases the chances that comprehensive health legislation will be enacted before long' (ibid.), chances already increased when the American Medical Association, a group notorious for its fierce opposition to all social reform in medicine, reversed course in May 1991 by endorsing a proposal which calls for a combination of government and business to provide all Americans with affordable coverage (see Philip Hilts, 'Demands to Fix U.S. Health Care Reach a Crescendo', *The New York Times* (19 May 1991), sect. 4, p. 1, and the *Montreal Gazette* editorial, 'U.S. Doctors See the Light' (17 May 1991), p. B2).

4. Health care has been brought to the centre of America's political stage ever since Democrat Harris Wofford defeated heavily favoured Republican Dick Thornburgh in a race for the US Senate last year. Wofford made advocacy of a national health insurance plan a central plank of his campaign (see Michael Prouse, 'Reform of US Health-Care System becomes Pressing Issue', *The Straits Times* (28 Nov. 1991), 25).

5. The share of the USA's gross national product absorbed by health care has more than doubled to 13% in the past three decades. This compares with 8–9% in other rich countries, including Canada where the government uses tax money to provide medical care to everyone at no charge. According to the US General Accounting Office (GAO), a Canadian-style national health pro-gramme would save $67 billion on bureaucracy in the first year alone (by eliminating the enormous overhead of insurance companies and relieving doctors and hospitals of most billing-related paperwork) and hold down increases through enforceable budgetary limits. Charles Bowsher, head of the non-partisan GAO, told Congress that 'The key lesson of the Canadian experience is that it is possible to have universal coverage of health care without incurring additional costs, if reform also includes simplification of the payment system and effective expenditure control' (see the article 'US Urged to Switch Health Systems', *Montreal Gazette* (5 June 1991), p. A8).

6. For a clear account of this division between contemporary feminists, see Iris Marion Young, 'Humanism, Gynocentrism, and Feminist Politics', *Hypatia: a Journal of Feminist Philosophy*, 3 (1985).

7. In the same vein, Susan Moller Okin writes: 'A just future would be one without gender. In its social structures and practices, one's sex would have no more relevance than one's eye color or the length of one's toes' (*Justice, Gender, and the Family* (New York: Basic Books, 1989), 181). It is difficult to imagine a dance-hall, even in a 'just future', where one's sex has no more relevance than the length of one's toes!

8. Prior to the 'liberal goal', a future without gender, gender hierarchy must of course be challenged (an aim which 'communitarian feminists' also endorse).

But Drucilla Cornell argues that striving to erase sexual difference (on the assumption that women are victims and only victims under the current gender system) cannot even challenge gender hierarchy because this stance reflects the very 'sexual shame' of women's 'sex' that keeps the feminine from being valued. Instead, Cornell advocates a programme of 'equivalent rights' which legally insists that the specificity of feminine sexual difference be valued (see her 'Sexual Difference: A Critique of MacKinnon's *Toward a Feminist Theory of the State*', *Yale Law Journal*, 100: 17 (May 1991), 2,250, 2,257.

For an account of the debate in feminist jurisprudence between 'rights theorists' who insist on the equal treatment of all individuals and 'difference theorists' who assert that the differences between men and women call for special treatment for women, see Deborah Rhode's *Justice and Gender* (Cambridge, Mass.: Harvard University Press, 1989).

9. A similar point can be made with respect to a society completely free from racial discrimination. While a liberal's vision of a 'just future' would mean a society where the various ethnic groups are randomly distributed within the various positions in society (one's race would have no more relevance than the length of one's toes), the communitarian would expect the historical experience of the various groups to have a significant influence in terms of which vocations individuals choose to pursue (or 'slip into'). A society X that doesn't discriminate against citizens of Chinese ancestry will still have a greater than average proportion of Chinese-X individuals in the restaurant business, given the special importance of food in Chinese culture.

10. A point also made by Michael Walzer in *The Company of Critics* (New York: Basic Books, 1988), 169.

11. Susan Moller Okin puts forward these arguments in *Justice, Gender, and the Family*, 66–7, 112.

12. Susan Moller Okin argues that the existence of disagreements between oppressors and oppressed undermines Walzer's theory of shared understandings: 'Contrary to Walzer's theory of shared understandings, in fact, oppressors and oppressed—when the voice of the latter can be heard at all—often disagree fundamentally' (ibid. 67). But Walzer never claimed that the oppressed necessarily accept the understandings of the oppressors, and he explicitly argues that slaves and masters in actual fact 'do not inhabit a world of shared meanings' (*Spheres of Justice* (Oxford: Basil Blackwell, 1983), 250 n.), a point which is probably also true of men and women in a patriarchal system. Moreover, the presence of disagreements between oppressors and oppressed does not mean that we should necessarily discard Walzer's theory, as there may still be shared meanings (latent or realized) bearing on some practices.

13. See the article 'Chinese Women Turned to Secret Script', *Montreal Gazette* (9 Oct. 1991), p. A1.

14. Ibid.
15. Susan Moller Okin makes these points in *Justice, Gender, and the Family*, 67–8.
16. Susan Moller Okin alludes to this sort of argument when she notes that the 'challenge of feminism' presents us with 'one of the most serious epistemological crises of our time' (ibid. 46). Charles Taylor, assuming that the epistemological crisis has been successfully resolved (at least at the level of theory), argues that feminist insights represent an 'epistemic gain' in modern moral growth (see his 'Comments and Replies', *Inquiry: An Interdisciplinary Journal of Philosophy*, 34: 2 (June 1991), 240). The full argument—one that provides a solution to this epistemological crisis by the invention or discovery of new concepts and the framing of new types of theory which meets MacIntyre's three requirements (see *Whose Justice? Which Rationality?* (London: Duckworth, 1988), 362), and shows that the crisis cannot be resolved by a return to patriarchy—still needs to be fleshed out.
17. Paradoxically, attempts to justify taken-for-granted freedoms might serve to undermine those freedoms. As it is, freedom of religion works pretty well in most liberal democracies, and there doesn't appear to be a need to 'fix what ain't broken'. Were Louise to tell people that their attachment to the value of freedom of religion rests on a distinction between true and false gods, militant atheists (for whom all gods are false) might well reconsider their (not well-thought-through) attachment to freedom for religion. Moreover, fundamentalists convinced of the truth of their religion might come to the conclusion that their religion is best served by prohibiting other religions and using state power for the cause of their own religion, rather than fighting for the freedom 'to hear the proponents of other religions'. Louise's argument for freedom of religion, then, will be unlikely to persuade those who do not already hold the belief that no religious (or atheist) dogma can reasonably be held with certainty (a belief already characteristic of a liberal outlook), and might well cause people who fall outside of that category but who none the less (implicitly, without having thought about it) uphold freedom of religion to jettison the latter value. In the same vein, Brian Barry argues that a person holding the view that religious teachings should not be matters of public policy must already have swallowed a large dose of liberalism (anyone holding their religious beliefs as though they were merely opinions that they should not seek to impose on anybody else through the machinery of the state must already have a sceptical attitude towards those beliefs), and that liberals would do better trying to discredit the beliefs of non-liberals rather than trying to persuade them to accept the principle of neutrality (see his 'How not to Defend Liberal Institutions', *British Journal of Political Science*, 20: 1 (Jan. 1990), 9–11, 14).
18. Similarly, Francis Fukuyama attributes the 'broadly felt sense of social malaise in the US and other Western societies today [to] the loss of community from

the breakdown of the family, the absence of any meaningful sense of local attachment and the fragmentation of national purpose' (see his article 'Soft Authoritarianism of Asia Challenges Western Democracy', *New Perspectives Quarterly* (Spring 1992)). Fukuyama differs from De la Patrie, however, in that he interprets the 'loss of community' to mean the absence of attachments to communities, whereas De la Patrie interprets this idea to mean the absence of (government-provided, in some cases) opportunities to act on deeply felt attachments to communities.

19. John Rawls's 'fanciful case' of a rational plan that establishes the good for a person, about which the state presumably ought to be non-judgmental (from *A Theory of Justice* (Cambridge, Mass.: The Belknap Press of Harvard University Press), 432–3).

20. Will Kymlicka's example in his *Contemporary Political Philosophy: An Introduction* (Oxford: Clarendon Press, 1990), 201. It follows from this example that liberals should object to recent measures by the British government to prop up the deficit-ridden Royal Shakespeare Company (see 'Shot in the Arm for UK Arts', *The Straits Times* (10 Nov. 1991), 8) even if only one UK citizen claims that professional wrestling is a more valuable activity than Shakespearean drama, and hence that it's unjust to subsidize theatre instead of wrestling.

21. The recent issue of *New Perspectives Quarterly* (Winter 1992) entitled 'Looking East: The Confucian Challenge to Western Liberalism' focuses on the challenge that the 'communitarian capitalism of East Asia' poses to Western liberal democracies.

22. A panel appointed by President Bush and Congress in 1988 has recently presented a report which calls for a new government agency to assess the future of key industries, monitor their foreign competitors, and develop policies to help critical industries stay competitive; large US companies such as IBM and Ford are trying to regain their strength by borrowing from Japan's *keiretsu* (business groups) enterprise model (see 'Learning from Japan', *Business Week* (27 Jan. 1992), 38–44); Eastman Kodak's Chemical Co. has recently scrapped the individual merit system in favour of a reward system based on teamwork (see the *New York Times* article, 'US Firms Trying to Get More out of Workers; Approval Systems being Revamped to Achieve this', repr. in *The Sunday Times* (Singapore) (26 Jan. 1992), 12).

23. Louise didn't say last time that she considers the threat to reflective processes to be 'the most serious problem facing our times', but she would have to hold that view in order to defend the (liberal) claim that policies which flow from our interest in having the capacity and opportunity to stand back and evaluate our way of life should trump other policies in cases of conflict.

24. See John Stuart Mill, 'On Liberty', in *Three Essays* (Oxford: Oxford University Press, 1975), 83.

Bibliography

ACKERMAN, BRUCE, *Social Justice in the Liberal State* (New Haven, Conn.: Yale University Press, 1981).

ANDERSON, BENEDICT, *Imagined Communities* (London: Verso, 1983).

ANDERSON, KEN; PICCONE, PAUL; SIEGEL, FRED; and TAVES, MICHAEL, 'Roundtable on Communitarianism', *Telos* (Summer 1988).

ANNAS, JULIA, *An Introduction to Plato's Republic* (Oxford: Clarendon Press, 1981).

—— 'MacIntyre on Traditions', *Philosophy and Public Affairs* (Fall 1989).

ARENDT, HANNAH, 'On Revolution', in Michael Sandel, ed., *Liberalism and its Critics* (Oxford: Basil Blackwell, 1984).

AUGUSTINE, ST, *Confessions*, trans. R. S. Pine-Coffin (London: Penguin Books, 1961).

AVINERI, SHLOMO, and DE-SHALIT, AVNER, eds., *Communitarianism and Individualism* (Oxford: Oxford University Press, 1992).

BAILEY, MICHAEL, and PILLARD, RICHARD, 'Homosexuality Seems to be Innate', *International Herald Tribune* (19 Dec. 1991).

BAIRD, ROBERT, and ROSENBAUM, STUART, eds., *Euthanasia: The Moral Issues* (Buffalo, NY: Prometheus Books, 1989).

BALFOUR, MICHAEL, *Withstanding Hitler in Germany: 1933–1945* (London: Routledge, 1988).

BARBER, BENJAMIN, *Strong Democracy: Participatory Politics for a New Age* (Berkeley, Calif.: University of California Press, 1984).

—— *The Conquest of Politics* (Princeton: Princeton University Press, 1988).

BARRY, BRIAN, 'How not to Defend Liberal Institutions', *British Journal of Political Science* (Jan. 1990).

—— Review of Michael Walzer's *Interpretation and Social Criticism* and *The Company of Critics*, *Philosophy and Public Affairs* (Fall 1990).

BBC2, 'The Hostages Speak', 20 Aug. 1990, 8.10 p.m.

BÉGIN, MONIQUE, *Medicine: Canada's Right to Health*, trans. David Hamel and Lucille Nelson (Toronto: Optimum Publishing International, 1988).

BELLAH, ROBERT; MADSEN, RICHARD; SULLIVAN, WILLIAM; SWIDLER, ANN; and TIPTON, STEVEN, *Habits of the Heart* (Berkeley, Calif.: University of California Press, 1985).

BERLIN, ISAIAH, 'Two Concepts of Nationalism: An Interview with Isaiah Berlin', *New York Review of Books* (21 Nov. 1991).

BETTELHEIM, BRUNO, *The Children of the Dream* (London: Thames and Hudson, 1969).

BLITZ, MARK, *Heidegger's Being and Time and the Possibility of Political Philosophy* (London: Cornell University Press, 1981).

BLOOM, ALLAN, *The Closing of the American Mind* (New York: Simon and Schuster, 1987).

BLOOR, DAVID, *Wittgenstein: A Social Theory of Knowledge* (London: Macmillan, 1983).

BONAVIA, DAVID, *The Chinese* (London: Penguin Books, 1989).

BOSWELL, JOHN, 'Gay History', *Atlantic Monthly* (Feb. 1989).

BOTSFORD, KEITH, 'Gays Go to Court to Seek Salvation', *Independent* (22 July 1989).

BROWN, DEREK, 'Mother Teresa Stands down after a Lifetime of Labour', *Guardian* (12 Apr. 1990).

BUCHANAN, ALLEN, 'Assessing the Communitarian Critique of Liberalism', *Ethics* (July 1989).

BURUMA, IAN, review of Tim Jeal's *The Boy-Man: The Life of Lord Baden-Powell*, *New York Review of Books* (15 Mar. 1990).

Business Week, 'Learning from Japan' (27 Jan. 1992).

Canada News, 'Cash Incentives for Large Families' (Aug. 1989).

CANEY, SIMON, 'Sandel's Critique of the Primacy of Justice: A Liberal Rejoinder', *British Journal of Political Science* (Oct. 1991).

—— 'Liberalism and Communitarianism: A Misconceived Debate', *Political Studies* (June 1992).

CAUDILL, W., and WEINSTEIN, H., 'Maternal and Infant Behaviour in Japan and in America', in C. S. Lavatelli and F. Stendler, eds., *Readings in Child Behaviour and Development* (New York: Harcourt and Brace, 1972).

CHANG, JUNG, *Wild Swans: Three Daughters of China* (New York: Simon and Schuster, 1991).

CHATWIN, BRUCE, *The Songlines* (London: Picador, 1987).

CHOMSKY, NOAM, *Language and Responsibility* (New York: Pantheon, 1977).

—— *Turning the Tide: U.S. Intervention in Central America and the Struggle for Peace* (Boston: South End Press, 1985).

—— and HERMAN, EDWARD, *Manufacturing Consent* (Boston: South End Press, 1988).

COHEN, JOSHUA, Review of 'Spheres of Justice', *Journal of Philosophy*, 83 (1986), repr. in Will Kymlicka, ed., *Justice in Political Philosophy* (Aldershot: Edward Elgar Ltd., 1992).

CORNELL, DRUCILLA, 'Sexual Difference: A Critique of MacKinnon's *Toward a Feminist Theory of the State*', *Yale Law Journal*, 100: 17 (May 1991).

CRANSTON, MAURICE, *Political Dialogues* (London: BBC, 1968).

CROWLEY, BRIAN LEE, *The Self, the Individual, the Community: Liberalism in the Political Thought of F. A. Hayek and Sydney and Beatrice Webb* (Oxford: Clarendon Press, 1987).

DANFORD, JOHN, *Wittgenstein and Political Philosophy* (Chicago: Chicago University Press, 1978).

DARNTON, ROBERT, 'What was Revolutionary about the French Revolution?', *New York Review of Books* (19 Jan. 1989).

DAVIS, GWYNN, 'Season of Discord', *Guardian* (15 Dec. 1989).

—— and MURCH, MERWYN, *Grounds for Divorce* (Oxford: Oxford University Press, 1988).

DE MOTT, BENJAMIN, review of Kenneth Lynn's *Hemingway, Atlantic Monthly* (July 1987).

DERRIDA, JACQUES, *De l'esprit* (Paris: Gallile, 1987).

DILLON, SAM, *Commandos: The CIA and Nicaragua's Contra Rebels* (New York: Henry Holt and Co., 1991).

DOPPELT, GERALD, 'Rawls' Kantian Ideal and the Viability of Modern Liberalism', *Inquiry* (Dec. 1988), 413–49.

—— 'Is Rawls' Kantian Liberalism Coherent and Defensible?', *Ethics*, 99 (July 1989), 815–51.

DOWNING, A. B., and SMOKER, BARBARA, eds., *Voluntary Euthanasia: Experts Debate the Right to Die* (London: Peter Owen, 1986).

DREYFUS, HUBERT, *Being-in-the-World: A Commentary on Heidegger's Being and Time, Division 1* (Cambridge, Mass.: MIT Press, 1991).

DUNN, JOHN, *Interpreting Political Responsibility* (Oxford: Polity Press, 1990).

DWORKIN, GERALD, 'Is More Choice Better than Less?', in J. Howie, ed., *Ethical Principles for Social Policy* (Carbondale, Ill.: Southern Illinois University Press, 1983).

DWORKIN, RONALD, 'Liberalism', in Stuart Hampshire, ed., *Public and Private Morality* (Cambridge: Cambridge University Press, 1978), 113–43.

—— review of Michael Walzer's *Spheres of Justice, New York Review of Books* (14 Apr. 1983).

—— *A Matter of Principle* (Cambridge, Mass.: Harvard University Press, 1985).

—— review of Peter Jenkins, *Mrs. Thatcher's Revolution: The Ending of the Socialist Era, New York Review of Books* (27 Oct. 1988).

—— 'Liberal Community', *California Law Review*, 77 (1989), 479–504.

EHRENREICH, BARBARA, 'On Feminism, Family and Community', *Dissent*, 30 (1983).

FALLOWS, JAMES, 'Japan: Playing by Different Rules', *Atlantic Monthly* (Sept. 1987).

FARIAS, VICTOR, *Heidegger et le Nazisme* (Lagrasse: Verdier, 1987).

FISH, STANLEY, *Self-Consuming Artifacts: The Experience of Seventeenth Century Literature* (Berkeley, Calif.: University of California Press, 1972).

FITZGERALD, FRANCIS, *Cities on a Hill* (London: Picador, 1987).

FRIEDMAN, MARILYN, 'Feminism and Modern Friendship: Dislocating the Community', *Ethics*, 99: 2 (1989), repr. in Shlomo Avineri and Avner de-Shalit, eds., *Communitarianism and Individualism* (Oxford: Oxford University Press, 1992).

FROST, ELLEN, *For Richer, for Poorer* (New York: Council on Foreign Relations, 1987).

FRYE, MARILYN, *The Politics of Reality: Essays in Feminist Theory* (Trumansburg: Crossing Press, 1983).

FUKUYAMA, FRANCIS, 'Soft Authoritarianism of Asia Challenges Western Democracy', *New Perspectives Quarterly* (Spring 1992).

GADAMER, HANS-GEORG, *Philosophical Hermeneutics*, trans. and ed. David E. Linge (Berkeley, Calif.: University of California Press, 1976).

GALSTON, WILLIAM, 'Community, Democracy, Philosophy: The Political Thought of Michael Walzer', *Political Theory* (Feb. 1989).

GEUSS, RAYMOND, *The Idea of a Critical Theory* (Cambridge: Cambridge University Press, 1981).

GODWIN, WILLIAM, *Enquiry Concerning Political Justice* (Oxford: Clarendon Press, 1971).

GOODIN, ROBERT, 'What is so Special about our Fellow Countrymen?', *Ethics* (July 1988).

GREENBERG, DAVID F., *The Construction of Homosexuality* (Chicago: University of Chicago Press, 1988).

GRESCHNER, DONNA, 'Feminist Concerns with the New Communitarians', in A. Hutchinson and L. Green, eds., *Law and the Community* (Toronto: Carswell, 1989).

GRIFFIN, JAMES, *Well-Being* (Oxford: Clarendon Press, 1986).

Guardian, 'Curtains for Tenant' (24 Mar. 1990).

—— 'Ryzhkov Warns of Soviet Break-up' (13 Sept. 1990).

—— 'Quickie Divorces Face Axe' (2 Nov. 1990).

GUTMANN, AMY, *Democratic Education* (Princeton, NJ: Princeton University Press, 1987).

—— 'Communitarian Critics of Liberalism', *Philosophy and Public Affairs* (Summer 1985).

HACKER, ANDREW, review of James Fallows's book *More Like Us: Making America Great Again*, *New York Review of Books* (30 Mar. 1989).

HAYMAN, RONALD, *Writing against: A Biography of Sartre* (London: Weidenfeld and Nicolson, 1986).

HEIDEGGER, MARTIN, *Being and Time*, trans. J. Macquarrie and E. Robinson (New York: Harper and Row, 1962).

—— 'A Dialogue on Language', in *On the Way to Language* (New York: Harper and Row, 1982).

HILTS, PHILIP, 'Demands to Fix U.S. Health Care Reach a Crescendo', *The New York Times* (10 May 1991).

HOCHSCHILD, JENNIFER L., *What's Fair* (Cambridge, Mass.: Harvard University Press, 1981).

HOLLANDER, XAVIERA, *The Happy Hooker* (London: Sphere Books, 1972).

HOLMES, STEPHEN, 'The Community Trap', *New Republic* (28 Nov. 1988).

—— 'The Permanent Structure of Anti-liberal Thought', in Nancy Rosenblum, ed., *Liberalism and the Moral Life* (Cambridge, Mass.: Harvard University Press, 1989).

IGNATIEFF, MICHAEL, *The Needs of Strangers* (Middlesex, England: Penguin Books, 1984).

International Financial Centres Organization of Montreal, 'Montreal: International Finance Centre', pamphlet.

International Herald Tribune, 'Heidegger and Nazism: The Dark Side of Being' (11 Dec. 1987).

JACKSON, TIM, 'Nothing Succeeds like 7-Eleven in Japan's Bizarre Retail System', *The Straits Times* (30 Oct. 1991).

JACOBS, JANE, *The Death and Life of American Cities* (New York: Random House, 1965).

KAFKA, FRANZ, *The Diaries of Franz Kafka 1910–23*, ed. Max Brod (London: Penguin Books, 1972).

—— *The Trial*, trans. D. Scott and C. Waller (London: Picador Classics, 1977).

KAPLAN, FRED, *Dickens: A Biography* (London: Hodder and Stoughton, 1988).

KEMP, PETER, 'Heidegger's Greatness and his Blindness', *Philosophy and Social Criticism* (Apr. 1989).

KENNY, ANTHONY, *The Legacy of Wittgenstein* (Oxford: Basil Blackwell, 1987).

KÜBLER-ROSS, ELIZABETH, *On Death and Dying* (London: Tavistock Publications, 1970).

KUKATHAS, CHANDRAN, and PETTIT, PHILIP, *Rawls: A Theory of Justice and its Critics* (Cambridge: Polity Press, 1990).

KULL, STEVEN, *Minds at War: Nuclear Reality and the Inner Conflicts of Defense Policymakers* (New York: Basic Books, 1988).

KYMLICKA, WILL, 'Liberalism and Communitarianism', *Canadian Journal of Philosophy*, 18 (1988).

—— 'Rawls on Teleology and Deontology', *Philosophy and Public Affairs* (Summer 1988).

—— 'Liberal Individualism and Liberal Neutrality', *Ethics* (July 1989).

—— *Liberalism, Community and Culture* (Oxford: Clarendon Press, 1989).

—— *Contemporary Political Philosophy: An Introduction* (Oxford: Clarendon Press, 1990).

—— 'The Ethics of Inarticulacy', *Inquiry* (June 1991).

—— 'Two Models of Pluralism and Tolerance', *Analyze & Kritik*, 14: 1 (1992).

LARMORE, CHARLES, *Patterns of Moral Complexity* (Cambridge: Cambridge University Press, 1987).

LASCH, CHRISTOPHER, review of John Kenneth White's *The New Politics of Old Values*, *New York Review of Books* (21 July 1988).

LEITHAUSER, BRAD, 'Iceland: A Nonesuch People', *Atlantic Monthly* (Sept. 1987).

LEPPMANN, WOLFGANG, *Rilke: A Life*, trans. Russell M. Stockman (Cambridge: Lutterworth Press, 1984).

LIPSET, SEYMOUR MARTIN, and SCHNEIDER, WILLIAM, *The Confidence Gap: Business, Labor and Government in the Public Mind* (New York: Free Press, 1983).

LUKACS, JOHN, 'In Love with Hitler', *New York Review of Books* (21 July 1988).

LUKAS, ANTHONY J., *Common Ground: A Turbulent Decade in the Lives of 3 American Families* (New York: Knopf, 1975).

LUKES, STEVEN, 'Making Sense of Moral Conflict', in Nancy Rosenblum, ed., *Liberalism and the Moral Life* (Cambridge, Mass.: Harvard University Press, 1989).

LYNN, KENNETH, *Hemingway* (New York: Simon and Schuster, 1987).

MACEDO, STEPHEN, *Liberal Virtues: Citizenship, Virtue, and Community in Liberal Constitutionalism* (Oxford: Clarendon Press, 1990).

McGILL, PETER, 'Japanese Fear "Store Wars" Threat from US', *Observer* (4 Mar. 1990).

MacINTYRE, ALASDAIR, *A Short History of Ethics* (London: Routledge, 1967).

—— *After Virtue*, 2nd edn. (Notre-Dame, Ind.: University of Notre-Dame Press, 1984).

—— 'Is Patriotism a Virtue?', Lindley Lecture, University of Kansas, 1984.

—— *Whose Justice? Which Rationality?* (London: Duckworth, 1988).

McLELLAN, DAVID, ed., *Karl Marx: Selected Writings* (Oxford: Oxford University Press, 1977).

MERNISSI, FATIMA, *Women and Islam: An Historical and Theological Inquiry* (Oxford: Blackwell, 1991).

MICHELS, ROBERT, *Political Parties* (New York: Free Press, 1962).

MILL, JOHN STUART, 'On Liberty', in *Three Essays* (Oxford: Oxford University Press, 1975).

MILLER, DAVID, 'The Ethical Significance of Nationality', *Ethics* (July 1988).

—— *Market, State and Community: Theoretical Foundations of Market Socialism* (Oxford: Clarendon Press, 1989).

—— 'Distributive Justice: What the People Think', *Ethics* (Apr. 1992).

MIZUNO, KOGEN, *Basic Buddhist Concepts*, trans. Charles Terry and Richard Gaye (Tokyo: Kosei Publishing Co., 1987).

Montreal Gazette, 'Haight-Ashbury Rejects Change in Struggle to Retain "60s" Heritage' (22 Oct. 1988).

—— 'Deficit Should be Priority: Poll' (28 Nov. 1988).

—— 'Seattle Finds High Cost to its Boom: Seeks to Limit Skyscrapers' (5 Dec. 1988).

—— 'US Doctors See the Light' (18 May 1991).

—— 'US Urged to Switch Health Systems' (5 June 1991).

—— 'Bouquets and Brickbats' (28 Sept. 1991).

—— 'Chinese Women Turned to Secret Script' (9 Oct. 1991).

Moscos, Charles, *A Call to Civic Service* (New York: Twentieth Century Fund/Free Press, 1988).

Mulhall, Stephen, 'The Theoretical Foundations of Liberalism', *European Journal of Sociology*, 28: 2 (1987).

—— *On Being in the World: Wittgenstein and Heidegger on Seeing Aspects* (London: Routledge, 1990).

—— and Swift, Adam, *Liberals and Communitarians* (Oxford: Basil Blackwell, 1992).

Nagel, Thomas, 'Locke Lectures', Oxford University, Hilary Term, 1990; published as *Equality and Partiality* (Oxford: Oxford University Press, 1991).

Neil, Patrick, and Paris, David, 'Liberalism and the Communitarian Critique: A Guide for the Perplexed', *Canadian Journal of Political Science* (Sept. 1990).

New York Times, 'Mercedes Sosa: A Voice of Hope' (9 Oct. 1988).

Okin, Susan Moller, 'Humanist Liberalism', in Nancy Rosenblum, ed., *Liberalism and the Moral Life* (Cambridge, Mass.: Harvard University Press, 1989).

—— 'Reason and Feeling in Thinking about Justice', *Ethics* (Jan. 1989).

—— *Justice, Gender, and the Family* (New York: Basic Books, 1989).

Pear, Robert, 'Why Bush Joined the Health-Care Debate, and why he had to Fudge the Details', *International Herald Tribune* (8–9 Feb. 1992).

Phillips, D. Z., and Winch, Peter, eds., *Wittgenstein: Attention to Particulars* (London: MacMillan, 1989).

Phillips, Roderick, *Putting Asunder: A History of Divorce in Western Society* (Cambridge: Cambridge University Press, 1988).

Pitkin, Hanna, *Wittgenstein and Justice* (Berkeley, Calif.: University of California Press, 1972).

Plant, Raymond, *Community and Ideology: An Essay in Applied Social Philosophy* (London: Routledge and Kegan Paul, 1974).

—— 'Community', in *The Blackwell Encyclopedia of Political Thought*, ed. David Miller (Oxford: Basil Blackwell, 1987).

—— *Modern Political Thought* (Oxford: Basil Blackwell, 1991).

Plante, D., 'In the Heart of Literary London', *New York Times Magazine* (11 Oct. 1988).

Posner, Ellen, 'A City that Likes itself', *Atlantic Monthly* (July 1991).

Prouse, Michael, 'Reform of US Health-Care System becomes Pressing Issue', *The Straits Times* (28 Nov. 1991).

Pullman, Geoffrey, *The Great Eskimo Vocabulary Hoax: And Other Irreverent Essays on the Study of Language* (Chicago: Chicago University Press, 1991).

Rahula, Walpola Sri, *What the Buddha Taught*, 2nd edn. (London: Gordon Fraser, 1967).

RASMUSSEN, DAVID, ed., *Universalism vs. Communitarianism* (Cambridge, Mass.: MIT Press, 1990).

RAWLS, JOHN, *A Theory of Justice* (Cambridge, Mass.: The Belknap Press of Harvard University Press, 1971).

—— 'Kantian Constructivism in Moral Theory', *Journal of Philosophy*, 77 (Sept. 1980).

—— 'Justice as Fairness: Political not Metaphysical', *Philosophy and Public Affairs* (Summer 1985).

—— 'The Idea of an Overlapping Consensus', *Oxford Journal of Legal Studies*, 7 (1987).

—— 'The Priority of Right and Ideas of the Good', *Philosophy and Public Affairs* (Fall 1988).

RAZ, JOSEPH, *The Morality of Freedom* (Oxford: Clarendon Press, 1986).

REED, CHRISTOPHER, 'Murderer to Die in "Liberal" State', *Guardian* (20 Mar. 1990).

REYNOLDS, CHARLES, and NORMAN, RALPH, eds., *Community in America: The Challenge of* Habits of the Heart (Berkeley, Calif.: University of California Press, 1988).

RHODE, DEBORAH, *Justice and Gender* (Cambridge, Mass.: Harvard University Press, 1989).

RICHARDSON, JOHN, *Existential Epistemology: A Heideggerian Critique of the Cartesian Project* (Oxford: Clarendon Press, 1986).

RICHLER, MORDECAI, *Home Sweet Home: My Canadian Album* (Toronto: McClelland and Stewart, 1984).

—— 'The New Yorker, Quebec, and Me', *Saturday Night* (May 1992).

RORTY, RICHARD, *Contingency, Irony and Solidarity* (Cambridge: Cambridge University Press, 1989).

ROSENBLUM, NANCY, 'Moral Membership in a Post-liberal State', *World Politics* (July 1984).

—— *Another Liberalism: Romanticism and the Reconstruction of Liberal Thought* (Cambridge, Mass.: Harvard University Press, 1987).

—— 'Pluralism and Self-Defense', in Nancy Rosenblum, ed., *Liberalism and the Moral Life* (Cambridge, Mass.: Harvard University Press, 1989).

ROTH, PHILIP, *Zuckerman Unbound* (London: Cape, 1981).

SANDEL, MICHAEL, *Liberalism and the Limits of Justice* (Cambridge: Cambridge University Press, 1981).

—— *Liberalism and its Critics* (Oxford: Basil Blackwell, 1984).

—— 'Morality and the Liberal Ideal', *New Republic* (7 May 1984).

—— 'Moral Argument and Liberal Toleration: Abortion and Homosexuality', *California Law Review*, 77 (1989).

SCHAMA, SIMON, *The Embarrassment of Riches: An Interpretation of Dutch Culture in the Golden Age* (New York: Knopf, 1987).

SHAPIRO, IAN, *The Evolution of Rights in Liberal Theory* (Cambridge: Cambridge University Press, 1986).

SHEEHAN, NEIL, *A Bright Shining Lie: John Paul Vann and America in Vietnam* (New York: Vintage Books, 1989).

SHER, GEORGE, 'Educating Citizens', *Philosophy and Public Affairs* (Winter 1989).

—— 'Three Grades of Social Involvement', *Philosophy and Public Affairs* (Spring 1989).

SINGER, PETER, *Hegel* (Oxford: Oxford University Press, 1983).

SMITH, ANTHONY, *The Ethnic Origins of Nations* (Oxford: Blackwell, 1986).

SOLZHENITSYN, ALEKSANDR, 'How we are to Rebuild Russia', *Komsomolskaya Pravda* (18 Sept. 1990) and *Literaturnaya Gazeta* (19 Sept. 1990).

STEINER, GEORGE, *Heidegger* (London: Fontana, 1978).

—— 'A Jew's Grief', *Harper's Magazine* (Oct. 1988).

STERBA, JAMES, ed., *Justice: Alternative Political Perspectives* (Belmont, Calif.: Wadsworth Publishing Co., 1980).

The Straits Times (Singapore), 'Shot in the Arm for UK Arts' (10 Nov. 1991).

—— 'Situation "can Explode into War" ' (10 Dec. 1991).

—— 'Rich are Richer while Poor are Poorer in US, Report Confirms' (7 Mar. 1992).

STROUD, BARRY, *The Significance of Philosophical Scepticism* (Oxford: Clarendon Press, 1984).

The Sunday Times (Singapore), 'US Firms Trying to Get More out of Workers: Approval Systems being Revamped to Achieve this' (26 Jan. 1992).

TAYLOR, CHARLES, *Hegel and Modern Society* (Cambridge: Cambridge University Press, 1979).

—— *Human Agency and Language: Philosophical Papers, 1* (Cambridge: Cambridge University Press, 1985).

—— *Philosophy and the Human Sciences: Philosophical Papers, 2* (Cambridge: Cambridge University Press, 1985).

—— 'Alternative Futures', in *Legitimacy, Identity and Alienation in Late Twentieth Century Canada* (Toronto: Knopff and Morton, 1986).

—— 'Irreducibly Social Goods', unpublished.

—— 'Overcoming Epistemology', in Kenneth Baynes, James Bohman, and Thomas McCarthy, eds., *After Philosophy: End or Transformation?* (Cambridge, Mass.: MIT Press, 1987).

—— 'Cross-Purposes: The Liberal–Communitarian Debate', in Nancy Rosenblum, ed., *Liberalism and the Moral Life* (Cambridge, Mass.: Harvard University Press, 1989).

—— *Sources of the Self: The Making of the Modern Identity* (Cambridge: Cambridge University Press, 1989).

—— 'Explanation and Practical Reason', Wider Working Paper WP72, World Institute for Development Economics Research (Helsinki, 1989).

TAYLOR, CHARLES, *The Malaise of Modernity* (Concord, Ontario: Anansi, 1991).

—— 'Comments and Replies' (to critics of *Sources of the Self*), *Inquiry: An Interdisciplinary Journal of Philosophy*, 34: 2 (June 1991).

TÖNNIES, FERDINAND, *Community and Association*, trans. C. Loomis (New York: Harper and Row, 1963).

Toronto Globe and Mail, 'Canadian Medicare Attracts Americans' (14 Feb. 1989).

TROUGHTON, TABITHA, 'A Fundamental Fight for Women', *Guardian* (20 Sept. 1990).

TULLY, JAMES, 'Wittgenstein and Political Philosophy: Understanding Practices of Critical Reflection', *Political Theory* (May 1989).

UPDIKE, JOHN, *Self-Consciousness: Memoirs* (London: André Deutsch, 1989).

WALLACH, JOHN, 'Liberals, Communitarians, and the Tasks of Political Theory', *Political Theory* (Nov. 1987).

WALZER, MICHAEL, *Spheres of Justice* (Oxford: Basil Blackwell, 1983).

—— *Interpretation and Social Criticism* (Cambridge, Mass.: Harvard University Press, 1987).

—— *The Company of Critics* (New York: Basic Books, 1988).

—— 'A Critique of Philosophical Conversation', *Philosophical Forum* (Fall–Winter 1989–90).

—— 'The Communitarian Critique of Liberalism', *Political Theory* (Feb. 1990).

WEBSTER, PAUL, 'Last Tango in La Coupole', *Guardian* (6 Jan. 1988).

WEINBERG, ROBERT, *Euthanasia, Suicide, and the Right to Die* (Grand Rapids, Mich.: William B. Eerdmans Publishing Co., 1989).

WEIR, ROBERT, ed., *Ethical Issues in Death and Dying* (New York: Columbia University Press, 1977).

WILSON, JAMES Q., and KELLING, GEORGE L., 'Making Neighbourhoods Safe', *Atlantic Monthly* (Feb. 1989).

WINCH, PETER, *The Idea of a Social Science and its Relation to Philosophy* (London: Routledge, 1958).

WITTGENSTEIN, LUDWIG, *Philosophical Investigations* (Oxford: Blackwell, 1953).

—— *On Certainty* (New York: Harper and Row, 1969).

YANKELOVICH, DANIEL, 'A Crisis of Moral Legitimacy?', *Dissent*, 21 (Fall 1974).

YOUNG, IRIS MARION, 'Humanism, Gynocentrism, and Feminist Politics', *Hypatia: A Journal of Feminist Philosophy*, 3 (1985).

—— *Justice and the Politics of Difference* (Princeton, NJ: Princeton University Press, 1990).

ZILLES, MICHAEL, 'Universalism and Communitarianism: a Bibliography', in David Rasmussen, ed., *Universalism vs. Communitarianism* (Cambridge, Mass.: MIT Press, 1990).

ZUCKERT, CATHERINE H., 'Martin Heidegger: His Philosophy and his Politics', *Political Theory* (Feb. 1990).

Index